John Gower

THE FRENCH BALADES

 MIDDLE ENGLISH TEXTS SERIES

The Middle English Texts Series is designed for classroom use. Its goal is to make available to teachers, scholars, and students texts that occupy an important place in the literary and cultural canon but have not been readily available in student editions. The series does not include those authors, such as Chaucer, Langland, or Malory, whose English works are normally in print in good student editions. The focus is, instead, upon Middle English literature adjacent to those authors that teachers need in compiling the syllabuses they wish to teach. The editions maintain the linguistic integrity of the original work but within the parameters of modern reading conventions. The texts are printed in the modern alphabet and follow the practices of modern capitalization, word formation, and punctuation. Manuscript abbreviations are silently expanded, and *u/v* and *j/i* spellings are regularized according to modern orthography. Yogh (ȝ) is transcribed as *g*, *gh*, *y*, or *s*, according to the sound in Modern English spelling to which it corresponds; thorn (þ) and eth (ð) are transcribed as *th*. Distinction between the second person pronoun and the definite article is made by spelling the one *thee* and the other *the*, and final *-e* that receives full syllabic value is accented (e.g., *charité*). Hard words, difficult phrases, and unusual idioms are glossed either in the right margin or at the foot of the page. Explanatory and textual notes appear at the end of the text, often along with a glossary. The editions include short introductions on the history of the work, its merits and points of topical interest, and brief working bibliographies.

This series is published in association with the University of Rochester.

Medieval Institute Publications is a program of
The Medieval Institute, College of Arts and Sciences

 WESTERN MICHIGAN UNIVERSITY

John Gower
THE FRENCH BALADES

Edited and Translated by
R. F. Yeager

TEAMS • Middle English Texts Series

MEDIEVAL INSTITUTE PUBLICATIONS
Western Michigan University
Kalamazoo

Library of Congress Cataloging-in-Publication Data

Gower, John, 1325?-1408.
[Traitié. English & French]
The French balades / edited and translated by R.F. Yeager.
p. cm. -- (Middle English texts series)
English and French on facing pages.
"Published for TEAMS (The Consortium for the Teaching of the Middle
Ages) in association with the University of Rochester."
Includes bibliographical references and index.
ISBN 978-1-58044-155-1 (pbk. : alk. paper)
I. Yeager, Robert F. II. Gower, John, 1325?-1408. Cinkante. English &
French. III. Title.
PQ1463.G98T7313 2011
841'.1--dc22
2010052306

ISBN 978-1-58044-155-1

P 5 4 3 2 1

❦ Contents

ACKNOWLEDGMENTS

The translations and commentary printed here have indebted me to few, but to those, deeply. Foremost among them is Brian Merrilees, who assiduously read everything, commented gently but always wisely and with extraordinary patience, and contributed as well the learned pages on Gower's particular Anglo-French *patois*. His encouragement, his excitement about the project, and his willingness to allow my many questions to find him in Canada, Normandy, or New Zealand were several times the margin by which the work went forward. Similarly, Robert S. Sturges' benignly proffered clarity about Gower's grammar in the *Traitié* was instrumental in convincing me at an early stage to carry on. Indispensable help at one level or another with questions related to manuscripts came from Derek Pearsall, A. S. G. Edwards, Dan Mosser, Ralph Hanna, Helen Cooper, Alastair Minnis, John Fleming, Eva Oledzka of Duke Humphrey's Library, Sandra Bailey of the library at Wadham College, the anonymous "Enquiry Officer" in Manuscripts and Special Collections at the University of Nottingham, Sam Block, and the most gracious staff at Fondation Bodmer. Kathryn D. Van Wert and John H. Chandler formatted the volume and prepared it for publication. Patricia Hollahan and Tom Krol at MIP saw the volume through the press. And, as is true for so many of us, I am doubly grateful to Russell A. Peck — immediately for his work with this volume and his good guidance as general factotum of TEAMS, but more generally (and profoundly) for his friendship over lo, these many years. We are all grateful to the NEH for helping to fund the series.

🌿 GENERAL INTRODUCTION

The English poet John Gower (d. 1408) has left substantial bodies of work in Middle English, Latin, and Anglo-French — all three, that is, of the major languages of his place and time. This accomplishment is truly remarkable, not only among poets in medieval England or on the Continent, but among poets generally, then or ever. It is hard to name anyone other than Gower who has done so, let alone in such quantity and with such skill. That Gower sought this singularity self-consciously, and was proud of it, requires no firmer evidence than a look at the tomb he designed for himself in Southwark Cathedral. Beneath his effigy's head lie three great books bearing the titles of his most important poems: *Vox Clamantis* (composed in Latin), *Confessio Amantis* (in Middle English), and *Speculum Meditantis* (better known by its French title, *Mirour de l'Omme*).[1] Gower's claim to be England's trilingual master *memoria in aeterna* is echoed in the short poem in Latin elegiacs, "Eneidos, Bucolis," attributed to an unidentified "Philosopher" in the manuscripts (but almost without doubt from Gower's own hand), in which Gower is found superior to Virgil, whose *Georgics*, *Bucolics*, and *Aeneid* were written — after all! — in Latin alone.[2] One can imagine conversations about choice of language taking place between Gower and his longtime friend Geoffrey Chaucer, with Gower firmly cautioning Chaucer not to tie his chance at immortality to a vernacular both poets considered to be woefully and whimsically mutable.[3]

Literary history has, of course, thus far proven Chaucer's the better wager. More the linguistic optimist, and an intellectual true to his times, Gower failed to foresee his country-men's rapid spiral into near-complete monolinguality. (The early fifteenth-century English rendering of the eighteen balades of the *Traitié selonc les auctours pour essampler les amantz*

---

[1] Thus the titles as they appear on the tomb today. We cannot be as certain that this order represents Gower's intention as we are that all three titles were so displayed at installation.

[2] The ascriptive headnote reads: "Carmen, quod quidam Philosophus in memoriam Iohannis Gower super consummacione suorum trium librorum forma subsequenti composuit, et eidem gratanter transmisit" ["A poem, which in remembrance of John Gower a certain philosopher composed in the following form and happily sent to the same man, to commemorate the completion of his three books"]. "Eneidos, bucolis" is known from five manuscripts: London, British Library, MS Cotton Tiberius A.iv; Glasgow, University of Glasgow Library, MS Hunter 59 (T.2.17); London, British Library, MS Harleian 6291; Oxford, All Souls College, MS 98; and Oxford, Bodleian Library, MS Fairfax 3, the latter two of which Gower is thought likely to have supervised in production. See further the discussion of "Eneidos, Bucolis" by Kuczynski in "Gower's Virgil," pp. 172–73.

[3] Chaucer famously expresses his concern about the mutability of English in *Troilus and Criseyde* V.1793–96; see further "Chaucers Wordes unto Adam, His Owne Scriveyn." For Gower, English seemed shaky, a language in need of support: as he points out in the *Confessio Amantis* Prol.22–23 "fewe men endite / In oure Englissh" (second recension).

1

marietz by the Yorkshireman Quixley, included in this volume, demonstrates how soon the need took hold.) In consequence, and clearly much against his wish, for several hundred years Gower's reputation has been based upon the *Confessio Amantis* and the comparatively brief "In Praise of Peace" — two of the finest Middle English poems, but amounting together to less than a third of his total *oeuvre*. The last half-century, however, has seen this situation remedied steadily, as one by one English translations of Gower's Latin and Anglo-French poems have appeared.[4] With the addition here of his two sets of balades, the *Traitié* and the *Cinkante Balades*, the complete poetry now is available to readers in both French and modern English.

It should be interesting, then, to see how future years will reassess Gower's achievement — whether posterity in the end will validate his bet on three languages to echo the "Philosopher's" judgment, or no. What, in any case, seems quite likely is that, had Gower chosen for his balades his premier native vernacular rather than French, the development of English letters might have taken a rather different course. Consider: Gower's *Traitié* and *Cinkante Balades* are the only extant *formes fixes* poems ("fixed forms," that is, fourteenth-century French lyrics, essentially the balade, rondeau, and virelai, developed as literary styles from thirteenth-century dances) that we can be assured were written by a native Englishman, those of "Ch" (and Chaucer's "many a song and many a leccherous lay" — presumably in French) notwithstanding.[5] More significant still is the conceptual unity of Gower's endeavors. Unlike the fifteen balades and chants in French of the otherwise-anonymous "Ch" — and unlike Chaucer's known Middle English "lyrics" as well — the eighteen balades that make up the *Traitié* and the fifty-four of the *Cinkante Balades* are not separate, occasional pieces, nor is their appearance together at all arbitrary. In each collection Gower wrote and arranged the poems to be read together and, as a composite grouping, to evince a determinable shape. Hence his use of "traitié" — "treatise" — as a collective term for the eighteen balades he addressed to married lovers. Although there is some obscurity about just what constituted a "treatise" in fourteenth-century English critical parlance, that Gower in this case was signaling an argument with an attempt to persuade is quite clear.[6] Married life is good, he says, adultery is bad, and here to prove it is a variety of cameos of the great and infamous, caught *in flagrante* and suffering the consequences. Thus technically we ought not think of the *Traitié selonc les auctours pour essampler les amantz marietz* as a "sequence," at least not in the sense of Petrarch's *Canzonière* or Sidney's *Astrophil and Stella*. The *Traitié*'s cameos develop no central characters, nor do they collectively narrate a larger story. The *Cinkante Balades*, however, do both. They therefore comprise a true poetic sequence, the first and

---

[4] For the Latin, see Gower, *Major Latin Works* and *Minor Latin Works*; the *Mirour de l'Omme* has been translated by Wilson. Of related interest is Itô's translation of the *Confessio Amantis* into modern Japanese. (*Koisuru Otokono Kokkai*, or lit. "Confessions of a Lover." My thanks to Toshi Takamiya for transcription and translation into English.)

[5] The poems of "Ch" have been edited by Wimsatt, *Chaucer and the Poems of "Ch"*; for Chaucer's remark, see his Retraction, line 1086.

[6] Strohm, "Some Generic Distinctions," similarly concludes that Chaucer understood a "tretys" to be "a 'tale'. . . neither 'storie' nor 'fable' in its rejection of plot" but "with its emphasis on reasoned exposition" (p. 326).

only one known by an Englishman[7] until Sidney's three hundred years later. Sidney wrote *Astrophil and Stella* looking over his shoulder at Petrarch's woeful song-and-sonnet "diary" of loving and losing Laura, and it is possible that a shadowy Petrarch lurks behind the *Cinkante Balades* as well. Certainly Chaucer's Englishing of "S'amor non è" (*Canzonière*, poem 132) as Troilus' song (*Troilus and Criseyde* I.400–20) suggests that Gower, too, despite our lack of evidence that he read Italian, could have been aware at least of the Petrarchan sequence, and learned from it how to embed a narrative within a collage of discreet poems.[8]

Whatever role, if any, Petrarch's *Canzonière* may have played in Gower's envisioning of the *Traitié* and the *Cinkante Balades*, it is nonetheless certain that, like their language, their major inspiration came from France, not Italy. Of the latter, one primary source, to be discussed below, was the vastly popular, multi-authored collection known as the *Cent Balades*. But most influential of all on Gower's balades, and of course on Chaucer's as well, were the examples of two contemporaries, Guillaume de Machaut and Eustache Deschamps, the latter of whom Chaucer, and perhaps Gower too, seems to have known.[9] Both Machaut and Deschamps composed in many poetic forms, but in the end their apparent preference for the balade gave that structure its decades-long vogue. It is not going too far to posit that together their works and theories about writing account for Gower's selection of balade form for the *Traitié*, the narrative arc of the *Cinkante Balades*, the faux epistolary style, the voices — perhaps even the personalities — of the Lover and his Lady, and the basic structure, in the *Traitié*, of three stanzas of seven lines each and no envoy, and in the *Cinkante Balades*, of three stanzas of eight lines each with a four-line envoy.

Indeed, it is difficult to overestimate how often Gower's balades bear the fingerprints of his two great French contemporaries. Commentary following in notes to specific lines will show, for example, that his admiration for centonic appropriation, so variously prominent in his Latin poetry, extended to his French lyrics as well — a fact that may lay to rest at last two stubborn, interconnected speculations about what prompted his balade-making in the first place. Several among the few early readers in modern times of Gower's balades found in them "evidence" — subject matter, images, sometimes even approximate lines — pointing to "troubadour influence."[10] The prospect that somehow Gower could have imagined himself a troubadour or a trouvère is urged by John H. Fisher, still Gower's most insightful critic in many respects, to posit Gower's membership in a London *puy*, a kind of poetic fraternity whose members strove each year to compose the finest poem in a predetermined genre, one

---

[7] I should acknowledge, however, that Charles of Orleans, though not English, composes in the mid-fifteenth century a balade sequence in Middle English that, like Pertrarch's *Canzonière*, develops a vague love plot.

[8] Single copies of poem 132 are known; for discussion and relevant bibliography see Barney's note to *Troilus and Criseyde* I.400 in the *Riverside Chaucer*. No evidence exists, it should be pointed out, to indicate that Gower read Italian.

[9] That Chaucer and Deschamps knew each other is strongly suggested by the latter's poem, the so-called "Letter to Chaucer," no. 138 in *Oeuvres Complètes de Eustache Deschamps*, 2:138–40. For discussion, see Wimsatt, *Chaucer and His French Contemporaries*, pp. 248–51, who also prints and translates Deschamps' balade 138.

[10] E.g., studies by Audiau, *Troubadours et l'Angleterre*, especially pp. 103–28; and Kar, *Thoughts on the Mediæval Lyric*, pp. 55–63.

of which was the balade.[11] To be sure *puys* were relatively common in France, even in the latter fourteenth century, and detailed records recovered by Fisher remain from a London *puy* active in the thirteenth century.[12] Short, however, of a fresh discovery linking Gower to something later (or, say, proof of his ability to own, or to read, Occitan books), it seems highly unlikely that troubadours, trouvères, or *puys* directly inspired any portion of either the *Traitié* or the *Cinkante Balades*. Indirectly, of course, they play a role via their contributions to the larger tradition of amorous verse drawn on by Machaut and Deschamps — and through these latter, it is best to think, ultimately on Gower too. But certainly nothing "troubadour" turns up in Gower's balades that cannot also be found, sometimes almost word for word, in the works of Deschamps, Machaut, and several of their French contemporaries.

Gower seems to have inhumed another lesson about the writing of balades from these poets as well, one worth mentioning since it is frequently overlooked, especially by new readers of his work. The *Traitié* and the *Cinkante Balades* stand apart not only because they are Gower's unique excursions into *formes fixes*, as far as we know, but also because there is no political cast to them at all. The *Mirour de l'Omme*, *Vox Clamantis*, and *Confessio Amantis* — the three great tomes decorating Gower's monument — all concern themselves pointedly with social and political reform. So too do the *Cronica Tripertita*, "In Praise of Peace," and most of his lesser verse in Latin. Clearly Gower put a high premium on this aspect of his art, and Petrarch's example — if whatever partial acquaintance with the *Canzonière* Gower might have had ran deep enough — would have taught him how to introduce social and institutional criticism into the mix of his balades, had he wished to do so. That nothing of the sort appears either in the *Traitié* or in the *Cinkante Balades* is therefore significant. It means that Gower had other, for him rather original, purposes for these poems. What these purposes may — or may not — have been will be addressed, along with matters of versification, dating, and manuscript provenance, in the separate discussions of each collection to follow.

---

[11] See Fisher, *John Gower: Moral Philosopher*, pp. 78–84.

[12] Fourteenth-century French *puys* are discussed by Wimsatt, *Chaucer and His French Contemporaries*, p. 277.

INTRODUCTION TO THE *TRAITIÉ*
SELONC LES AUCTOURS POUR ESSAMPLER LES AMANTZ MARIETZ

THE SUBJECT OF THE *TRAITIÉ*

At first glance perhaps it appears superfluous to inquire after the subject of a "treatise, following the authorities, as an example for married lovers." In his description of its contents, Gower seems to have been quite clear about what he intended the *Traitié* to do. Nonetheless, certain anomalies exist that may further clarify, and so influence, our understanding of Gower's subject. There are, for example, two quite different versions of the prose heading from which G. C. Macaulay borrowed his title for these balades. The longer one, in Oxford, Bodleian Library MS Fairfax 3 and similar manuscripts, runs as follows:

> Because the preceding poem in English [i.e., the *Confessio Amantis*] was by way of example of the foolishness of those in particular who love in a courtly manner, now the subsequent treatise will be in French, for all the world generally, following the authorities, as an example for married lovers, in order that they might be able to protect the promise of their sacred spousal through perfect loyalty, and truly hold fast to the honor of God.[1]

This, the more extensive wording, raises a number of issues of interest, not the least of them, especially from the perspective of establishing a date of composition for the *Traitié*, being the firm connection of the *Traitié* with the *Confessio*. The statement also unmistakably contrasts two kinds of love between men and women: the "foolish," "courtly" sort (exemplified, it would appear, in the *Confessio* — a not unimportant commentary on that poem) with the love of a husband and a wife, united *salvement* — "truly" (although with more than a hint, perhaps, also of "safely," "salvifically," or "in good health") — in the eyes of God. Intriguingly, it contrasts two languages as well — the English of the *Confessio* with the French of the *Traitié* — and for a particular reason: to Gower, apparently, "François" was a universal, "for all the world generally," not a regional, language. And it is a language, if we take him as this word — see the envoy of *Traitié* XVIII — of which he felt himself no master. Does this mean that Gower expected a broader readership for the *Traitié* than for the *Confessio*? I suspect it does, as I have argued elsewhere, and this is interesting and important in itself.[2] And among other things, it may lend further support to the earlier dating of the *Traitié*, since as the 1390s progressed Gower's focus on England and English issues increased

---

[1] "Puisqu'il ad dit ci devant en Englois par voie d'essample la sotie de cellui qui par amours aime par especial, dirra ore apres en François a tout le monde en general un traitié selonc les auctours pour essampler les amantz mariez, au fin q'ils la foi de lour seintes espousailes pourront par fine loialté guarder, et al honour de dieu salvement tenir." Text from Gower, *Complete Works*, 1:379.

[2] See Yeager, "John Gower's Audience" pp. 92–93.

commensurately, at the expense of his attention to noninsular events. (One thinks immediately of the *Cronica Tripertita* — but it is no less possible, and probably more significant, to view his decision to write the *Confessio* in English as a milder, less partisan marker of this same shift in concern.) We may note further here as well the appeal to *les auctours* — "the authorities" — which itself prompts inquiry. Specific allusions to doctrinal and classical sources will be pursued as they appear, line by line, in the notes. But interestingly foregrounded, too, is the broader question: what did Gower mean by "authorities"? In the case of the *Traitié*, would the term have been applied to include (as I believe it likely did) contemporary masters of versification — Machaut, Deschamps, Froissart, and the chevalier poets of the *Livre de Cent Ballades*, aristocrats such as Jean de Saint-Pierre, and Oton de Graunson? Hints may lie here that, carefully exhumed and weighed, can further our advancing archaeology of Gower's literary-critical lexicon.

But surely the most meaningful portions of the *Traitié*'s descriptive heading, in both the longer and shorter versions, are, first, the attention called there to the role of God as the cause — the origin, the root, effectively — of marriage as a viable, indeed the most *desirable*, human condition; and second, Gower's pointed insistence that "lovers" and "marriage" are not — *simpliciter* — contradictory notions.[3] Perhaps for modern readers, whose vision of marriage begins with love and (with luck) evolves into one form of religious service or another, these issues seem unprovocative in the extreme, even to the degree of unnoticeability. Nevertheless, making the case for each of them is clearly Gower's subject in the *Traitié*. And conceivably he had good reason — or reasons.

As to the first — that is, God's preferment of marriage: a block of patristic and subsequent, dogmatic opinion proffered the claim that ideally virginity, not marriage, was the highest state of aspiration for the human soul. Gower expresses this position through Genius, who remarks to Amans in Book V (lines 6388–90) of the *Confessio Amantis*, "Virginité is for to preise, / Which, as th'Apocalips recordeth, / To Crist in hevene best acordeth."[4] Yet to assert, as Gower does throughout the *Traitié*, that God intended people to multiply, and moreover to base that claim on reason, is scarcely a radical position. (Indeed, insisting on God's opposition to carnal intercourse was a primary heresy of the Albigensians, condemned repeatedly beginning in 1025.)[5] Humankind is constituted, after all, of spirit *and* flesh; and in Eden before the Fall, where God established the first marriage, his intention was a harmony

---

[3] The shorter version, as found in Glasgow, University of Glasgow Library, MS Hunter 59 (T.2.17) and related manuscripts, is as follows: "Cest un traitie quel Johan Gower ad fait selonc les auctours touchant lestat de matrimoine dont les amantz marietz se pourront essampler a tenir la foi de lour seintes espousailes." ["This is a treatise which John Gower made, following the authorities, concerning the matrimonial state, whereof married lovers might be able to take examples for themselves and hold fast to the promise of their holy spousal."]

[4] See also the Latin stanza heading the same section: "Ut Rosa de spinis spineto prevalet orta, / Et lilii flores cespite plura valent, / Sic sibi virginitas carnis sponsalia vincit, / Eternos fetus que sine labe parit." ["As risen rose outshines the thorny bush, / And lily's flowers are valued more than earth, / So maidenhood, surpassing carnal vows, / Wins out, and spotless bears eternal fruit."] The translation is by Echard and Fanger, *Latin Verses*, p. 65.

[5] The Albigensians, or Cathars, were neo-Manichaean dualists who held the body to be evil and a prison to the pure soul (hence "Cathar," from *katharos*, "pure"), the liberation of which was the purpose of every life. Suicide was justified; engendering offspring served only the dark power. See Holmes, *Holy Heretics*; and more recently Barber, *Cathars*.

of both in the sinless procreation of Adam and Eve.[6] The problem facing postlapsarian humanity, in the orthodox view of the medieval Church, was adjudicating the legitimate requisites of soul and flesh: procreation was both necessary and good, as was physical desire, provided that serving God was the wished-for end product of every carnal act. Intention, *ergo*, was all, and the assessment and direction of intent toward the lawful was the role appropriate to reason. In the *Confessio Amantis*, high on Gower's list of purposes is to demonstrate through fictive example that love, thoughtfully weighed in reason's balance and leading to fruitful relations between man and woman, is highly pleasing to God.[7] In the *Traitié*, this is *the* purpose, minus, largely, the reliance on fictive example. Despite their "lyric" form, the balades of the *Traitié* comprise a true "treatise" (hence, probably, Gower's use of the term): that is, a rational argument, logically assembled, poem by poem, to define "honeste" marriage and justify its centrality to God's greater plan for human life.

Thus for Gower "love" and "marriage" are by no means exclusionary conditions, certain twentieth-century scholars to the contrary.[8] Taking as serious (rather than tongue-in-cheek humor, as is more likely) the assertions of Andreas Capellanus, among others, that married couples could not be lovers — of each other — these scholars extrapolated an antipathy to marriage that they believed ran commonly in late medieval thought.[9] One result for Gower, who so openly champions marriage throughout his works, albeit with special vehemence in the *Traitié*, was his condemnation by the critics as a regressive conservative (if not a prude) in matters of the heart. Yet a better word for Gower's stance in the *Traitié*, even than conservative, is orthodox. Certainly neither here nor elsewhere in his work does he ever speak against love's power, importance, or the fulfillment it provides in its properly sanctioned incarnation. And there is another, more valuable result of the criticism of Gower's staunch defense of married lovers, especially as found in the *Traitié*: it suggests a reason for their writing. To choose a form associated with frivolous love to promote its opposite is characteristically Gowerian — n.b., his wish to demonstrate to the poetic community at home and abroad that he, too, was master of the balade, if as always in his own particular way.

MANUSCRIPTS

- F: Oxford, Bodleian Library, MS Fairfax 3, fols. 186v–190. [Primary base text for these poems, collated by Macaulay with S, G, and T. Also contains *Confessio Amantis* and various minor Latin poems.]
- S: Oxford, All Souls College, MS 98, fols. 132–135. [Also contains *Vox Clamantis*, *Cronica Tripertita*, and various minor Latin poems.]
- T: London, British Library, MS Additional 59495 (formerly MS Trentham Hall), fols. 33–39. [Also contains "In Praise of Peace," "Rex celi deus," *Cinkante Balades*, "Ecce patet tensus," "Henrici quarti." Also: London, British Library, MS Additional 59496, a transcript commissioned in 1764 by the then-owner of Add. 59495, Granville Leveson-Gower, second Earl Gower.]

---

[6] On this and subsequent points of marital doctrine, see Kelly, *Love and Marriage*.

[7] The point is made eloquently and at length by Peter Nicholson in *Love and Ethics*.

[8] E.g., Lewis, *Allegory of Love*.

[9] This is the true (if frequently misunderstood) meaning of the "First Rule of Love," that "Marriage is no real excuse for not loving." See Andreas Capellanus, *Art of Courtly Love*, p. 184.

- G: Glasgow, University of Glasgow Library, MS Hunter 59 (T.2.17), fols. 124v–128. [Also contains *Vox Clamantis*, *Cronica Tripertita*, and various minor Latin poems. Apparently derived from S.]
- H: London, British Library, MS Harley 3869, fols. 186v–190. [Also contains *Confessio Amantis* and various minor Latin poems. Identical to F.]
- B: Oxford, Bodleian Library, MS Bodley 294, fols. 197v–199v. [Also contains *Confessio Amantis* and various minor Latin poems.]
- Tr: Cambridge, Trinity College, MS R.3.2, fols. 148–152. [Also contains *Confessio Amantis* and various minor Latin poems.]
- W: Oxford, Wadham College, MS 13, fols. 442v–446v. [*Traitié* incomplete. Also contains *Confessio Amantis*.]
- Bo: Geneva, Foundation Bodmer, MS 178. [Also contains *Confessio Amantis* and various minor Latin poems; formerly Morwich, Keswick Hall, MS Gurney 121. Identical to F.]
- Λ: Nottingham, University Library, Wollaton Library Collection, MS WLC LM 8, fols. 201–203v. [Also contains *Confessio Amantis*.]
- A: London, British Library, MS Arundel 364, fol. 223. [Fragment on leaf inserted into Nicholas Love's *Meditationes Vitae Christi*.]
- Y: New Haven, Yale University, Beinecke Library, Osborn Collection, MS fa.1, fols. 196–199. [Also contains *Confessio Amantis*.]
- P: Princeton, Princeton University, Firestone Library, Robert H. Taylor Collection, MS Taylor 5, fols. 187–191. [Also contains *Confessio Amantis*.]

TRANSLATION

- London, British Library, MS Stowe 951, fols. 313–322. [Quixley. Also contains English versions of John of Hildesheim's *Historia trium regum* ("History of the Three Kings") and the *Speculum vitae* ("Mirror of Life"), attributed to William of Nassington.]

VERSIFICATION AND DATING

All eighteen balades of the *Traitié* follow the same formal pattern of three stanzas of seven lines each and no envoy, except the eighteenth, which adds a fourth stanza of seven lines, perhaps intended as an envoy (but see below). Rhyming is ABABBCC consistently throughout — what is known, when found in Middle English poetry, as "rime royal."[10] The end rhymes deserve particular attention, as they demonstrate Gower's concern about detail and a measure of his poetic skill. Each balade in the *Traitié* has but three rhymes — that is, e.g., in IV, line-endings of *-emte* (AA), *-ouses* (BBB), *-orde* (CC) in each stanza. Such limitation is not unusual for balades in French, given the accessibility of rhymes, especially in comparison to English. Gower, however, seems purposely to have set himself a more difficult task in the *Traitié* by seeking a *different* rhyming triad for each of the eighteen balades. The rhymes of I–VI should illustrate: I: *-ure* (AA), *-age* (BBB), *-able* (CC); II: *-ence* (AA), *-ant* (BBB), *-our* (CC); III: *-a* (AA), *-itz/is* (BBB), *-ue* (CC); IV: *-emte* (AA), *-ouses* (BBB), *-orde* (CC);

---

[10] A useful discussion of Gower's treatment of rime royal in French and English, and in comparison with Chaucer's, is Itô's chapter "Gower and Rime Royal" in his *John Gower, the Medieval Poet*, pp. 101–18.

V: *-on* (AA), *-ire* (BBB), *-este* (CC); VI: *-oine* (AA), *-é* (BBB), *-ure* (CC). To be sure, there are occasional repetitions of one or another rhyme, as follows: I and XVII have *-age* as, respectively, B and C rhymes; IV and XVIII have *-orde* as, respectively, A and C rhymes; V, XII, and XVI have *-on* as, respectively, A, A, and B rhymes; VI, VIII, and XII have B rhymes in *-é*; IX, XV, and XVIII have C rhymes in *-ie*. The rhymes of the remaining six balades (II, III, VII, X, XIII, XIV) are unique, however, so that, taken together, Gower's rhymes in the *Traitié* point toward a thought-out program of variation, apparently unnecessary except to demonstrate the poet's artfulness.

DATING THE *TRAITIÉ*

The artfulness of the *Traitié* is perhaps worth interrogating further, specifically in light of our uncertainty about its date of composition. Noting that in the Latin verses following balade XVIII "in all the copies" (except, that is, B), Gower describes himself as "old in years" ("vetus annorum") and entering into the "order of husbands" ("ordine sponsorum") — a nuptial on record as having taken place in 1398 — Macaulay logically posited that "it would seem that the *Traitié* belongs to the year 1397."[11] This date, along with the corollary assumption that Gower wrote the *Traitié* in celebration of his own marriage, has found general acceptance for many years. Yet difficulties with both should be pointed out, beginning with the apparent incongruity of Gower finding in his new marriage inspiration for the *Traitié*, which is, after all, an altogether blistering indictment of adultery. Not that it couldn't happen — but it doesn't seem likely. Nor can we be sure that Gower's later Latin verses, necessarily work of 1397–98, were written at the same time as the *Traitié*. Contiguous appearance in a manuscript — even several manuscripts over which Gower may have had oversight — is no proof of coterminal composition. And finally, one might wonder whom Gower had in mind as the ideal reader of the *Traitié*? It would take quite a leap to decide that his bride, one Agnes Groundolf, had skills up to the task, although, as we know very little about her, perhaps she did. But would Gower have put himself to the extra trouble of so successfully varying his rhyme schemes just to shine in the eyes of his wife?

If not, however, and if indeed Gower wrote the *Traitié* at a time other than when he married, when might that have been? In the absence of stronger evidence, where might we turn for clues? One possibility is the versification itself.[12] Lacking envoys, as they do, the balades of the *Traitié* resemble the earlier style of Machaut (d. 1377) whose work remained rooted in musical composition, to which envoys were relatively unsuited. Deschamps, in *L'Art de Dictier* (ca. 1392), his widely-read "how-to" treatise on writing verse, distinguished between what he called "artificial music" (that is, made with instruments or singing voice) and "natural music," or lyric poetry, intended as now for unaccompanied reading, silently or aloud. "Those who make natural music," Deschamps concluded, "generally don't know . . . how to give their lyrics artful melody."[13] An admitted "natural music maker," Deschamps shortly after Machaut's death set out — self-consciously, it is thought — to play to his strength

---

[11] Gower, *Complete Works*, 1:lxxxiii–iv.

[12] For fuller discussion, see Yeager, "John Gower's Audience."

[13] "[E] que les faiseurs d'icelle [musique naturele] ne saichent pas . . . donner chant par art de notes a ce qu'ilz font"; see Deschamps, *L'Art de Dictier*, pp. 60–68 (at p. 62).

by separating verse from music permanently.[14] His impact on the balade was profound. It seems to have been his preferred mode: his collected *Oeuvres* contain more than a thousand. Most conclude with the envoy that served as his trademark, and subsequently through his influence became the standard for the form. Gower may or may not have read *L'Art de Dictier* — we lack proof either way — but about whether in general he knew the work of Deschamps (who after all composed a balade, *avec envoi*, for Chaucer ca. 1385–91) there can be little doubt.[15] The absence of envoys from the *Traitié*, then, suggests an earlier rather than a later date for these poems, and weakens the case for Gower's marriage in 1398 as the cause.

It seems likely too that the manuscripts, as well as the particular exempla singled out in the *Traitié*, provide other clues about the moment of their writing. The manuscript evidence is of two sorts. First, in the twelve known manuscripts containing the balades of the *Traitié*, they are preceded in nine by the *Confessio Amantis*, in two by the *Vox Clamantis* and *Cronica Tripertita*, and in one they appear alongside the *Cinkante Balades* and "In Praise of Peace."[16] Moreover, just as in the *Confessio*, Latin prose commentary was written for the *Traitié* poems (even Quixley's fifteenth-century translation retains it), directing our reading of the balades and of the longer *Confessio* in precisely the same ways. Among Gower's poems only the *Traitié* and the *Confessio* are so glossed. Both presentational elements suggest the close association of *Traitié* and *Confessio* in Gower's mind, if not necessarily demonstrating their near-simultaneous composition.

The suggestion, however, is further strengthened by content, as well: ten of the eighteen balades in the *Traitié*, i.e., all of them containing exempla, have their narratives replicated, usually in greater detail, in the *Confessio Amantis*. Nothing we know would have prevented Gower from using either work as a base for narratives in another with decades in between, but Occam's razor points toward a different conclusion. Thus it seems plausible, even, indeed, more than likely, that the balades of the *Traitié* and the *Confessio* date from approximately the same time: not later than 1390, and possibly as early as 1385.[17]

---

[14] See Wimsatt, *Chaucer and His French Contemporaries*, chap. 1: "Natural Music in Middle French Verse and Chaucer," pp. 3–42, especially pp. 12–16; and, further, Butterfield, *Poetry and Music*.

[15] As Wimsatt notes, no consensus exists concerning when Deschamps wrote his balade to Chaucer. Wimsatt himself settles on "late 1380s"; see *Chaucer and His French Contemporaries*, p. 248.

[16] Excluding the fragment leaf in Nicholas Love from the count.

[17] Fisher, *John Gower: Moral Philosopher*, p. 116, offers 1385 as a probable beginning point for the *Confessio*. Russell A. Peck holds to 1386; see the chronology in his edition, *Confessio Amantis*, 1:59.

 **TRAITIÉ**

Puisqu'il ad dit ci devant en Englois par voie d'essample la sotie de cellui qui par amours aime par especial, dirra ore apres en François a tout le monde en general un traitié selonc les auctours pour essampler les amantz marietz, au fin q'ils la foi de lour seintes espousailes pourront par fine loialté guarder, et al honour de dieu salvement tenir.

I

Le creatour de toute creature,
Qui l'alme d'omme ad fait a son ymage,   *(see note)*
Par quoi le corps de reson et nature
Soit attempré per jouste governage,
5   Il done al alme assetz plus d'avantage;
Car il l'ad fait discrete et resonable,
Dont sur le corps raison ert conestable.

En dieu amer celle alme ad sa droiture,
Tant soulement pour fermer le corage
10   En tiel amour u nulle mesprisure
De foldelit la poet mettre en servage
De frele char, q'est toutdis en passage:
Mais la bone alme est seinte et permanable;
Dont sur le corps raison ert conestable.

15   En l'alme gist et raison et mesure,
Dont elle avera le ciel en heritage;
Li corps selonc la char pour engendrure
Avera la bone espouse en mariage;
Qui sont tout une chose et un estage,
20   Qe l'un a l'autre soient entendable:
Dont sur le corps raison ert conestable.

II

De l'espirit l'amour quiert continence,   *(see note)*
Et vivre chaste en soul dieu contemplant;
Li corps par naturele experience
Quiert femme avoir, dont soir multipliant;
5   Des bones almes l'un fait le ciel preignant,

12

 TRAITIÉ

Because the preceding poem in English [i.e., *Confessio Amantis*] was by way of example of the foolishness of those in particular who love in a courtly manner, now the subsequent treatise will be in French, for all the world generally, following the authorities, as an example for married lovers, in order that they might be able to protect the promise of their sacred spousal through perfect loyalty, and truly hold fast to the honor of God.

I   The Creator of every creature,
                 Who made the soul of man in His image,
                 In order that the body by reason and nature
                 Might be ruled with just governance,
5   Gave superiority to the soul;
                 Because He made it discreet and rational,
                 Reason is therefore constable over the body.

                 This soul in its rectitude loves God,
                 Exclusively to firm the heart
10   In such love that no misdeed
                 Of foul delight is able to put it in service
                 Of the weak flesh, which is always passing away:
                 But the good soul is holy and eternal;
                 Therefore reason is constable over the body.

15   In the soul lie reason and measure,
                 Because it will inherit heaven;
                 The body, in accord with the flesh, for engendering
                 Will have a good spouse in marriage;
                 Each has one essence and one condition,
20   To which the one or the other should be obedient:
                 Therefore reason is constable over the body.

II   From the spirit Love seeks continence,
                 And to live chaste, contemplating God alone;
                 The body by natural experience
                 Seeks to have a female, so that it might multiply;
5   With good souls the one seeks to make heaven replete,

Et l'autre emplist la terre de labour:
Si l'un est bon, l'autre est assetz meilour.

A l'espirit qui fait la providence
Ne poet failir de reguerdon suiant.
10   Plus est en l'alme celle intelligence,
Dont sanz null fin l'omme en serra vivant,
Qe n'est le corps en ses fils engendrant;
Et nepourqant tout fist le creatour:
Si l'un est bon, l'autre est assetz meilour.

15   A l'espirit dieus dona conscience,
Par quelle om ert du bien et mal sachant.
Le corps doit pas avoir la reverence,
Ainz ert a l'alme et humble et obeissant;
Mais dieus, qui les natures vait creant,
20   Et l'un et l'autre ad mis en son atour:
Si l'un est bon, l'autre est assetz meilour.

III   Au plus parfit dieus ne nous obligea,
☞   Mais il voet bien qe nous soions parfitz.   *(see note)*
Cist homme a dieu sa chasteté dona,
Et cist en dieu voet estre bons maritz:
5   S'il quiert avoir espouse a son avis,
Il plest a dieu de faire honeste issue
Selonc la loi de seinte eglise due.

Primerement qant mesmes dieus crea
Adam et Eve en son saint paradis,
10   L'omme ove la femme ensemble maria,
Dont ait la terre en lour semense emplis:
Lors fuist au point celle espousaile empris
Du viele loi, et puis, qant fuist venue,
Selonc la loi de seinte eglise due.

15   Et puisque dieus qui la loi ordina
En une char ad deux persones mis,
Droitz est qe l'omme et femme pourcela
Tout un soul coer eiont par tiel devis,
Loiale amie avoec loials amis:
20   C'est en amour trop belle retenue
Selonc la loi de seinte eglise due.

IV   Ovesque amour qant loialté s'aqueinte,
☞   Lors sont les noeces bones et joiouses;   *(see note)*

The other fills the earth with its labor:
If the one is good, the other is that much better.

From the spirit which does this, Providence
Cannot withhold a subsequent reward.
10 This understanding is greater in the soul,
By which a man will be alive eternally, without end,
Than in the body engendered in its sons;
And nonetheless, the Creator makes it all:
If the one is good, the other is that much better.

15 To the spirit God gives a conscience,
By which a man is aware of good and evil.
The body should not have reverence
But — on the contrary — be humble and obedient to the soul;
Yet God alone, who creates every nature,
20 Has given to one and the other its condition:
If the one is good, the other is that much better.

III   God does not compel us to be altogether perfect,
But He strongly desires that we be perfect.
One man promises chastity to God,
And another wishes to be well married:
5   If he seeks to have an agreeable wife,
It pleases God to create honest issue
According to the law set out by Holy Church.

In the beginning when God created
Adam and Eve in His holy paradise,
10 He married man and woman together,
By which means the earth filled with their offspring:
Thus, marriage was made at that time,
Under the Old Law, and since then, whenever it has taken place,
According to the law set out by Holy Church.

15 And since God who ordained the law
Placed two persons in one flesh,
It is meet that the male and the female therefore
Should have one single heart by that devising,
The loyal wife with the loyal husband:
20 Love is a most beautiful companionship,
According to the law set out by Holy Church.

IV   When Love acquaints itself with Loyalty,
Then weddings are good and joyous;

Mais li guilers, qant il se fait plus queinte,
Par falssemblant les fait sovent doubtouses,
5   A l'oill qant plus resemblont amorouses:
C'est ensi come de stouppes une corde,
Qant le penser a son semblant descorde.

Celle espousaile est assetz forte et seinte,
D'amour u sont les causes vertuouses:
10   Si l'espousaile est d'avarice enceinte,
Et qe les causes soient tricherouses,
Ja ne serront les noeces graciouses;
Car conscience toutdis se remorde,
Qant le penser a son semblant descorde.

15   Honest amour, q'ove loialté s'aqueinte,
Fait qe les noeces serront gloriouses;
Et qui son coer ad mis par tiele empeinte,
N'estoet doubter les changes perilouses.
Om dist qe noeces sont aventurouses;
20   Car la fortune en tiel lieu ne s'accorde,
Qant le penser a son semblant descorde.

V   Grant mervaile est et trop contre reson,
Q'om doit du propre chois sa femme eslire,
☞   Et puis confermer celle eleccion   (see note)
Par espousaile, et puis apres desdire
5   Sa foi, qant il de jour en jour desire
Novell amour assetz plus qe la beste:
Sa foi mentir n'est pas a l'omme honeste.

De l'espousailes la profession
Valt plus d'assetz qe jeo ne puiss descrire:
10   Soubtz cell habit prist incarnacion
De la virgine cil q'est nostre Sire:
Par quoi, des toutes partz qui bien remire,
En l'ordre de si tresseintisme geste
Sa foi mentir n'est pas a l'omme honeste.

15   De l'espousailes celle beneiçoun
Le sacrement de seinte eglise enspire:
C'est un liens, sanz dissolucioun
Q'om doit guarder; car quique voldra lisre
Le temps passé, il avera cause a dire,
20   Pour doubte de vengeance et de moleste,
Sa foi mentir n'est pas a l'omme honeste.

But the beguilers, when they make themselves most cunning,
Often create doubts by dissembling,
5   When to the eye they most resemble lovers:
It is thus like a rope of tow,
When the thought and its semblance disagree.

That marriage is strongest and most sanctified,
In which the causes of love are virtuous:
10   If the marriage is impregnated by Avarice,
And its causes are treacherous,
Then no nuptials will be gracious;
Because the conscience always is remorseful,
When the thought and its semblance disagree.

15   Honest love, which acquaints itself with loyalty,
Creates marriages that are glorious;
And whosoever sets his heart guided by such an impulse,
Need not be afraid of dangerous changes.
It is said that marriages are adventurous,
20   Because Fortune in such a case is discordant —
When the thought and its semblance disagree.

V   It is a great marvel and altogether against reason,
That a man should by his own choice select a wife,
And then confirm that election
By marriage, and immediately after disavow
5   His promise, when day after day he desires
Fresh love, more even than a beast does:
He who falsifies a promise is no honest man.

The profession of marriages
Is worth more than I am able to describe.
10   Under that guise He took incarnation
From the Virgin, He who is our Lord:
Because — let anyone take a second look at all aspects —
By command of so supremely sacred an act,
He who falsifies a promise is no honest man.

15   That benediction of marriages
Inspires the sacrament of Holy Church:
It is a bond, without dissolution,
Which one should protect; because whosoever might wish to understand
The times past, he will have cause to say,
20   For fear of vengeance and torment,
He who falsifies a promise is no honest man.

VI   Nectanabus, qui vint en Macedoine
☞   D'Egipte, u qu'il devant ot rois esté,   *(see note)*
               Olimpeas encontre matrimoine,
               L'espouse au roi Philipp, ad violé,
5   Dont Alisandre estoit lors engendré:
               Mais quoique soit du primere envoisure,
               Le fin demoustre toute l'aventure.

               Cil q'est de pecché pres sa grace esloigne:
               Ceo parust bien, car tiele destinée
10   Avint depuis, qe sanz nulle autre essoine
               Le fils occist, le pere tout de grée.
               Ore esgardetz coment fuist revengé
               D'avolterie celle forsfaiture:
14   Le fin demoustre toute l'aventure.

☞   Rois Uluxes pour plaire a sa caroigne   *(see note)*
               Falsoit sa foi devers Penolopé;
               Avoec Circes fist mesme la busoigne,
               Du quoi son fils Thelogonus fuist née,
               Q'ad puis son propre piere auci tué.
20   Q'il n'est plesant a dieu tiele engendrure,
               Le fin demoustre toute l'aventure.

VII   El grant desert d'Ynde superiour
☞   Cil qui d'arein les deux pilers fichoit,   *(see note)*
               Danz Hercules, prist femme a son honour
               Qe file au roi de Calidoine estoit;
5   Contre Achelons en armes conquestoit
               La belle Deianire par bataille.
               C'est grant peril de freindre l'espousaile.

               Bien tost apres tout changea cell amour
               Pour Eolen, dont il s'espouse haoit:
10   Celle Eolen fuist file a l'emperour
               D'Eurice, et Herculem tant assotoit,
               Q'elle ot de lui tout ceo q'avoir voloit.
               N'ert pas le fin semblable au comensaile;
               C'est grant peril de freindre l'espousaile.

15   Unqes ne fuist ne ja serra null jour,
               Qe tiel pecché de dieu vengé ne soit:
               Car Hercules, ensi com dist l'auctour,
               D'une chemise, dont il se vestoit,
               Fuist tant deceu, qu'il soi mesmes ardoit.

VI   Nectanabus — who came into Macedonia
      From Egypt, where earlier he had been king —
      Olimpeas, contrary to matrimony,
      The wife of King Philip, he ravished,
5   From which Alexander was then engendered:
      But whatever the first pleasure might be,
      The end reveals the full story.

      He who is close to sin sends grace fleeting.
      This appears clearly from such a destiny
10   As happened long thereafter: without any other cause,
      The son killed the father willfully.
      Now observe how was avenged
      This transgression of adultery:
      The end reveals the full story.

15   King Ulysses, to pleasure his carcass,
      Falsified his oath to Penelopé;
      With Circe he enacted the same business,
      From which his son Thelegonus was born,
      Who also afterwards killed his own father.
20   Such engendering is not pleasing to God:
      The end reveals the full story.

VII   In the vast desert of India the Greater,
      He who established therein the two pillars,
      Master Hercules, for his honor, took a woman
      Who was the daughter of the king of Caledonia;
5   At arms against Achelons he won
      The beautiful Deianira in battle.
      Great peril it is to break a marriage.

      Shortly thereafter his love changed entirely
      In favor of Eolen, so that he hated his wife:
10   This Eolen was the daughter of the emperor
      Of Euricie, and she made such a fool of Hercules
      That she had from him everything she wanted.
      The end is not like the beginning:
      Great peril it is to break a marriage.

15   Never has there been nor will there ever be a day
      When such sin would not be avenged by God:
      Because Hercules, so says the author,
      By a shirt in which he dressed himself,
      Was so completely deceived that he burned himself up.

20   De son mesfait porta le contretaille;
          C'est grant peril de freindre l'espousaile.

VIII   Li prus Jason, q'en l'isle de Colchos
☞   Le toison d'or par l'aide de Medée   *(see note)*
            Conquist, dont il d'onour portoit grant los,
            Par tout le monde en court la renomée,
5   La joefne dame ove soi ad amenée
            De son paiis en Grece, et l'espousa.
            Freinte espousaile dieus le vengera.

            Qant Medea meulx quide estre en repos
            Ove son mari, et q'elle avoit porté
10   Deux fils de lui, lors changea le purpos,
            El quel Jason primer fuist obligé:
            Il ad del tout Medeam refusé,
            Si prist la file au roi Creon Creusa.
            Freinte espousaile dieux le vengera.

15   Medea, q'ot le coer de dolour clos,
            En son corous, et ceo fuist grant pité,
            Ses joefnes fils, quex ot jadis enclos
            Deinz ses costées, ensi come forsenée
            Devant les oels Jason ele ad tué.
20   Ceo q'en fuist fait pecché le fortuna;
            Freinte espousaile dieus le vengera.

IX   Cil avoltiers qui fait continuance
            En ses pecchés et toutdis se delite,
☞   Poi crient de dieu et l'ire et la vengeance: *(see note)*
            Du quoi jeo trieus une Cronique escrite
5   Pour essampler; et si jeo le recite,
            L'en poet noter par ceo qu'il signifie,
            Horribles sont les mals d'avolterie.

            Agamenon, q'ot soubtz sa governance
            De les Gregois toute la flour eslite,
10   A Troie qant plus fuist en sa puissance,
            S'espouse, quelle estoit Climestre dite,
            Egistus l'ot de fol amour soubgite,
            Dont puis avint meinte grant felonie:
            Horribles sont les mals d'avolterie.

15   Agamenon de mort suffrist penance
            Par treson qe sa femme avoit confite;

20   For his misdeed he bore the retribution;
               Great peril it is to break a marriage.

VIII   The noble Jason — he who on the isle of Colchos
               The golden fleece with the aid of Medea
               Won (for which he gained great fame for honor,
               Renowned of everyone in court) —
5   Brought the young lady with him
               From her country into Greece, and married her.
               A broken marriage God will avenge.

               When Medea most trusted to be at peace
               With her husband, and when she had borne
10   Two sons by him, then he changed his purpose
               Toward her, to whom Jason was first bound:
               He rejected Medea outright,
               And took Creusa, daughter of Creon the king.
               A broken marriage God will avenge.

15   Medea, who had her heart closed by sadness,
               In her rage — and this was a great pity! —
               Her young sons, whom she had formerly enclosed
               Within her sides, just like a madwoman
               Killed them, right before Jason's eyes.
20   Such is the fortune of him who committed sin.
               A broken marriage God will avenge.

IX   Those adulterers who persevere
               In their sins, and always delight themselves,
               Little fear the anger or the vengeance of God:
               About which I find a chronicle written
5   As an example; and thus I tell it,
               So that one may be able to note what it signifies:
               Horrible are the evils of adultery.

               When Agamemnon, who had under his governance
               All the select flower of the Greeks,
10   Was at Troy at the height of his power,
               His wife, who was called Climestre,
               Egistus had subjected to foul love,
               From which afterward a great crime arose:
               Horrible are the evils of adultery.

15   Agamemnon suffered death as penance
               Through the treachery which his wife had arranged;

                Dont elle apres morust sanz repentance:
                Son propre fils Horestes l'ad despite,
                Dont de sa main receust la mort subite;
20   Egiste as fourches puis rendist sa vie:
                Horribles sont les mals d'avolterie.

X   La tresplus belle q'unqes fuist humeine,
☞   L'espouse a roi de Grece Menelai,   *(see note)*
                C'estoit la fole peccheresse Heleine,
                Pour qui Paris primer se faisoit gai;
5   Mais puis tornoit toute sa joie en wai,
                Qant Troie fuist destruite et mis en cendre:
                Si haut pecché covient en bass descendre.

☞   Tarquins auci, q'ot la pensé vileine,   *(see note)*
                Q'avoit pourgeu Lucrece a son essai,
10   Sanz null retour d'exil receust la peine;
                Et la dolente estoit en tiel esmai,
                Qe d'un cotell s'occist sanz null deslai:
                Ceo fuist pité, mais l'en doit bien entendre,
                Si haut pecché covient en bass descendre.

15   Mundus fuist prince de la Court Romeine,
☞   Qui deinz le temple Ysis el mois de Maii   *(see note)*
                Pourgeust Pauline, espouse et citezeine:
                Deux prestres enbastiront tout le plai.
                Bani fuist Munde en jugement verai,
20   Ysis destruit, li prestres vont au pendre:
                Si haut pecché covient en bass descendre.

XI   Albins, q'estoit un prince bataillous,
                Et fuist le primer roi de Lombardie,
☞   Occist, com cil qui fuist victorious,   *(see note)*
                Le roi Gurmond par sa chivalerie;
5   Si espousa sa file et tint cherie,
                La quelle ot noun la belle Rosemonde.
                Cil qui mal fait, falt qu'il au mal responde.

                Tiel espousaile ja n'ert gracious,
                U dieus les noeces point ne seintifie:
10   La dame, q'estoit pleine de corous
                A cause de son piere, n'ama mie
                Son droit mari, ainz est ailours amie;
                Elmeges la pourgeust et fist inmonde.
                Cil qui mal fait, falt qu'il au mal responde.

For which she died without repenting:
Her legitimate son Horestes hated her,
And immediately she received death at his hand;
20   Thereafter Egistus on the gallows gave up his life:
Horrible are the evils of adultery.

X   The most beautiful woman who ever was human,
The wife of the king of Greece, Menelaus,
Was the mad sinner Helen,
On account of whom Paris at first was joyful;
5   But thereafter all his joy turned to woe,
When Troy was destroyed and burned to ash:
Thus high sin must needs be brought low.

Tarquin also, who had villainous ideas,
Who had lain with Lucrece, to her danger,
10   Received the punishment: exile without return;
And the sorrowing woman was in such dismay,
That she with a knife killed herself without delay;
That was a pity, but it must be understood:
Thus high sin must needs be brought low.

15   Mundus was a prince in the Roman court,
Who within the temple of Isis in the month of May
Lay with Paulina, wife and citizen:
Two priests contrived the entire affair.
Mundus was banished, in a true judgment,
20   Isis destroyed, the priests went to the gallows;
Thus high sin must needs be brought low.

XI   Albinus, who was a warlike prince,
And the first king of Lombardy,
Killed, when victorious
Through his knighthood, King Gurmond;
5   He married his daughter and held her dear —
She who was called the beautiful Rosamunde:
One who does evil invokes an evil response.

Such a marriage is never gracious,
Wherever God does not sanctify the wedding at all:
10   The lady, who was full of anger
On account of her father, loved not at all
Her legal husband, but was another's beloved;
Helmege lay with her uncleanly.
One who does evil invokes an evil response.

15   Du pecché naist le fin malicious,
      Par grief poison Albins perdist la vie:
      Elmeges ove sa dame lecherous
      Estoient arsz pour lour grant felonie;
      Le duc q'ot lors Ravenne en sa baillie
20   En son paleis lour jugement exponde:
      Cil qui mal fait, falt qu'il au mal responde.

XII   Le noble roi d'Athenes Pandeon
           Deux files ot de son corps engendré,
☞   Qe Progne et Philomene avoient noun: *(see note)*
           A Tereüs fuist Progne mariée,
5   Cil fuist de Trace roi; mais la bealté
           De l'autre soer lui fist sa foi falser.
           Malvois amant reprent malvois loer.

           De foldelit contraire a sa reson
           Cil Tereüs par treson pourpensée
10   De Philomene en sa proteccion
           Ravist la flour de sa virginité,
           Contre sa foi, qu'il avoit espousée
           Progne sa soer, qui puis se fist venger:
           Malvois amant reprent malvois loer.

15   Trop fuist cruele celle vengeisoun:
           Un joefne fils qu'il ot de Progne né
           La miere occist, et en decoccion
           Tant fist qe Tereüs l'ad devorée;
           Dont dieus lui ad en hupe transformée,
20   En signe qu'il fuist fals et avoltier:
           Malvois amant reprent malvois loer.

XIII   Seint Abraham, chief de la viele loi,
           De Chanaan pour fuïr la famine
☞   Mena Sarrai sa femme ovesque soi   *(see note)*
           Tanq'en Egipte, u doubta la covine
5   De Pharao, qui prist a concubine
           Sarrai s'espouse, et en fist son voloir.
           En halt estat fait temprer le pooir.

           Cist Abraham, qui molt doubta le roi,
           N'osa desdire, ainz suffrist la ravine,
10   Pour pes avoir et se tenoit tout coi:
           Dont il fuist bien; du roi mais la falsine
           De son pecché par tiele discipline

15   From sin an evil end is born:
          Through grievous poison Albinus lost his life;
          Helmege and his lecherous lady
          Were burned for their great felony.
          The duke who had Ravenna in his charge
20   In his palace pronounced their judgment:
          One who does evil invokes an evil response.

XII   The noble king of Athens, Pandion,
          Had engendered two daughters of his body,
          Who were called Philomena and Progne:
          Progne was married to Tereus,
5   Who was king of Thrace; but the beauty
          Of the other sister caused him to falsify his oath.
          A wicked lover receives a wicked reward.

          With mad delight contrary to reason
          This Tereus, with malice aforethought,
10   From Philomena, who was in his protection,
          Ravished the flower of her virginity,
          Contrary to his oath, with which he had espoused
          Progne her sister, who thereafter avenged herself:
          A wicked lover receives a wicked reward.

15   This vengeance was most cruel:
          A lovely son, whom Progne had borne,
          The mother killed, and in a concoction
          Caused Tereus to devour his son;
          Thereafter God transformed him into a hoopoe,
20   As a sign that he was a false adulterer:
          A wicked lover receives a wicked reward.

XIII   The blessed Abraham, head of the Old Law,
          Out of Canaan in order to flee the famine
          Led Sarrai his wife with him
          Into Egypt, where he feared the designs
5   Of Pharaoh, who seized as a concubine
          Sarrai his wife, and with her worked his will.
          Power in high estate must be controlled.

          Abraham, who greatly feared the king,
          Dared say nothing, but endured the rapine,
10   In order to have peace, and maintained silence:
          Thereafter he was well; but the king's falsehood,
          His sin, with such punishment

Dieus chastioit, dont il poait veoir,
En halt estat fait temprer le pooir.

15   Soubdeinement, ainz qe l'en scieust pour quoi,
        Par toute Egipte espandist la morine;
        Dont Pharao, q'estoit en grant effroi,
        Rendist l'espouse, et ceo fuist medicine.
        A tiel pecché celle alme q'est encline,
20   Pour son delit covient au fin doloir:
        En halt estat fait temprer le pooir.

XIV   Trop est humaine char frele et vileine;
          Sanz grace nulls se poet contretenir:
☞   Ceo parust bien, sicom le bible enseine,   *(see note)*
          Qant roi David Urie fist moertrir
5   Pour Bersabée, dont il ot son plesir:
          Espouse estoit, mais il n'en avoit guarde;
          N'ert pas segeur de soi qui dieus ne guarde.

          La bealté q'il veoit ensi lui meine,
          Qu'il n'ot poair de son corps abstenir,
10   Maisqu'il chaoit d'amour en celle peine,
          Dont chastes ne se poait contenir:
          L'un mal causoit un autre mal venir,
          L'avolterie a l'omicide esguarde:
          N'ert pas segeur de soi qui dieus ne guarde.

15   Mais cil, qui dieus de sa pité remeine,
          David, se prist si fort a repentir,
          Q'unqes null homme en ceste vie humeine
          Ne receust tant de pleindre et de ghemir:
          Merci prioit, merci fuist son desir,
20   Merci troevoit, merci son point ne tarde.
          N'ert pas segeur de soi qui dieus ne guarde.

XV   Comunes sont la cronique et l'istoire
          De Lancelot et Tristrans ensement;
☞   Enqore maint lour sotie en memoire,   *(see note)*
          Pour essampler les autres du present:
5   Cil q'est guarni et nulle garde prent,
          Droitz est qu'il porte mesmes sa folie;
          Car beal oisel par autre se chastie.

          Tout temps del an om truist d'amour la foire,
          U que les coers Cupide done et vent:

God chastised, that he was able to understand:
Power in high estate must be controlled.

15 Suddenly, before he knew why,
Throughout all Egypt spread the murrain;
Then Pharaoh, who was greatly frightened,
Returned the wife, and that was the medicine.
The soul so disposed to do such sin,
20 For its delight sorrow must be its end.
Power in high estate must be controlled.

XIV Human flesh is exceedingly frail and base;
Without grace no one is able to defend himself:
That is apparent, as the Bible teaches,
When King David of Uriah became a murderer
5 For Bersabee; whereupon he had his pleasure:
Wife she was, but he cared not;
He has no security, whom God does not protect.

The beauty which he saw thus led him,
He who did not have the power to forbear his body,
10 But he fell into such pain of love —
Thus he was powerless to keep himself chaste.
The one evil causes another evil to come:
Adultery looks forward to murder.
He has no security, whom God does not protect.

15 But he whom God in His pity restored,
David, himself very forthrightly acted to repent,
So that — as no man ever in this human life —
He welcomed such mourning and groaning:
He prayed for mercy, mercy was his desire,
20 Mercy he found, mercy his point did not delay.
He has no security, whom God does not protect.

XV Common are the chronicle and the history
Of Lancelot and Tristan both;
Even yet their hubris remains in memory,
By way of an example to others in the present:
5 He who is warned and takes no care,
It is just that he himself carry the same folly:
Because the beautiful bird by means of another corrects itself.

All year long one finds the fair of love,
Where Cupid buys and sells hearts:

10   Deux tonealx ad, dont il les gentz fait boire,
        L'un est assetz plus douls qe n'est pyment,
        L'autre est amier plus que null arrement:
        Parentre deux falt q'om se modefie,
        Car beal oisel par autre se chastie.

15   As uns est blanche, as uns fortune est noire;
        Amour se torne trop diversement,
        Ore est en joie, ore est en purgatoire,
        Sanz point, sanz reule et sanz governement:
        Mais sur toutz autres il fait sagement,
20   Q'en fol amour ne se delite mie;
        Car beal oisel par autre se chastie.

XVI   Om truist plusours es vieles escriptures
          Prus et vailantz, q'ont d'armes le renoun,
☞   Mais poi furont q'entre les envoisures   *(see note)*
          Guarderont chaste lour condicion.
5   Cil rois qui Valentinians ot noun
          As les Romeins ceo dist en son avis,
          Qui sa char veint, sur toutz doit porter pris.

          Qui d'armes veint les fieres aventures,
          Du siecle en doit avoir le reguerdoun;
10   Mais qui du char poet veintre les pointures,
          Le ciel avera trestout a sa bandoun.
          Agardetz ore la comparisoun,
          Le quell valt plus, le monde ou Paradis:
          Qui sa char veint, sur toutz doit porter pris.

15   Amour les armes tient en ses droitures,
          Et est plus fort, car la profession
          De vrai amour surmonte les natures
          Et fait om vivre au loi de sa reson:
          En mariage est la perfeccioun;
20   Guardent lour foi cils q'ont celle ordre pris:
          Qui sa char veint, sur toutz doit porter pris.

XVII Amour est dit sanz partir d'un et une;
          Ceo voet la foi plevie au destre main:
          Mais qant li tierce d'amour se comune,
☞   Non est amour, ainz serra dit barguain.   *(see note)*
5   Trop se decroist q'ensi quiert avoir guain,
          Qui sa foi pert poi troeve d'avantage,
          A un est une assetz en mariage.

10   He has two casks, from which he makes men drink,
    One is sweeter than piment,
    The other more bitter than any ink:
    Between the two falls the man who controls himself,
    Because the beautiful bird by means of another corrects itself.

15   Toward one white, toward another Fortune is black;
    Love changes very diversely:
    One is joyful, another is in purgatory,
    Without purpose, without rule and without government:
    But above all others he acts sagely
20   Whom wanton love delights not at all;
    Because the beautiful bird by means of another corrects itself.

XVI   One finds often in ancient writings
    The brave and valiant, who have renown of arms,
    But few there are who between the snares
    Guard their chaste condition.
5   That king who was named Valentinian
    To the Romans gave his advice:
    Who overcomes his flesh, over all ought he bear the glory.

    He who by arms overcomes fierce adventures
    Ought to have the reward of the age;
10   But he who is able to overcome the stings of the flesh
    Will have heaven quickly in its power.
    Take heed now of the comparison:
    Which is worth more, the world or Paradise?
    Who overcomes his flesh, over all ought he bear the glory.

15   Love takes up arms in its uprightness,
    And is more robust, because the profession
    Of true love surmounts natures
    And makes one live according to the law of reason:
    In marriage is perfection;
20   They guard their faith who have this order taken.
    Who overcomes the flesh, over all ought he bear the glory.

XVII   Love is said [to be] a man and a woman without parting;
    This the faith pledged with the right hand requires:
    But when a third party shares love,
☞   It is not love — rather, it is called a business transaction.   *(see note)*
5   He loses too much, who seeks to have gain,
    Who loses his faith finds little profit,
    For one man one woman is enough in marriage.

      N'est pas compaigns q'est comun a chascune;
      Au soule amie ert un ami soulain:
10   Mais cil qui toutdis change sa fortune,
      Et ne voet estre en un soul lieu certain,
      Om le poet bien resembler a Gawain,
      Courtois d'amour, mais il fuist trop volage:
      A un est une assetz en mariage.

15   Semblables est au descroisçante lune
      Cil q'au primer se moustre entier et plain,
      Qant prent espouse, ou soit ceo blanche ou brune,
      Et quiert eschange avoir a l'endemain:
      Mais qui q'ensi son temps deguaste en vain
20   Doit bien sentir au fin de son passage,
      A un est une assetz en mariage.

XVIII   En propreteé cil qui del or habonde
☞   Molt fait grant tort s'il emble autri monoie: *(see note)*
               Cil q'ad s'espouse propre deinz sa bonde
               Grant pecché fait s'il quiert ailours sa proie.
5   Tiels chante, "c'est ma sovereine joie,"
               Qui puis en ad dolour sanz departie:
               N'est pas amant qui son amour mesguie.

               Des trois estatz benoitz c'est le seconde,
               Q'au mariage en droit amour se ploie;
10   Et qui cell ordre en foldelit confonde
               Trop poet doubter, s'il ne se reconvoie.
               Pource bon est qe chascun se pourvoie
               D'amer ensi, q'il n'ait sa foi blemie:
               N'est pas amant qui soun amour mesguie.

15   Deinz son recoi la conscience exponde
               A fol amant l'amour dont il foloie;
               Si lui covient au fin qu'il en responde
               Devant celui qui les consals desploie.
               O come li bons maritz son bien emploie,
20   Qant l'autre fol lerra sa fole amie!
               N'est pas amant qui son amour mesguie.

☞   Al universiteé de tout le monde   *(see note)*
               Johan Gower ceste Balade envoie;
               Et si jeo n'ai de François la faconde,
25   Pardonetz moi qe jeo de ceo forsvoie:
               Jeo sui Englois, si quier par tiele voie

It is not a companion who is common to everyone;
For a single beloved there shall be a single lover:
10   But he who always changes fortune,
And is not able to be in one single place steadfast,
That one rightly can resemble Gawain,
Courtly in love, but wholly fickle:
For one man one woman is enough in marriage.

15   He is similar to the waning moon
That at first shows itself whole and full,
When he takes a spouse, whether she be fair or dark,
And seeks to have a substitute the next day:
But he who wastes his time thus in vain
20   Will have to realize at the end of his passage,
For one man one woman is enough in marriage.

XVIII   Proprietarily, he who by right has gold
Does great wrong if he steals another's money:
Just so he who has a proper spouse in his bond
Does great sin if he seeks his prize elsewhere.
5   Many a one sings, "It is my sovereign joy,"
Who thereafter will have sorrow without remove:
He is not a lover who his love misguides.

Of the three estates, blessed is the second,
That to marriage in lawful love yields itself;
10   And whoever confounds that order in sinful pleasure
It is extremely doubtful that he will lead himself back.
Therefore it is good that each prepare himself
To love thus, who has not tarnished his promise:
He is not a lover who his love misguides.

15   In privacy the conscience sets forth
To the wanton lover the love to which he plays the fool;
Thus at last he is obliged to respond to it
Before the One who unfolds the counsels.
Oh how the good husband puts his goodness to use,
20   While the wanton other deserts his wanton lover!
He is not a lover who his love misguides.

To the community of the entire world
John Gower this Balade sends:
And if I do not have eloquence in French,
25   Pardon me when I go astray with it:
I am English — thus I seek in such a way

Estre excusé; mais quoique nulls en die,
L'amour parfit en dieu se justifie.

[Latin verses following the balades:]

Quis sit vel qualis sacer ordo connubialis
Scripsi, mentalis sit amor quod in ordine talis.
Exemplo veteri poterunt ventura timeri;
Cras caro sicut heri leuiter valet ilia moueri.
5   Non ita gaudebit sibi qui de carne placebit,
Quin corpus flebit aut spiritus inde dolebit:
Carne refrenatus qui se regit inmaculatus,
Omnes quosque status precellit in orbe beatus,
Ille deo gratus splendet ad omne latus.

To be excused; but whatever anyone may say about it,
Perfect love justifies itself in God.

[Latin verses following the balades:]

For whomsoever the sacred order of marriage may be,
I write, so that there may be such spiritual love in the order.
We may fear what is to come by the example of what is past;
Tomorrow as yesterday the flesh may be lightly stirred.
5   Thus he will not honor himself who will please the flesh:
Either the body laments or the spirit suffers because of it;
He who will reign immaculate must restrain the flesh.
And he whose blessed status will surpass all,
He will shine, wholly and broadly pleasing to God.

EXPLANATORY NOTES TO THE *TRAITIÉ*
SELONC LES AUCTOURS POUR ESSAMPLER LES AMANTZ MARIETZ

ABBREVIATIONS: B: Oxford, Bodleian Library, MS Bodley 294; *CA*: Gower, *Confessio Amantis*, ed. Peck; **F**: Oxford, Bodleian Library, MS Fairfax 3; **G**: Glasgow, University of Glasgow Library, MS Hunter 59 (T.2.17); **Mac**: Macaulay, ed., *The Complete Works of John Gower*; *MO*: Gower, *Mirour de l'Omme*, trans. Wilson; **S**: Oxford, All Souls College, MS 98; **T**: London, British Library, MS Additional 59495 (Trentham).

A note on capitalization: in these translations capitalization generally adheres to Macaulay's practice, which replicates forms in the manuscripts. Wherever capitalization may help the modern reader better comprehend Gower's intention — as for example, in the case of theological concepts (e.g., "Creator," *Traitié* I.1; "Providence," *Traitié* II.8) or allegorical figures (e.g., "Love," *Traitié* II.1; "Holy Church," *Traitié* III.7; "Danger," *Cinkante Balades* XXIII.10) — capitalization is added here.

Heading   *Puisqu'il . . . salvement tenir.* Found in those manuscripts, like F, when the *Traitié* follows *CA* ("ci devant en Englois"). Heading in F (with collation of B) reads:

> Puisqu'il ad dit ci devant en Englois par voie d'essample la sotie de cellui qui par amours aime par especial, dirra ore apres en François a tout le monde en general un traitié selonc les auctours pour essampler les amantz marietz, au fin q'ils la foi de lour seintes espousailes pourront par fine loialté guarder, et al honour de dieu salvement tenir. ["Because the preceding poem in English was by way of example of the foolishness of those in particular who love in a courtly manner, now the subsequent treatise will be in French, for all the world generally, following the authorities, as an example for married lovers, in order that they might be able to protect the promise of their sacred spousal through perfect loyalty, and truly hold fast to the honor of God."]

Alternate heading: Found in those manuscripts when the *Traitié* follows other poems, most frequently the *Vox Clamantis*, as in G. Heading in G (with collation of S and T) reads:

> Cest vn traitie quel Johan Gower ad fait selonc les auctours touchant lestat de matrimoine dont les amantz marietz se pourront essampler a tenir la foi de lour seintes espousailes. ["This is a treatise which John Gower made, following the authorities, concerning the matrimonial state, whereof married lovers might be able to take example for themselves and hold fast to the promise of their holy spousals."]

Heading line 3   *les auctours*. Macaulay (Mac, 1:lxxxiv) translates "authors." Our difference is perhaps marginal: Gower's concern is to "authorize" the positions he takes regarding marriage.

la foi. Lit. "faith" — and so Macaulay (Mac, 1:lxxxiv) who intends, I think, to emphasize the sanctity of the ceremony ("seintes espousailes"). In fourteenth-century England, however, a couple's shared promise sufficed alone to constitute legitimate marriage: no additional ceremony was necessary; see Gratian, *Decretum* 2.30.5.9, and Kelly, *Love and Marriage*, p. 165.

I LE CREATOUR DE TOUTE CREATURE

2 ff.   ☞ **Latin marginalia** in F: *Qualiter creator omnium rerum deus hominem duplicis nature, ex anima racionali et humana carne, in principo nobilem creauit; et qualiter anima ex sue crear cionis priuilegio supercorpus dominium possidebit.* ["How God the creator of all things in the beginning made man noble, with a double nature, rational from the soul and carnal from the body; and how the soul by virtue of its privileged creation with reason will have dominion over the body."]

3–4   *Par quoi le corps . . . governage*. On the propriety of reason's rule over the body, see Aquinas, *Summa Theologica* Q.75.a.6.; see also *Cinkante Balades* L.

8–12   *En dieu amer . . . frele char*. On the just capacity of the soul to protect the body through its firm love of God, see Aquinas, *Summa Theologica* Q.9.a.6.

19   *chose*. Lit. "thing, being."

20   *Qe l'un a l'autre soient entendable*. I.e., within their respective realms each holds authority.

II DE L'ESPIRIT L'AMOUR QUIERT CONTINENCE

2 ff.   ☞ **Latin marginalia** in F: *Qualiter spiritus, vt celum impleatur, castitatem affectat, et corpus, vt genus humanum in terra multiplicetur, coniugii copulam carnaliter concupiscit.* ["How the spirit, by heaven made full, honors chastity, and the body, in order that humankind be multiplied on earth, carnally desires the bond of marriage."]

5   *l'un fait le ciel preignant*. Gower alludes here to the notion that humankind will replenish with *bones almes* ("good souls") the absence in heaven caused by the fall of Lucifer and his cohorts. This idea is prominent in *CA*; see especially 8.30–36. The one (*l'un*) refers to the male.

7   *Si l'un est bon, l'autre est assetz meilour*. Following strictly the sequence in this stanza of "l'espirit" and "li corps" / "l'un" and "l'autre" the refrain would suggest that the soul's goodness is bettered by that of the body; but see I, above, and note 17–18, below.

17–18   *Le corps . . . obeissant.* While the hierarchy is clear, and orthodox — soul over body — the ambiguity of the refrain smacks of the intentional, as a bridge to the subsequent balade (III).

III AU PLUS PARFIT DIEUS NE NOUS OBLIGEA

2 ff.   ☞ **Latin marginalia** in F: *Qualiter virginalis castitas in gradu suo matrimonio prefertur: ambo tamen sub sacre conversacionis disciplina deo creatori placabilia consistunt.* ["How, by the virginal, chastity is preferred in place of marriage: nevertheless, both, under the sacred discipline of regular intercourse created by God, become acceptable."]

10   *ove.* Lit. "with."

19   *Loiale amie avoec loials amis.* Lit. "Loyal lover (female) with loyal lover (male)": no equivalent exists in Modern English for Gower's inflected forms.

20   *retenue.* Lit. "retinue, following," invoking the feudal vow of loyal service, vassalage. Macaulay (Mac, 1:463, note VIII.17) glosses as "engagement"; see *Cinkante Balades* VIII.17, XV.14. Note the considerable play here on "loiale/loials/loi" and in IV following.

IV OVESQUE AMOUR QANT LOIALTÉ S'AQUEINTE

2 ff.   ☞ **Latin marginalia** in F: *Qualiter honestas coniugii non ex libidinis aut auaricie causa, set tantummodo quod sub lege generacio ad cultum dei fiat, primordia sua suscepit.* ["How the virtue of marriage takes her origin not of lust or avarice, but only under the law of generation, as the reverence of God decrees."]

6   *C'est ensi come de stouppes une corde.* ["It is thus like a rope of tow."] On the worthlessness of straw (tow), see *CA* 5.5623 and 5.5626; cited in Whiting (*Chaucer's Use of Proverbs*, p. 297) as a proverbial phrase.

10   *d'avarice enceinte.* I.e., marriages contracted for gain.

V GRANT MERVAILE EST ET TROP CONTRE RESON

3 ff.   ☞ **Latin marginalia** in F: *Qualiter matrimonii sacramentum, quod ex duorum mutuo consensu sub fidei iuramento firmius astringitur, propter diuine vindicte offensam euitandam nullatenus dissolui debet.* ["How the sacrament of marriage, which is more firmly bound together by a mutual consent of two people under an oath of faith, ought under no circumstances whatsoever be loosened, a deadly offense worthy of divine retribution."]

10–11   *Soubtz cell habit . . . Sire.* I.e., the wedding of Mary and Joseph preceded the Incarnation, and was a true marriage; see Aquinas, *Summa Theologica*, Q.29.a.1–2.

15–16   *De l'espousailes . . . enspire.* That the marriage of man and woman was a sacramental mirroring of Christ's spiritual union with the Church originates in Paul (Ephesians 5:22–32: "Sacramentum hoc magnum est, ego autem dico in Christo et in Ecclesia," at 32), was defended by Augustine (*De bono coniugii*, 24; *De nuptiis et concupiscentia* I.10) and dogmatized by Innocent IV in 1208; later biblical literalists, including Lollards (and Wyclif specifically, see, e.g., *Of Wedded Men and Wives*), denied the necessity of clerical participation — which may underlie Gower's admonitory tone here.

15   *l'espousailes.* Macaulay (Mac, 1:470, note V.8) observes "this use of 'li' as fem. plur. is rather irregular."

20   *moleste.* Perhaps merely "trouble, vexation," but compare "propter divine vindicte" in the associated marginal gloss.

VI NECTANABUS, QUI VINT EN MACEDOINE

1   *Nectanabus.* Gower's major source is Thomas of Kent's *Roman de toute chevalerie*, supplemented by the *Historia Alexandri de preliis*; see Macaulay's note (Mac, 3:519); see also *CA* 6.1789–2366.

2 ff.   ☞ **Latin marginalia** in F: *Nota hic contra illos qui nuper sponsalia sua violantes in penam grauis vindicte dilapsi sunt. Et primo narrat qualiter Nectanabus rex Egipti ex Olimpiade vxore Philippi regis Macedonie magnum Alexandrum in adulterio genuit, qui postea patrem suum fortuito casu interfecit.* ["Note this, against those who, lately violating their espousal, by retribution perish in grave punishment. And first it is told how Nectanabus, king of Egypt, begot in adultery upon Olympias, wife of Philip, king of Macedonia, the great Alexander, who later through an act of fortune killed his father."]

6   *envoisure.* Lit. "joy, disport, enjoyment"; Macaulay (Mac, 1:471, note VI.6) translates "trickery, deceit"; but see XVI.3, below.

10   *sanz nulle autre essoine.* Following Macaulay, "cause" (Mac, 1:471, note VI.10); but lit. "hindrance, difficulty."

15ff.   ☞ **Latin marginalia** in F: *Qualiter Vluxes Penolope sponsus in insula Cilli Circen ibidem reginam adulterando Thelogonum genuit, qui postea propriis manibus patrem suum mortaliter iaculo transfodit.* ["How Ulysses the husband of Penelope on the island of Sicily adulterously begot upon Circe the queen Thelogonus, who later with his own hands mortally transfixed his own father with a spear."]

15   *Rois Uluxes.* See *CA* 6.1391–1781; *MO* lines 16673–92.

         caroigne. Lit. "carrion, corpse."

17   *mesme la busoigne.* Compare "la besoigne d'amors"=sexual intercourse; i.e., Ulysses
          and Nectanabus commit the same sin, with the same results.

VII EL GRANT DESERT D'YNDE SUPERIOUR

1   *El grant desert d'Ynde superiour.* "Greater India" for Gower meant essentially the
          subcontinent, including Afghanistan; see Pliny, *Natural History*, V.iv. On the
          desert, Gower's source undoubtedly was the *Epistola Alexandri ad Aristotelem*.

2 ff.   ☞ **Latin marginalia** in F: *Qualiter Hercules, qui Deianiram regis Calidonie filiam
          desponsauit, ipsam postea propter amorem Eolen Euricie Imperatoris filiam a se penitus
          amouit. Vnde ipse cautelis Achelontis ex incendio postea periit.* ["How Hercules, who
          married Deianira, daughter of the king of Caledonia, later banished her utterly
          from himself on account of loving Eolen, daughter of the emperor of Eurice. For
          that, by a trick of Achelons, he later perished in flames."] *cautelis Achelonis.* I.e.,
          the shirt poisoned with the centaur Nessus' blood (Ovid, *Heroides* IX), not by
          agency of Achelons.

2   *Cil qui d'arein les deux pilers fichoit.* See Chaucer's Sir Thopas, *Canterbury Tales*
          VII[B^2]2117–18.

3–6   *Hercules . . . Deianire.* See *Cinkante Balades* XLIII; *CA* 2.2145–2307, especially
          2259 ff.; Ovid, *Heroides* IX.

5   *Achelons.* See *CA* 4.2068.

11   *D'Eurice.* Macaulay (Mac, 1:471, note VII.11) states: "'Euricie' in the Latin margin;
          compare 'The kinges dowhter of Eurice,' *CA* 2.2267. It is taken as the name of
          a country, but no doubt this results from a misunderstanding of some such ex-
          pression as Ovid's 'Eurytiodosque Ioles,' 'of Iole the daughter of Eurytus,' taken
          to mean 'Eurytian Iole.'"

17   *l'auctour.* I.e., Ovid.

VIII LI PRUS JASON, Q'EN L'ISLE DE COLCHOS

1–2   *Jason . . . Medée.* See *MO* lines 3725–30; *CA* 5.3247–4237; *Cinkante Balades* XLIII;
          Ovid, *Heroides* XII.

2 ff.   ☞ **Latin marginalia** in F: *Qualiter Iason vxorem suam Medeam relinquens Creusam
          Creontis regis filiam sibi carnaliter copulauit; vnde ipse cum duobus filiis suis postea
          infortunatus decessit.* ["How Jason, giving up his wife Medea, carnally coupled with
          Creusa, daughter of king Creon; for that he later perished, miserable, along with
          two of his sons."]

20   *Ceo q'en fuist fait pecché le fortuna.* "Such is the fortune of him who committed sin";
          or perhaps "He who commits sin risks this."

IX CIL AVOLTIERS QUI FAIT CONTINUANCE

3 ff.   ☞ **Latin marginalia** in F: *Qualiter Egistus, Climestram regis Agamenontis vxorem adulterando, ipsum regem in lecto noctanter dormientem proditorie interfecit, cuius mortem Orestes filius eius crudelissime vindicauit.* ["How Egistus, having committed adultery with Climestra, wife of king Agamenon, at night treacherously killed that king, sleeping in bed; whose death his son Orestes avenged most cruelly."] *in lecto noctanter dormientem.* A detail not found in Benoît de Ste.-More, *Roman de Troie*, but in Guido della Colonna's *Historia destructionis Troiana*: see Macaulay's note (Mac, 2:499).

8–12   *Agamenon . . . Climestre . . . Egistus.* See *CA* 3.1885–2195; Gower's primary source is Benoît, *Roman de Troie*, lines 27925–90, 28155–28283, and 28339–28402.

X LA TRESPLUS BELLE Q'UNQES FUIST HUMEINE

2 ff.   ☞ **Latin marginalia** in F: *Qualiter ex adulterio Helene vxoris Menelai regis Troia magna in cineres conuersa pro perpetuo desolata permansit.* ["How through the adultery of Helen, the wife of king Menelaus, great Troy, turned to ashes, remained forever forsaken."]

2–4   *Menelai . . . Heleine . . . Paris.* See *Cinkante Balades* XIIII, XL.

8 ff.   ☞ **Latin marginalia** in F: *Qualiter ob hoc quod Lucrecia Rome Collatini sponsa vi oppressa pre dolore interiit, Tarquinus ibidem rex vna cum Arronte filio suo, qui sceleris auctores extiterant, pro perpe tuo exheredati exilium subierunt.* ["How, because of the fact that Lucrecia, wife of Collatin, oppressed by force in Rome, died in anguish, King Tarquin, together with Arrontes his son, originators of the crime, were ruined, were cast down, permanently disinherited."]

8–9   *Tarquins . . . Lucrece.* See *CA* 7.4754–5123. Gower's source is Ovid, *Fasti* II.687–720.

15–17   *Mundus . . . Pauline.* See *CA* 1.761–1059. Macaulay (Mac, 2:470) suggests Vincent of Beauvais' *Speculum Historiale* VII.iv as Gower's source.

16 ff.   ☞ **Latin marginalia** in F: *Qualiter Mundus Romane milicie princeps nobilem Paulinam in templo Isis decepit; vnde ipse cum duobus presbiteris sibi confederatis iudicialiter perierunt.* ["How the Roman general and prince Mundus deceived the noble Paulina in the temple of Ysis; for that he justly perished, along with the two priests, his confederates."]

18   *enbastiront tout le plai.* Macaulay (Mac, 3:471, note X.18) observes: "The word 'plait' or 'plee' means properly a process at law, hence a process or design of any kind: 'bastir un plait' is the same thing as 'faire un plait,' used of designing or proposing a thing."

XI ALBINS, Q'ESTOIT UN PRINCE BATAILLOUS

1–13   *Albins . . . Rosemonde . . . Elmeges.* See *CA* 1.2459–2646. Gower's source seems to have been Godfrey of Viterbo's *Pantheon* XVII; see Macaulay's note (Mac, 2:476–77).

3 ff.   ☞ **Latin marginalia** in F: *Qualiter Helmeges miles Rosemundam regis Gurmondi filiam Albinique primi regis Longobardorum vxorem adulterauit: vnde ipso rege mortaliter intoxicato dictam vxorem cum suo adultero dux Rauenne conuictos pene mortis adiudicauit.* ["How the knight Helmeges committed adultery with Rosemunda, daughter of King Gurmond and wife of Albinus, distinguished king of the Lombards: for that the duke of Ravenna doomed him and his adulterous partner, the wife at whose order he mortally poisoned the king, together to the penalty of death."]

3   *com cil qui fuist victorious.* Lit. "in the manner of one who was victorious."

17–18   *sa dame lecherous . . . Estoient arsz.* In *CA* no hint is given of Rosemund's lechery; her motive is simply vengeance and her means political. Their death is brought about by poison, as in the Latin marginalia 3 ff., rather than by burning as the French text says here.

XII LE NOBLE ROI D'ATHENES PANDEON

1–4   *Pandeon . . . Progne . . . Philomene . . . Tereüs.* See *CA* 5.5551–6047. Gower's source is Ovid, *Metamorphoses* VI.424–674.

3 ff.   ☞ **Latin marginalia** in F: *Qualiter Tereus rex Tracie Prognem filiam Pandeon regis Athenarum in vxorem duxit, et postea Philomenam dicte vxoris sue sororem virginem vi oppressit. Vnde dicte sorores in peccati vindictam filium suum infantem ex Progne genitum variis decocionibus in cibos transformatum comedere fecerunt.* ["How Tereus, king of Thrace, took Progne, daughter of Pandeon, king of Athens, to wife, and afterward forcibly oppressed the virginity of her sister, Philomena. For that the two sisters, in revenge for the sin, made [him] eat his infant son by Progne, transformed by diverse boilings into food."]

9   *treson.* Lit. "treason, treachery."

19   *hupe.* See *CA* 5.6041, where Tereus is transformed into "a lappewincke mad." Both the hoopoe (*Upupa epops*) and the lapwing (*Vanellus vanellus* — probably, since it is more common) have distinctive but similar crests and could be confused. Interestingly, in the context of infanticide, is *Physiologus'* description of the hoopoe: "There is a bird called the hoopoe; if the young see their parents grow old and their eyes dim, they preen the parents' feathers and lick their eyes and warm their parents beneath their wings and nourish them as a reciprocation just as they nourished their chicks, and they become new parents of their own parents" (trans. Curley, pp. 14–15); see also "Epopus" in *Bestiary* (trans. White, pp. 131–32); but compare with "Upupa" (*Bestiary*, trans. White, p. 150); also "the

Hoopoe," which "lines its nest with human dung. The filthy creature feeds on stinking excrement. He lives on this in graves. . . . If anybody smears himself with the blood of this bird on his way to bed, he will have nightmares about suffocating devils" (*Bestiary*, trans. White, p. 150). See also *MO* line 8869.

XIII SEINT ABRAHAM, CHIEF DE LA VIELE LOI

1–5   *Abraham . . . Sarrai . . . Pharao*. See Genesis 12:10–20.

3 ff.   ☞ **Latin marginalia** in F: *Qualiter pro eo quod Pharao rex Egipti Sarrai vxorem Abrahe ob carnis concupiscenciam impudice tractauit, pestilencia per vniuersum Egiptum peccatum vindcauit.* ["How, because Pharaoh, king of Egypt, on account of desire of the flesh, treated Sarai the wife of Abraham shamelessly, pestilence avenged the sin throughout all Egypt."]

16   *la morine.* "the murrain," i.e., a plague especially affecting animals.

XIV TROP EST HUMAINE CHAR FRELE ET VILEINE

3 ff.   ☞ **Latin marginalia** in F: *Qualiter ob peccatum regis Dauid, de eo quod ipse Bersabee sponsam Vrie ex adulterio impregnauit, summus Iudex infantem natum patre penitente sepulcro defunctum tradidit.* ["How because of sin of the king David, who himself adulterously impregnated Bethsabee, wife of Urias, the greatest Judge consigned the child born to the penitent father dead to the grave."] *summus Iudex infantem . . . tradidit.* See 2 Kings 12:14–23.

4–5   *David . . . Urie . . . Bersabée.* See 2 Kings 11:1–27 and 12:1–13.

XV COMUNES SONT LA CRONIQUE ET L'ISTOIRE

Macaulay (Mac, 1:472, note XV.1–10) notices "losses at the beginnings of these lines in the Fairfax MS are as follows: Comun / De lan / Enqore ma / Pour essamp / Cil q'est gu / Droitz est / Car be / To / U que / Deu."

2   *Lancelot . . . Tristrans.* See *CA* 8.2500–01; *Cinkante Balades* XLIII.

3 ff.   ☞ **Latin marginalia** in F: *Qualiter ob hoc quod Lanceolotus Miles probatissimus Gunnoram regis Arthuri vxorem fatue permauit, eciam et quia Tristram simili modo Isoldam regis Marci auunculi sui vxorem violare non timuit, Amantes ambo predicti magno infortunii dolore dies suos extremos clauserunt.* ["How because the most honored knight Lancelot by fate inordinately loved Gunnora, the wife of King Arthur and also because Tristram feared not to violate in a similar way Isold the wife of his uncle King Mark, it was foretold that both lovers ended their days in extreme misery."]

7   *Car beal oisel par autre se chastie.* Macaulay (Mac, 1:472, note 7) compares *MO* line
           7969.

10–13   *Deux tonealx . . . se modefie.* See Boethius, *Consolation of Philosophy*, II.pr.2; *Roman
           de la Rose*, lines 6783–96 and 10597–10603. The origin is Homer, *Iliad* XXIV.527
           ff. See also *CA* 6.330–90.

15   *As uns est blanche, as uns fortune est noire.* ["Toward one white, toward another
           Fortune is black."] Fortuna was frequently portrayed as having a divided face,
           half black and half white.

XVI OM TRUIST PLUSOURS ES VIELES ESCRIPTURES

3 ff.   ☞ **Latin marginalia** in F: *Qualiter Princeps qui sue carnis concupiscenciam exuperat
                pre ceteris laudabilior existit. Narrat enim quod cum probus Valentinianus Imperator
                octogenarius in armis floruit, et suorum preliorum gesta coram eo publice decantabantur,
                asseruit se de victoria sue carnis, cuius ipse motus illecebros extinxerat, magis letari, quam
                si ipse vniuersas mundi partes in gladio belliger subiugasset.* ["How the Prince who
                overcame his fleshly desire lived the more praised among [all] others. It tells also
                how the wise octogenarian Emperor Valentinian flourished in arms, and, his
                deeds of battle having been sung openly by the public, he claimed for himself
                victory of his flesh, whose illicit urgings he himself abolished — a greater thing
                to be killed, than if he subjugated every part of the world waging war with a
                sword."]

5   *Valentinians.* See *CA* 5.6395–6416; *MO* line 17089. Macaulay (Mac, 3:507)
           suggests the *Epistola Valerii ad Rufinum* as Gower's source. Valentinian I (A.D.
           364–75) seems the most likely of the three emperors by that name to have been
           the origin of this apocryphal story.

XVII AMOUR EST DIT SANZ PARTIR D'UN ET UNE

2   *Ceo voet la foi plevie au destre main* ["The brave and valiant, who have renown of
           arms"]. I.e., in the acknowledged gesture of an oath; see *Cinkante Balades* XXIII,
           stanza 1.

4 ff.   ☞ **Latin marginalia** in F: *Nota hic quod secundum iura ecclesie, vt sint duo in carne
                vna tantum ad sacri coniugii perfeccionem et non aliter expediens est.* ["Take note here
                the fact that according to the laws of the church, two may be one in the flesh only
                through the perfection of holy matrimony, and not otherwise is it permitted."]

4   *barguain.* "Business transaction" is a bit flat, given the intensity of Gower's feeling
           on this point. Perhaps "arbitrage" would be a better equivalent as the Old
           French word has been adopted by corporate America to define the "simultaneous
           purchase and sale of the same equivalent security in order to profit from price

discrepancies," which gets well at the manipulation of marriage in a bull market for gain that Gower finds so perverse.

9   *ert.* Both future and conditional forms express imperative, apparently as needed for the meter; see *MO* line 17689.

12   *Gawain.* Macaulay (Mac, 1:472, note XVII.13) remarks, "This is the traditional character of Gawain 'the Courteous.'" See Thompson and Busby, *Gawain*, pp. 52–62, on Gawain's amorousness and promiscuity in numerous French and English romances.

XVIII EN PROPRETEÉ CIL QUI DEL OR HABONDE

1   *En propreteé.* Lit. "particularity, the particular, property." The intent seems to be to create a contrast between stealing gold — i.e., the realm of property — and stealing a wife, the latter the more sinful since it involves violating a vow.

2 ff.   ☞ **Latin marginalia** in F: *Nota hic secundum auctores quod sponsi fideles ex sui regiminis discreta bonitate vxores sibi fidissimas conseruant. Vnde ipsi ad inuicem congaudentes felicius in domino conualescunt.* ["Take note here according to the authors that faithful husbands, because of the moral goodness of their governance, had maintained wives most faithful to them. Whence they themselves, mutually rejoicing the more together, gained strength in God."]

3   *deinz sa bonde.* I.e., joined in matrimony; compare "marriage bond."

8   *Des trois estatz.* The three estates of human life: virginity, chaste marriage, and chaste widowhood.

17   *en.* The antecedent is "la conscience."

18   *celui qui.* I.e., God the Judge.

22 ff.   ☞ **Latin marginalia** in F: *Hic in fine Gower, qui Anglicus est, sua verba Gallica, si que incongrua fuerint, excusat.* ["Here in conclusion Gower, who is English, excuses (apologizes for) his French words, those that may have been discordant."]

TEXTUAL NOTES TO THE *TRAITIÉ*
SELONC LES AUCTOURS POUR ESSAMPLER LES AMANTZ MARIETZ

ABBREVIATIONS: B: Oxford, Bodleian Library, MS Bodley 294; **F**: Oxford, Bodleian Library, MS Fairfax 3 (base text); **G**: Glasgow, University of Glasgow Library, MS Hunter 59 (T.2.17); **Mac**: Macaulay, ed., *The Complete Works of John Gower*; **S**: Oxford, All Souls College, MS 98; **T**: London, British Library, MS Additional 59495 (Trentham).

Macaulay notes: "The text is that of F with collation of S, G, and T. A full collation of B is given for the heading and it is occasionally cited afterwards" (Mac, 1:379).

Macaulay notes: "S T are imperfect at the beginning" (Mac, 1:379).

Heading	*Pusiqu'il.* F: *Pvsquil.*
	ci. B: *cy.*
	Englois. B: *englois.*
	cellui. B: *celluy.*
	François. B: *franceis.*
	un. F: *une.*
	selonc les. B: *solonc les.*
	pour essampler. B: *pur ensampler.*
	foi. B: *foy.*
	seintes. B: *seints.*
	pourront. B: *purront.*
1 ff.	(Latin marginalia) *possidebit.* B: *possidebat.*

I LE CREATOUR DE TOUTE CREATURE

7	*raison ert conestable.* G: *Raison ert Conestable.*
12	*De.* G: *Du.*
14, 21	*raison ert conestable.* G: *Raison ert Conestable.*
15	*raison.* G: *reson.*

II DE L'ESPIRIT L'AMOUR QUIERT CONTINENCE

9	Mac: "The text of T begins here."
13	*tout.* T: *toute.*

III AU PLUS PARFIT DIEUS NE NOUS OBLIGEA

4	Mac: "The text of S begins here."
5	*quiert.* So S, T, G. F: *quier.*
7	*seinte.* S, T: *seint.*
14	*seinte.* S: *seint.*
	eglise. F, G: *esglise.*
21	*eglise.* F: *esglise.*

IV OVESQUE AMOUR QANT LOIALTÉ S'AQUEINTE

1 ff.	(Latin marginalia) *libidinis.* S: *libidine.*
3	*li.* G, B: *lui.*
	guilers. S, T, G: *guiliers.*
6	*come.* S, T: *com.*
20	*s'accorde.* S, T: *saacorde.*

V GRANT MERVAILE EST ET TROP CONTRE RESON

1	*mervaile.* S: *merveile.*
3	*puis.* T: *puiss.*
13	*tresseintisme.* T: *tressentisme.*
15	*l'espousailes.* T: *lespousails.*
	beneiçoun. S: *beneiceon.* G: *beneicon.*
16	*eglise.* S: *esglise.*
17	*dissolucioun.* S: *dissolucion.*
20	*vengeance.* T: *vengance.*

VI NECTANABUS, QUI VINT EN MACEDOINE

7, 14, 21	*demoustre.* T: *demonstre.*
8	*esloigne.* S, G: *eloigne.*
9	*destinée.* S: *destine.*
10	*sanz.* S omits.

VII EL GRANT DESERT D'YNDE SUPERIOUR

2	*d'arein.* T: *darrein.*
4	*de.* S omits.
6	*bataille.* T: *bataile.*
8	*cell.* T: *celle.*
10	*file.* T: *fille.*
16	*vengé.* S, G: *vengee.*
19	*tant.* S omits.
	qu'il. S, G: *qil.*
20	*contretaille.* S, G, T: *contretaile.*

VIII Li prus Jason, q'en l'isle de Colchos

3	*los.* T: *loos.*
10	*lui.* T: *luy.*
11	*quel.* S, G: *quell.* T: *quelle.*
15	*clos.* T: *cloos.*
17	*quex.* T: *queux.*
18	*come.* S, T: *com.*

IX Cil avoltiers qui fait continuance

1 ff.	(Latin marginalia) *Climestram.* S, T, G: *Clemestram.*
4	*Cronique.* S: *croniqe.*
6	*ceo.* F: *se.*
	qu'il. S, T, G: *qil.*
17	*repentance.* S: *repentace.*
18	*Horestes.* T: *Orestes.*

X La tresplus belle q'unqes fuist humeine

3	*C'estoit.* S: *Estoit.*
4	*qui.* T: *quoi.*
	se. S omits.
5	*wai.* T: *way.*
7	*haut.* T: *halt.*
8	*Tarquins.* T: *Tarquinus.*
	pensé. S, T, G: *pensee.*
10	*null.* T: *nul.*
12	*cotell.* So F, T, G. S: *coutell.*
14	*haut.* T: *halt.*
15 ff.	(Latin marginalia) *Paulinam.* So T, (by correction) G. F, S: *Paulinum.*
18	*enbastiront.* T: *embastiront.*
19	*jugement.* S, T, G: *juggement.*
20	*prestres.* S, T, G: *prestre.*
21	*haut.* T: *halt.*

XI Albins, q'estoit un prince bataillous

1 ff.	(Latin marginalia) *Helmeges.* S: *Elmeges.*
	Gurmondi. S, G: *Gurumundi.*
	Albinique. F: *Abbinique.*
5	*file.* T: *fille.*
8	*Tiel.* T: *Ciel.*
9	*seintifie.* T: *seintefie.*
12	*ailours.* S: *aillours.*
18	*Estoient.* S, T, G: *estoiont.*
	arsz. S: *ars.*

19   *q'ot.* T: *quot.*
20   *jugement.* S, T, G: *juggement.*

XII LE NOBLE ROI D'ATHENES PANDEON

1 ff.   (Latin marginalia) *transformatum.* S, T, B: *transmutatum.*
3   *avoiont.* T: *avoient.*
6   *lui.* T: *li.*
16   *né.* T: *nee.*
18   *devorée.* T: *devouree.*
19   *transformée.* T: *transforme.*
20   *qu'il fuist.* T: *qui fuist.*

XIII SEINT ABRAHAM, CHIEF DE LA VIELE LOI

7   *halt.* F: *haut.*
8   *molt . . . roi.* T: *moult . . . Roy.*
10   *coi.* T: *coy.*
11   *falsine.* F: *falsisine.*
17   *effroi.* T: *esfroi.*
19   *celle.* T: *cel.*

XIV TROP EST HUMAINE CHAR FRELE ET VILEINE

1 ff.   (Latin marginalia) *Bersabee.* S: *Bersabe.*
            sepulcro. So F, B. S, T, G: *sepulture.*
1   *humaine.* T: *lumaine.*
3   *le bible.* S: *la Bible.* T, G: *la bible.*
            enseine. S: *enseigne.*
8   *q'il.* S, G: *quil.*
9   *Qu'il.* S: *Qil.*
12   *un autre.* F: *lautre.*

XV COMUNES SONT LA CRONIQUE ET L'ISTOIRE

Macaulay notes: "Owing to a slight damage to the leaf the beginnings of the first ten lines and a few syllables of the marginal summary are wanting in F" (1:389). See headnote to the explanatory notes for XV, p. 41 above.

1 ff.   (Latin marginalia) *extremos.* S, G: *exremos.*
1   *l'istoire.* S, G: *lestoire.*
4   *du.* S, G: *de.*
6   *sa.* T: *la.*
8   *truist . . . foire.* T: *trust . . . ffoire.*
14   *oisel.* T: *oiseal.*

XVI OM TRUIST PLUSOURS ES VIELES ESCRIPTURES

1	*es.* So S, G, B. T: *et.* F: *de.*
6	*Romeins.* T: *Romeines.*
10	*poet.* S: *poeit.*
12	*Agardetz.* G: *Agardes.*
	comparisoun. S, G: *comparison.*
19	*perfeccioun.* S, G: *perfeccion.*
20	*celle.* S: *cell.*

XVII AMOUR EST DIT SANZ PARTIR D'UN ET UNE

1 ff.	(Latin marginalia) *duo.* F: *due.*
6	*troeve.* T: *troue.*
16	*primer.* F: *primere.*
	moustre. T: *monstre*(?).

XVIII EN PROPRETEÉ CIL QUI DEL OR HABONDE

2	*s'il.* S: *cil.*
4	*ailours.* T: *aillours.*
12	*Pource.* S, T, G: *Pourceo.*
	pourvoie. S, G: *purvoie.*
13	*q'il.* S, G: *quil.*
	n'ait. G: *naid.*
14	*soun.* So F. S, T, G: *son.*
19	*come.* T: *com.*
23	*Johan.* S, G: *Iehan.*
25	*forsvoie.* G: *forvoie.*

Introduction to the *Cinkante Balades*

Title

The title by which these poems are known descends from Thomas Warton, who in the eighteenth century discovered Gower's sequence and first published four of "the Cinkante Balades or fifty French Sonnets" he found in a manuscript then belonging to Earl Gower (a relation in name only).[1] Warton himself seems to have obtained this number, and hence his title, from the damaged heading preceding Balade I: "Si apres sont escrites en françois Cinkante balades, quelles . . . d fait, dont les . . . ment desporter" ("Here following are written in French fifty balades, which . . . made, in order to entertain the . . ."). In fact, the "Cinkante" balades in London, British Library, MS Additional 59495 amount to what would have been fifty-four, including two dedicating the rest to Henry IV (the second of which is defective), two both numbered "IIII," one assumes by mistake, and a final balade addressed to the Virgin. The latter, while fully within the window of style and amorous language established by the sequence, seems nonetheless to have been intended as a coda, in that it directs love at last toward heaven and away from earthly concerns. Despite the various additions, there can be little doubt, for reasons discussed below, that Gower deliberately chose to announce that his sequence included fifty balades. Warton's title, in other words, is thus more apt than he imagined.

The Structure and Subject of the *Cinkante Balades*

Gower's *Cinkante Balades* approaches love and its assorted quandaries from several directions. As does Petrarch in the *Rime*, Gower offers a narrative of an (ultimately unsuccessful) love affair as seen *en pastiche* through the eyes of a first-person lover whose poems to and about his lady explore the range of his feelings. As in the *Livre de Cent Ballades*, questions of loyalty and temptation arise, to be dealt with variously; and, as in Christine de Pizan's *Cent Ballades d'Amant et de Dame*, the lady has her say (XLI–XLIV), responding in her own voice to the lover, rejecting his suit, and eventually turning toward another lover, who greets her (XLV) and she accepts him (XLVI). Seasonally topical balades (e.g., March in XIII, May in XV, winter and Christmas in XXXII and XXXIII, St. Valentine's Day in XXXIV and XXXV, May again in XXXVI and XXXVII) allow us to patch together a chronology of the affair (it seems to last two years or a bit less); poems about separation and return (e.g., XXV, XXIX), brought about by slanderous gossip, generate misunderstanding initially but devolve into reconciliation; iconic characters from the *Roman de la Rose* (e.g., Danger, Cupid),

---

[1] See Warton, *History of English Poetry*, sect. xix (especially p. 333).

chivalric romance (e.g., Lancelot, Tristan, Partenope), and Boethian traditions (Lady Fortune) make central contributions to the poetic vocabulary. As one might expect from Gower, classical figures (e.g., Ulysses, Alceone and Ceix, Hector, Hercules) make their entrances and exits as well.

These elements Gower has clustered variously in line with what seems to have been a structural plan. At least as presented in our sole witness, British Library, MS Additional 59495, he apparently wanted to mark off the first four balades, which a marginal note explains "are made especially for those who wait on their loves in expectation of marriage" ("sont fait especialement pour ceaux q'attendont lours amours par droite mariage"), from the remainder, dedicated in a second marginal note, "for everyone, according to the properties and conditions of Lovers who are diversely serving subjects to the fortune of love" ("a tout le monde, selonc les propretés et les condicions des Amantz, qui sont diversement travailez en la fortune d'amour"). Macaulay called attention to this division early on; and under further scrutiny, a subtle pattern is discernible on a larger scale into which the bifurcation, marked in the manuscript, can fit. Clearly the lover's narrative (V–XLVII) is intended as a kind of tutelary drama, his feelings and poetic language providing exemplary lessons in the sensations, art, and uncontrollable outcomes of an affair. This second section, by far the greatest, is followed by two (or possibly three) others. Balades XLVIII–L seem to abandon the fiction, progressively stepping away from drama into philosophical speculation. Although hardly similar in appearance when placed side-by-side, these three balades establish a kind of structural balance, or parallel, with I–IV, those identified as being for love stories leading to marriage. The voice of XLVIII–L is, nevertheless, new to the sequence, characterized no longer in imaginary first person but now turned authorial and definitive about the inter-relationship of legitimate love with honor, reason, and the higher purposes of God. It is, in fact, a recognizably "Gowerian" voice, one discernible throughout his works, and it prepares us for what may or may not be a fourth posture in the final balade. Thus when the "I" returns to claim both voice and sentiment in LI, that it should bring closure to the sequence by redirecting love away from mortal women toward the "Virgin and mother" ("Virgine et miere") as the vessel most replete and deserving, most able and eager to respond selflessly to love in kind, the move to supramundane distance and profound amorous commitment on a heavenly plane comes as scant surprise. It is, in a sense, Gower's "Troilus moment" — but significantly unburdened, in its affirmation and hopefulness, by Troilus' bitter laughter back and downward from the eighth sphere. Even more closely, then, LI recalls the tenth and final section of the *Mirour de l'Omme*, in which the poet seemingly *in propria persona* invokes the love and pardon of the "doulce Miere la Vierge gloriouse" ("the sweet mother the glorious Virgin"). The two compared highlight Gower's strategy in the *Cinkante Balades*: very likely, so that for his careful readers there should be no *revelatio post mortem* regarding love — always his primary subject, work after work — he took up the French challenge (always the nationalist, even in humility!) of the *Livre de Cent Ballades*, transforming it and making it his own.

DATING

Macaulay pointed out in 1899 that "the date at which the *Cinkante Balades* were composed cannot be determined with certainty," and no evidence has surfaced since to alter his statement concretely.[2] Various theories have been offered over the years by various hands, and these for purposes of discussion can be gathered into three groups: (1) the *Cinkante Balades* were the work of Gower the young man; (2) they were all written at various times throughout his long life; (3) they were written when Henry IV acceded to the throne in 1399 or immediately after, as a special gift for the new monarch.[3] Each of these rests upon certain assumptions, and each is therefore vulnerable to significant objections. The argument for juvenilia, for example, accepts as a given that all first-person statements must be autobiographical.[4] The "jeo" of the *Cinkante Balades* is, thus, Gower himself, and since (the assumption continues) only a man in the grip of passion could be so moved — and passion being the exclusive province of the young — the poems are, ergo, the work of Gower's youth. This may be so, of course, but perhaps in the postmodern present little more need be said by way of response than to note that, were the *Cinkante Balades* truth instead of fiction, it would mark an all-time first for literature.

More attractive on the surface, certainly, is the second claim, that the sequence represents a gathering of poems written over a lifetime. Not only did this seem reasonable to George Lyman Kittredge in 1909, who first offered the notion that Gower composed the balades over the course of his long life, but also more credible, because for Kittredge it had somewhere behind it the presence of Petrarch notching up the *Rime sparse* year by year. Notions of Petrarch's self-revelation in the *Rime*, however — for note, this theory presumes autobiography too — by now have shifted a good deal as scholars have traced how Petrarch edited and reordered the poems to shape his larger project, writing new pieces "after the fact" as narrative gaps occurred.[5] Post-hoc arrangement of any sort is itself a creative act, and necessarily, in addition to occluding the identity of "Laura," it transforms even "real" events into fiction. Moreover, we know today to look toward Machaut and Deschamps — supreme fictionists — as guiding inspiration for Gower's balades.

The third argument, too, that the *Cinkante Balades* were composed ca. 1399–1400 to celebrate Henry IV's coronation, should give us pause on grounds of likelihood and veracity, in at least equal measure. Essentially the supposition stands or falls upon the belief that the love-narrative told by the *Cinkante Balades* proper, the dedicatory two balades to Henry, and the concluding rime royal stanza lauding England's good fortune at his accession were written of a piece. However, nothing either in the poems themselves or in the extant

---

[2] Gower, *Complete Works*, 1:lxxii.

[3] Warton initially offered the first view, that of youthful composition, and it is the line taken by Fisher as well (*John Gower: Moral Philosopher*, pp. 73–74); Kittredge promoted the second, of lifelong labor (see *Date of Chaucer's Troilus and Other Chaucer Matters*, p. 76); Macaulay — although he hedges his bets a trifle ("it seems certain that at least some of the balades were composed with a view to the court of Henry IV," Gower, *Complete Works*, 1:lxxiii) — appears to favor 1399, as does Itô (*John Gower, the Medieval Poet*, pp. 158–59).

[4] In Gower's case, this assumed autobiography has extended for some readers to the first-person narrator in the *Mirour de l'Omme* (lines 27340–41) whose confession of youthful follies includes writing love poetry ("les fols ditz d'amours") which he sang while dancing ("en chantant je carolloie"). Warton seems to have imagined these to be Gower's references to his extant balades — but practically speaking the suggestion is risible for several reasons, not the least of which is the complete unsingability of Gower's balades.

[5] On Petrarch's extensive adding and reordering, with consequent difficulties for dating individual poems, see Wilkins, *Petrarch's Later Years*, especially pp. 258–60.

evidentiary records of Gower's life establishes or requires, even tangentially, their co-terminal composition. And yet, upon reflection, the yoking together of a laudatory political *hommage* and the amorous fiction of the sequence seems to demand justification, either in the work or in biography. If all of the poems we today call the *Cinkante Balades* were written to celebrate Henry's accession, what made Gower think that love would especially have delighted the usurper as by force and duplicity he seized the crown and power in 1399? Rather better, one supposes, is to recognize that this argument for dating confuses the writing of the *Cinkante Balades* with the preparation of the manuscript from which we know them, a manuscript that British Library, MS Additional 59495 replicates and that, in its more elaborate presentation version, very likely did commemorate Henry's coronation, if not with the composition of all of its parts, then certainly in their collection and assemblage.

To uncouple the *Cinkante Balades* proper, perhaps including LI, the paean to the Virgin, from the two dedicatory balades to Henry and the concluding rime royal stanza to England under his new rule is to open the way to consider moments other than the coronation for the writing of the sequence. As I have argued elsewhere, one such likely moment is 1391–93, when the nobility on both sides of the Channel were yet under the sway of the *Livre de Cent Ballades*.[6] A collection of a hundred balades as the title implies, the *Cent Ballades* were the joint effort of the *crème de la crème* of chivalric France.[7] Begun by Jean de Saint-Pierre, seneschal d'Eu, in the late 1380s, the *Livre* is a love-debate in two parts. The first fifty poems comprise a dialogue between a young knight and an old, variously about the ways of war and love. Together they agree that love and loyalty are more or less interchangeable terms. In the second fifty, however, the young knight is distracted by a woman, La Guignarde ("she who desires"), who tells him that loyal lovers are fools, in essence because false ones have more fun. The young knight appeals to the wisdom of others, eliciting answers from Philippe d'Artois, count of Eu, the younger Boucicaut, and Jean de Cresécque. An open request is made in a separate balade to lovers generally to help resolve the issue. By 1390, thirteen of France's most celebrated had written in response, for present purposes significantly including Guillaume de Tignonville, a friend of Deschamps and Christine de Pizan, and François d'Auberchicourt, whose father Eustache had fought with the Black Prince in Spain, and whose relation Jean, a longtime Lancastrian retainer and confidant of John of Gaunt, probably was known to Chaucer and Gower. In 1390, when young Henry, then earl of Derby, was jousting at the tournament of St. Inglevert in Normandy with his French compeers, including virtually all of the poets of the *Cent Ballades* and most of the prominent respondents, the *Livre* was the rage of Paris, and a topic doubtless of much talk (and friendly competition) during the many festivities which marked the premier French-English armigeral exercise of the later truce.[8]

For a brief period, writing in response to the *Cent Ballades* possessed a certain cachet: it suggested an inner circle, not only of poetic talent but also of social, aesthetic, and nationalistic arrival. Hence the Savoyard Oton de Graunson, poet, influential friend of Chaucer (who called Graunson "flour of hem that make in Fraunce" in the *Complaint of Venus*, lines 75–76) as well as John of Gaunt (and Gower?), directly links his own balades ca.

---

[6] See Yeager, "John Gower's Audience," pp. 89–91.

[7] See the edition, and especially the introduction, of Raynaud, *Les Cent Ballades*.

[8] On young Henry's presence at the St. Inglevert tourney, and his movements thereafter, see Kirby, *Henry IV of England*, especially pp. 28–34.

1391 in defense of lovers' loyalty to the *Cent Ballades*; and Christine de Pizan, newly widowed and needing a career to support herself and her children, at the same time wrote her own sequence, *Cent Ballades d'Amant et de Dame*, apparently in order to establish herself as a credible poet, worthy of patronage.[9] Until 1393 at least, it would hardly be an exaggeration to imagine on both sides of the Channel other writers measuring themselves by the *Livre de Cent Ballades*.

That by 1391 Chaucer and Gower were familiar with the reputation of the collection (if not indeed with the full *Livre* itself), and its significance as a benchmark of poetic prowess, while difficult to demonstrate, is thus nonetheless extremely likely. That Henry of Derby, however, knew the *Livre de Cent Ballades* and its poets at St. Inglevert in 1390, and that he probably admired both, seems beyond doubt — as does the obvious influence of the popular French collection on the title, language, and matter of Gower's *Cinkante Balades*. A plausible scenario for the composition of Gower's sequence, then, would involve Gower's awareness of Henry's interest in the competitive drama surrounding the *Livre de Cent Ballades*, at its peak in 1391; his wish to please a Lancastrian patron; and his lifelong effort to establish his poetic reputation. That Gower, like Oton de Graunson, Christine de Pizan, and the various noble French respondents, should have accepted the challenge of the *Livre de Cent Ballades* in 1390–93 appeals to a clearer logic than does the assumption of Henry's coronation as a prompting occasion for love balades. That at this time he presented the *Cinkante Balades* as a separate, unified work to Henry, then earl of Derby, and that Henry was pleased, cannot be proven, but the gift from Henry to Gower of a collar of S's and Lancastrian swans in 1393 is perhaps suggestive.[10] Usually this gift is credited to Gower's giving Henry a copy of the *Confessio Amantis*, but for this there is no evidence — and in any case such a present might not have struck Henry as sufficiently new to prompt reward, since a *Confessio* in some form was possibly in the hands of Gaunt and his children by 1386–87.[11] Moreover, Henry's prior familiarity with (and presumed fondness for) the *Cinkante Balades* would explain their inclusion in British Library, MS Additional 59495, the contents of which were certainly assembled, but not necessarily written, as an accession present. So viewed, the appeal of the pieces we know from British Library, MS Additional 59495 — in addition to whatever magnificence the original presentation copy must have had — would be the convenient gathering between two covers of Gower's poems written explicitly to or for Henry up to, and on, the coronation. On balance, then, the best probable date for the composition of the *Cinkante Balades* is 1391–93.

MANUSCRIPT

The *Cinkante Balades* is still known only in a single manuscript, now in the possession of the British Library.

---

[9] On Oton de Graunson, see Braddy, *Chaucer and the French Poet*; on Christine de Pizan, see Willard, *Christine de Pizan*.

[10] On the gift, see Fisher, *John Gower: Moral Philosopher*, pp. 25–26.

[11] On the dedication to Henry "Derbeie Comes" see Nicholson, "Dedications of Gower's *Confessio Amantis*"; on the possibility that Gaunt's family had an early copy, or a copy-in-progress, of the *Confessio* when they embarked for Castille in 1386, see Yeager, "Gower's Lancastrian Affinity."

• T: London, British Library, MS Additional 59495 (formerly MS Trentham Hall), fols. 11v–33. [This manuscript also contains "To King Henry IV In Praise of Peace," "Rex celi deus," "Ecce patet tensus," *Traitié selonc les auctours pour les amantz marietz*, and "Henrici quarti."]

VERSIFICATION

Six stanza patterns exist in the *Cinkante Balades*, two of them dominant: the two dedicatory poems to Henry included, twenty-four have three stanzas of seven lines, each rhyming ABABBCC ("rime royal") with an envoy BCBC (dedicatory I, III, IIII, *IIII, VI–VIII, X, XI, XIII, XXVII, XXVIII, XXX, XXXIII, XXXV–XXXVIII, XLIV–XLIX); seventeen have three stanzas of eight lines, each rhyming ABABBCBC with an envoy BCBC (I, II, V, XII, XV, XVI, XXIII, XXV, XXVI, XXIX, XXXI, XXXIV, XL–XLIII, L); seven have three stanzas of eight lines, each rhyming ABABBABA with an envoy BABA (XVII, XIX, XX, XXI, XXII, XXIIII, XXIX); three have three stanzas of seven lines, each rhyming BABABAA with an envoy BABA (XIV, XVIII, XLV); one (dedicatory II) has four stanzas of eight lines, each rhyming ABABBCBC with an envoy BCBC; one (IX) has five stanzas of eight lines, each rhyming ABABBABA, with envoy BABA; one has three stanzas of seven lines, each rhyming ABABBCC, but lacking an envoy; and one (LI) has three stanzas each rhyming ABABBCBC, but in place of an envoy proper has an added stanza in rime royal addressed to "gentile Engleterre," under the new reign of Henry IV. This was, perhaps, intended as an envoy to the sequence as a whole, or (more likely) written later when, as the contents of British Library, MS Additional 59495 suggest, the works it contains were collected and arranged for presentation as an unique group to Henry after the usurpation. (See "Dating," above.) Although, presumably by necessity even in French, Gower repeats rhyming triads in the *Cinkante Balades* more often than in the *Traitié*, he seems nonetheless to have paid pointed attention here at least to their sequence: that is, only occasionally do triads containing the same rhymes occur in proximity to each other, e.g., when the "A" rhyme of XXXIX is replicated as the "B" rhyme of XL.[12] In general in the *Cinkante Balades* as in the *Traitié*, Gower's rhymes are pure, with but a few fudges here and there, e.g., rhymes on "-entz" and "-ens" in I, or on "-ra," "-a," and "-ça" in II. The practice implicates both a closeness of sound in Gower's dialect, and/or rhyming by sight.

Certainly the latter — visual as well as aural rhyming — seems supported by Gower's metrical habits in the balades and in the *Mirour de l'Omme*. As Macaulay has noted,

> The balade form is of course taken from Continental models, and the metre of the verse is syllabically correct like that of the *Mirour*. As was observed however about the octosyllabic line of the *Mirour*, so it may be said of the ten-syllable verse here, that the rhythm is not exactly like that of the French verse of the Continent. The effect is due . . . to the attempt to combine the English accentual with the French syllabic measure.[13]

---

[12] Note, however, that Itô has argued for conscious linkages between balades, based on lineal echoes, e.g., in XII, XIII and XIV, respectively, "the third lines of the envoys resemble one another: 'Q'a moi, qui sui del tout soubtz vostre cure'; 'Si porte ades le jolif mal sanz cure'; 'Par quoi soubtz vostre grace jeo languis'. And it is likely that the last was a mixture of the first two." See his chapter "*Cinkante Balades*: A Garland for a New King" in *John Gower, the Medieval Poet*, pp. 156–80, especially p. 166.

[13] Gower, *Complete Works*, 1:lxxiv.

In effect, rhythmically too Gower seems to be exercising his "good eye" rather than his "good ear": counting — a visual mode of composition — rather than *hearing* his numbers, a conclusion not surprising about a bookish poet writing in a second, learned language. Gower's apology for his French in the final stanza of *Traitié* XVIII is interesting in this regard: "Et si jeo n'ai de François la faconde, / Pardonetz moi qe jeo de ceo forsvoie: / Jeo sui Englois, si quier par tiele voie / Estre excusé" ("And if I do not have eloquence in French, / Pardon me when I go astray with it: / I am English — thus I seek in such a way / To be excused"). While on one level pro forma, in the manner of most humility topoi, and concerned with language facility generally, on another it may also acknowledge his recognition of his own metrical *ausländigkeit*.

❧ Cinkante Balades

[DEDICATION TO KING HENRY THE FOURTH]

I
       Pité, prouesse, humblesse, honour roial
       Se sont en vous, mon liege seignour, mis
       Du providence q'est celestial.
       Noz coers dolentz par vous sont rejoïs;
5   Par vous, bons Roys, nous susmes enfranchis,
       Q'ainçois sanz cause fuismes en servage:
       Q'en dieu se fie, il ad bel avantage.

       Qui tient du ciel le regne emperial
       Et ad des Rois l'estat en terre assis,
10   Ceo q'il ad fait de vostre original
       Sustiene ades contre vos anemis;
       Dont vostre honour soit sauf guardé toutdis
       De tiel conseil que soit et bon et sage:
       Q'en dieu se fie, il ad bel avantage.

15   Vostre oratour et vostre humble vassal,
       Vostre Gower, q'est trestout vos soubgitz,
       Puisq'ore avetz receu le coronal,
       Vous frai service autre que je ne fis,
       Ore en balade, u sont les ditz floriz,
20   Ore en vertu, u l'alme ad son corage:
       Q'en dieu se fie, il ad bel avantage.

       O gentils Rois, ce que je vous escris
       Ci ensuant ert de perfit langage,
       Dont en latin ma sentence ai compris:
25   Q'en dieu se fie, il ad bel avantage.

[Latin verses following #1 above:]

       O recolende, bone, pie Rex Henrice, patrone,
       Ad bona dispone quos eripis a Pharaone;
       Noxia depone, quibus est humus hec in agone,

CINKANTE BALADES

[DEDICATION TO KING HENRY THE FOURTH]

I
    Mercy, prowess, humility, regal honor
    Belong to you, my liege lord, sent
    By Providence that is celestial.
    Our sorrowing hearts because of you are joyful;

5
    Thanks to you, good King, we are set free,
    Who before were in servitude without cause:
    Whoso trusts in God, he has the best of it.

    O you who hold from heaven imperial reign
    And are appointed to the status of king on earth,

10
    May He who did this from your origin
    Sustain [you] continually against your enemies;
    Wherefore may your honor be safeguarded always
    By such counsel as may be good and wise:
    Whoso trusts in God, he has the best of it.

15
    He who prays for you and your humble vassal,
    Your Gower, who is entirely your subject,
    Since now you have received the crown,
    I do you a service different from what I have done before,
    Now in balade, where the flower is of poetry,

20
    Now in virtue, where the soul has its heart:
    Whoso trusts in God, he has the best of it.

    Oh gentle King, this which I write for you —
    What follows here uses polished language,
    Whose message I have written in Latin:

25
    Whoso trusts in God, he has the best of it.

[Latin verses following #1 above:]

    O venerable, good, and pious King Henry, patron,
    Set up for good things those whom you rescue from Pharaoh.
    Remove from them what is harmful, for whom this land is in conflict,

Regni persone quo viuant sub racione;
5   Pacem compone, vires moderare corone,
Legibus impone frenum sine condicione,
       Firmaque sermone iura tenere mone.
Rex confiramtus licet vndique magnificatus,
H. aquile pullus, quo nunquam gracior vllus,
10   Hostes confregit que tirannica colla subegit:
H. aquile cepit oleum, quo regna recepit,
Sic veteri iuncta stipiti noua stirps redit vncta.
Nichil proficient inimicus in eo, et filius iniquitatis non apponet nocere ei.
Dominus conservet eum, et viuificet eum, et beatum faciat eum in terra, et non
15   tradat eum in animam inimicorum eius.

II   A vous, mon liege Seignour natural,
Henri le quarte, l'oure soit benoit
Qe dieu par vous de grace especial
Nous ad *re* . . . .   *(see textual notes)*
5   Ore est *be* . . . . . .
Ore *est* . . . .
Par *d* . . . .
          . . . .

C . . . .
10   *D* . . . .
O . . . .
O . . . .
P . . . .
V . . . .
15   *A* . . . .
Ca . . . .

Du . . . .
Ainz graunt   . . . .
Car tiel amour q'est   . . .
20   Quant temps vendra joious louer reçoit:
Ensi le bon amour q'estre soloit
El temps jadis de nostre ancesserie,
Ore entre nous recomencer om doit
Sanz mal pensier d'ascune vileinie.

25   O noble Henri, puissant et seignural,
Si nous de vous joioms, c'est a b[on droit]:
Por desporter vo noble Court roia[l]
Jeo frai balade, et s'il a vous plerro[it],
Entre toutz autres joie m'en serroit:

	So that the people of the realm may live under the rule of reason.
5	Establish peace, moderate the powers of the crown,
	Bridle the laws unconditionally,
	Confirm rights by your command, admonish your people to keep them.
	Although you are confirmed king and glorified on all sides
	H[enry] son of the eagle, than whom no one is ever more graceful,
10	Has broken his enemies, and subjugated tyrannical necks.
	H[enry] the eagle has captured the oil, by which he has received the rule of the realm,
	Thus the new stock returns, anointed and joined to the old stem.

Let nothing adverse grow in him, and may the son of injustice not approach to hurt him. May the Lord preserve him, and vivify him, and make him blessed

15   on earth, and surrender him not into the power of his enemies.

II	To you, my benevolent liege lord,
	Henry the Fourth, the hour was blessed
	When God through you by special grace
	We to *re* . . . . . .
5	Now is *be* . . . . . .
	Now *is* . . . . . .
	Through *d* . . . . .
	. . . . . .
	C . . . .
10	*D* . . . .
	O . . . .
	O . . . .
	P . . . .
	V . . . .
15	*A* . . . .
	Ca . . . . . .
	Du . . . .
	Thus great . . . . .
	Because such love that is . .
20	When the time comes receive joyous praise:
	Thus the good love which existed
	Long ago, in the former time of our ancestors,
	Now, between us, let us begin again
	Without thinking villainy of any.
25	O noble Henry, powerful and lordly,
	If we rejoice in you, it is a h[appy duty]:
	In order to entertain your noble Court roya[l]
	I make a balade, and if it pleas[es] you,
	Amid all others it will be a joy to me:

30   Car en vous soul apres le dieu aïe
        Gist moun confort, s'ascun me grieveroit.
        Li Rois du ciel, monseignour, vous mercie.

        Honour, valour, victoire et bon esploit,
        Joie et saunté, puissance et seignurie,
35   Cil qui toutz biens as bones gentz envoit
        Doignt de sa grace a vostre regalie.

[CINKANTE BALADES]

Si apres sont escrites en françois Cinkante balades, quelles . . . *d* fait, dont les
. . . *ment* desporter.

I   .   .   .   .   .   .   esperance
            .   .   .   .   .   .   attens
            .   .   .   .   .   .   -*ance*
            .   .   .   .   .   .
5   .   .   .   .   .   .
            .   .   .   .   .   .
            .   .   .   .   .   .
            [Mon coer remaint toutditz en vostre grace.]

            .   .   .   .   .   .
10   .   .   .   .   .   .
            .   .   .   .   .   .
            .   .   .   .   .   gementz
            .   .   .   .   .   -*ssetz* mon purpens:
            Car qoi qu'om dist d'amer en autre place,
15   Sanz un soul point muer de toutz mes sens
            Moun coer remaint toutditz en vostre grace.

        Si dieus voldroit fin mettre a ma plesance,
        Et terminer mes acomplissementz,
        Solonc la foi et la continuance
20   Que j'ai gardé sanz faire eschangementz,
        Lors en averai toutz mez esbatementz:
        Mais por le temps, quoique fortune enbrace,
        Entre lez biens du siecle et les tormentz
        Mon coer remaint toutdits en vostre grace.

25   Par cest escrit, ma dame, a vous me rens:
        Si remirer ne puiss vo bele face,
        Tenetz ma foi, tenetz mes serementz;
        Mon coer remaint toutditz en vostre grace.

30   Because in you alone after the aid of God
     Lies my comfort, should anyone harm me.
     May the King of heaven, my lord, reward you.

     Honor, valor, victory and good success,
     Joy and health, power and lordship —
35   May He who sends all good to good people
     Give of His grace to your reign.

[CINKANTE BALADES]

Here following are written in French fifty balades, which . . . *d* made, of which
. . . *ment* to disport.

I   . . . . . . hope
     . . . . . . remain
     . . . . . . *.ance*
     . . . . . .
5   . . . . . .
     . . . . . .
     . . . . . .
     [My heart remains always in your grace.]

     . . . . . .
10   . . . . . .
     . . . . . .
     . . . . . . groaning
     . . . . . . my purpose well enough:
     Because whatever one speaks about love elsewhere,
15   Without changing my feelings a single jot
     My heart remains always in your grace.

     If God wished to put an end to my happiness
     And terminate all my activities,
     In accord with the faith and the continuity
20   Which I have kept without alteration,
     Then I shall have all of my pleasures:
     But for the meantime, whatever Fortune may embrace,
     Between the good things of the world and the torments
     My heart remains always in your grace.

25   By means of this writing, my lady, I give myself to you:
     If I am unable to look again upon your fair face,
     My faith holds, my oaths hold;
     My heart remains always in your grace.

II   L'ivern s'en vait et l'estée vient flori,
           De froid en chald le temps se muera,
           L'oisel, qu'ainçois avoit perdu soun ny,
           Le renovelle, u q'il s'esjoiera:
5   De mes amours ensi le monde va,
           Par tiel espoir je me conforte ades;
           Et vous, ma dame, croietz bien cela,
           Quant dolour vait, les joies vienont pres.

           Ma doulce dame, ensi come jeo vous di,
10   Saver poetz coment moun coer esta,
           Le quel vous serve et long temps ad servi,
           Tant com jeo vive et toutditz servira:
           Remembretz vous, ma dame, pour cela
           Q'a moun voloir ne vous lerrai jammes;
15   Ensi com dieus le voet, ensi serra,
           Quant dolour vait, les joies vienont pres.

           Le jour qe j'ai de vous novelle oï,
           Il m'est avis qe rien me grievera:
           Porceo, ma chiere dame, jeo vous pri,
20   Par vo message, quant il vous plerra,
           Mandetz a moi que bon vous semblera,
           Du quoi moun coer se poet tenir en pes:
           Et pensetz, dame, de ceo q'ai dit pieça,
           Quant dolour vait, les joies vienont pres.

25   O noble dame, a vous ce lettre irra,
           Et quant dieu plest, jeo vous verrai apres:
           Par cest escrit il vous remembrera,
           Quant dolour vait, les joies vienont pres.

III   D'ardant desir celle amorouse peigne
           Mellé d'espoir me fait languir en joie;
           Dont par dolçour sovent jeo me compleigne
           Pour vous, ma dame, ensi com jeo soloie.
5   Mais quant jeo pense que vous serretz moie,
           De sa justice amour moun coer enhorte,
           En attendant que jeo me reconforte.

           La renomée, dont j'ai l'oreile pleine,
           De vo valour moun coer pensant envoie
10   Milfoitz le jour, u tielement me meine,
           Q'il m'est avis que jeo vous sente et voie,
           Plesante, sage, belle, simple et coie:

II   The winter goes and the flowery summer comes,
     From cold to hot the weather changes,
     The bird, which had lost its nest,
     Rebuilds it, where it will rejoice:
5   The world goes thus, matching my love —
     With such hope I comfort myself continually;
     And you, my lady, believe well that,
     When sadness goes, joys come soon after.

     My sweet lady, thus as I tell you,
10   You can know how my heart will be,
     Which serves you and has served a long time,
     And always will serve as long as I live:
     Remember, my lady, because of this
     Of my own will I shall never leave you;
15   Just as God wishes, so it will be,
     When sadness goes, joys come soon after.

     The day when I have heard news of you,
     Nothing, it seems to me, will grieve me:
     Therefore, my dear lady, I pray you,
20   By your messenger, when it may please you,
     Send to me whatever you will,
     So that my heart will be able to keep itself in peace:
     And think, lady, about that which was said before,
     When sadness goes, joys come soon after.

25   O noble lady, to you this letter will go,
     And when God pleases, I shall see you afterwards.
     By this writing you will remember:
     When sadness goes, joys come soon after.

III This loving punishment of burning desire
     Mingled with hope sickens me with joy:
     Thus from sweetness often I complain
     On your account, my lady — just so am I accustomed.
5   But when I think that you will be mine,
     My heart exhorts Love for its justice,
     Awaiting the time when I shall be comforted.

     The renown, of which my ears are full,
     Of your worth transports my pensive heart
10   A thousand times a day, where it so guides me
     That it seems to me that I feel and see you,
     Pleasant, wise, beautiful, innocent and tranquil:

Si en devient ma joie ades plus forte,
En attendant que jeo me reconforte.

15   Por faire honour a dame si halteigne
A toutz les jours sanz departir me ploie;
Et si dieus voet que jeo le point atteigne
De mes amours, que jeo desire et proie,
Lors ai d'amour tout ceo q'avoir voldroie:
20   Mais pour le temps espoir moun coer supporte,
En attendant que jeo me reconforte.

A vous, ma dame, ensi come faire doie,
En lieu de moi ceo lettre vous apporte;
Q'en vous amer moun coer dist toute voie,
25   En attendant que jeo me reconforte.

IIII   D'entier voloir sanz jammes departir,
Ma belle, a vous, en qui j'ai m'esperance,
En droit amour moun coer s'ad fait unir
As toutz jours mais, pour faire vo plesance:
5   Jeo vous asseur par fine covenance,
Sur toutes autres neez en ceste vie
Vostre amant sui et vous serrez m'amie.

Jeo me doi bien a vous soul consentir
Et doner qanque j'ai de bienvuillance;
10   Car pleinement en vous l'en poet sentir
Bealté, bounté, valour et sufficaunce:
Croietz moi, dame, et tenetz ma fiaunce,
Qe par doulçour et bone compaignie
Vostre amant sui et vous serretz m'amie.

15   De pluis en pluis pour le tresgrant desir
Qe j'ai de vous me vient la remembrance
Q'en mon pensant me fait tant rejoïr,
Qe si le mond fuist tout en ma puissance,
Jeo ne querroie avoir autre alliance:
20   Tenetz certain qe ceo ne faldra mie,
Vostre amant sui et vous serretz m'amie.

Au flour des flours, u toute ma creance
D'amour remaint sanz nulle departie,
Ceo lettre envoie, et croi me sanz doubtance,
25   Vostre amant sui et vous serretz m'amie.

So thence always my joy becomes all the stronger,
Awaiting the time when I shall be comforted.

15   To do honor to a lady so superior
I exert myself every day, unswervingly;
And if God wishes that I attain the peak
Of my love, which I desire and pray for,
Then I'll have from love all that I might wish to have.
20   But for the time, hope supports my heart,
Awaiting the time I shall be comforted.

For you, my lady, thus like this I must do —
In place of myself this letter I give you;
Herein my heart continually speaks love to you,
25   Awaiting the time I shall be comforted.

IIII   With a whole desire, unswervingly,
My beautiful one, for you, in whom I have my hope,
In true love my heart has united itself
Forevermore in order to do your pleasure;
5   I assure you by a perfect covenant,
Above all others born into this life
Your lover I am and you will be my beloved.

I must rightly be in agreement with you alone
And give whatever I have of good will;
10   Because in you one may sense amply
Beauty, bounty, virtue, and sufficiency:
Believe me, lady, and depend upon my assurance,
Because for sweetness and good company
Your lover I am and you will be my beloved.

15   More and more, on account of the very great desire
I have for you, memory comes to me,
Which, in my heart, makes me rejoice,
So that if the world were entirely in my power,
I would not seek to have another alliance:
20   Hold certain that this will not diminish a jot:
Your lover am I and you will be my beloved.

To the flower of flowers, where all my faith
Of love remains without any leave-taking,
Take this letter, and believe me without any doubt,
25   Your lover am I, and you will be my beloved.

IIII*   Sanz departir j'ai tout mon coer assis
                   U j'aim toutditz et toutdis amerai;
                   Sanz departir j'ai loialment promis
                   Por toi cherir tancome jeo viverai;
5   Sanz departir ceo qe jeo promis ai
                   Jeo vuill tenir a toi, ma debonaire;
                   Sanz departir tu es ma joie maire.

                   Sanz departir jeo t'ai, m'amie, pris,
                   Q'en tout le mond si bone jeo ne sai;
10   Sanz departir tu m'as auci compris
                   En tes liens, dont ton ami serrai;
                   Sanz departir tu m'as tout et jeo t'ai
                   En droit amour por ta plesance faire;
                   Sanz departir tu es ma joie maire.

15   Sanz departir l'amour qe j'ai empris
                   Jeo vuill garder, qe point ne mesprendray;
                   Sanz departir, come tes loials amis,
                   Mon tresdouls coer, ton honour guarderai;
                   Sanz departir a mon poair jeo frai
20   Des toutes partz ceo qe toi porra plaire;
                   Sanz departir tu es ma joie maire.

                   De coer parfit, certain, loial et vrai
                   Sanz departir en trestout mon affaire
                   Te vuil amer, car ore est a l'essai;
25   Sanz departir tu es ma joie maire.

V   Pour une soule avoir et rejoïr
                   Toutes les autres laisse a noun chaloir:
                   Jeo me doi bien a tiele consentir,
                   Et faire honour a trestout moun pooir,
5   Q'elle est tout humble a faire mon voloir:
                   Jeo sui tout soen et elle est toute moie,
                   Jeo l'ai et elle auci me voet avoir;
                   Pour tout le mond jeo ne la changeroie.

                   Qui si bone ad bien la devera cherir,
10   Q'a sa valour n'est riens qe poet valoir:
                   Jeo di pour moi, quant jeo la puiss sentir,
                   Il m'est avis qe jeo ne puiss doloir.
                   Elle est ma vie, elle est tout mon avoir,
                   Elle est m'amie, elle est toute ma joie,
15   Elle est tout mon confort matin et soir;
                   Pour tout le mond jeo ne la changeroie.

IIII*   Unswervingly I have taken you, my beloved,
Where I love always, and always will love;
Unswervingly I have loyally promised
To cherish you as long as I may live;
5   Unswervingly that which I have promised
I intend to hold to for you, my bountiful one:
Unswervingly you are my greatest joy.

Unswervingly I have prized you, my beloved,
In all the world I know none so good;
10   Unswervingly you have taken me so
In your bonds, and so I shall be your lover;
Unswervingly you have me wholly and I have you
In true love to do you pleasure;
Unswervingly you are my greatest joy.

15   Unswervingly the love I have undertaken
I wish to guard, I shall not at all take wrongfully;
Unswervingly, as your loyal lover,
My very sweet heart, I shall guard your honor;
Unswervingly to the best of my ability I shall do
20   In every way that which will be pleasing to you;
Unswervingly you are my greatest joy.

With perfect heart, certain, loyal and true
Unswervingly in all of my affairs
I intend to love you, because now is the trial;
25   Unswervingly you are my greatest joy.

V   In order to have and give joy to one alone,
Leave all the others without a second thought:
I myself must agree with that utterly,
And do honor with all of my power,
5   Because she is utterly humble to do my desire.
I am completely hers and she is all mine
I have her and she also wishes to have me;
For all the world I'll not exchange her.

Whosoever has such goodness ought to cherish it well,
10   Because its worth is nothing that he can deserve:
I say for myself, when I am able to feel so,
It seems to me that I cannot feel pain.
She is my life, she is all my riches,
She is my beloved, she is all of my joy,
15   She is all my comfort morning and evening;
For all the world I'll not exchange her.

La destinée qe nous ad fait unir
Benoite soit; car sanz null decevoir
Je l'aime a tant com coer porra tenir,
20   Ceo prens tesmoign de dieu qui sciet le voir:
Si fuisse en paradis ceo beal manoir,
Autre desport de lui ja ne querroie;
C'est celle ove qui jeo pense a remanoir,
Pour tout le mond jeo ne la changeroie.

☞   Ceste balade en gré pour recevoir,   *(see note)*
26   Ove coer et corps par tout u qe jeo soie,
Envoie a celle u gist tout mon espoir:
Pour tout le mond jeo ne la changeroie.

VI   La fame et la treshalte renomée
☞   Du sens, beauté, manere et gentilesce,   *(see note)*
Qe l'en m'ad dit sovent et recontée
De vous, ma noble dame, a grant leesce
5   M'ad trespercié l'oreille et est impresse
Dedeinz le coer, par quoi mon oill desire,
Vostre presence au fin qe jeo remire.

Si fortune ait ensi determinée,
Qe jeo porrai veoir vo grant noblesce,
10   Vo grant valour, dont tant bien sont parlée,
Lors en serra ma joie plus expresse:
Car pour service faire a vostre haltesse
J'ai grant voloir, par quoi mon oill desire,
Vostre presence au fin qe jeo remire.

15   Mais le penser plesant ymaginée,
Jesqes a tant qe jeo le lieu adesce,
U vous serretz, m'ad ensi adrescée,
Qe par souhaid Milfoitz le jour jeo lesse
Mon coer aler, q'a vous conter ne cesse
20   Le bon amour, par quoi moun oill desire,
Vostre presence au fin que jeo remire.

Sur toutes flours la flour, et la Princesse
De tout honour, et des toutz mals le Mire,
Pour vo bealté jeo languis en destresce,
25   Vostre presence au fin qe jeo remire.

VII   De fin amour c'est le droit et nature,
Qe tant come pluis le corps soit eslongée,

The fate which has made us one
Be blessed! Because without any deceit
I love her as much as a heart can hold:
20   About that take witness from God who knows the truth.
If one might dwell in such a beautiful paradise,
Never would he long for other entertainment;
She it is with whom I think to remain,
For all the world I'll not exchange her.

25   This balade receive in pleasure,
With one heart and body wholly wherever I may be —
I send it to her where lies my whole hope:
For all the world I'll not exchange her.

VI   The fame and highest renown
Of mind, beauty, manners and gentility,
That often have been described to me and recounted
About you, my noble lady, with great delight
5   Have pierced my ear and are impressed
Within my heart, for which reason my eye desires
That I may look on you in person forever.

If Fortune has so determined
That I may be able to see your great nobility,
10   Your great worth, of which such good is spoken,
Then my greatest joy will be realized:
Because to do service for your highness
I greatly wish, for which reason my eye desires
That I may look on you in person forever.

15   But that pleasant imagined thought,
Until whenever I reach the place
Where you may be, has directed me,
So that through desire a thousand times a day I allow
My heart to go, which does not cease to speak to you
20   Of my loyal love: for this reason my eye desires
That I may look on you in person forever.

Above all flowers the flower, and the Princess
Of all honor, and of all ills the Physician —
For your beauty I languish in distress,
25   That I may look on you in person forever.

VII   Of *fin amour* it is the law and the nature,
That the more distant the body,

Tant plus remaint le coer pres a toute hure,
Tanqu'il verra ceo qu'il ad desirée.
5   Pourceo sachetz, ma tresbelle honourée,
De vo paiis qe jeo desire l'estre,
Come cil qui tout vo chivaler voet estre.

De la fonteine ensi come l'eaue pure
Tressalt et buile et court aval le prée,
10   Ensi le coer de moi, jeo vous assure,
Pour vostre amour demeine sa pensée;
Et c'est toutdits sanz repos travailée,
De vo paiis que jeo desire l'estre,
Come cil qui tout vo chivaler voet estre.

15   Sicome l'ivern despuile la verdure
Du beal Jardin, tanque autresfoitz Estée
L'ait revestu, ensi de sa mesure
Moun coer languist, mais il s'est esperée
Q' encore a vous vendrai joious et lée;
20   De vo paiis qe jeo desire l'estre,
Come cil qui tout vo chivaler voet estre.

Sur toutes belles la plus belle née,
Plus ne voldrai le Paradis terrestre,
Que jeo n'ai plus vostre presence amée,
25   Come cil qui tout vo chivaler voet estre.

VIII   D'estable coer, qui nullement se mue,
S'en ist ades et vole le penser
Assetz plus tost qe falcon de sa Mue;
Ses Eles sont souhaid et desirer,
5   En un moment il passera la mer
A vous, ma dame, u tient la droite voie,
En lieu de moi, tanque jeo vous revoie.

Si mon penser saveroit a sa venue
A vous, ma doulce dame, reconter
10   Ma volenté, et a sa revenue
Vostre plaisir a moi auci conter,
En tout le mond n'eust si bon Messager;
Car Centmillfoitz le jour jeo luy envoie
A vostre court, tanque jeo vous revoie.

15   Mais combien qu'il ne parle, il vous salue
Depar celui q'est tout le vostre entier,
Q'a vous servir j'ai fait ma retenue,

The heart at all times remains even further away,
Until it may see that which it has desired.
5   Therefore know, my very beautiful, honorable one,
I desire your country for my home,
As he who would be your knight completely.

Thus, as the pure water from the fountain
Leaps and bubbles and courses down the meadow,
10   Thus this heart of mine, I assure you,
For your love experiences its hope;
And it is always laboring without rest.
I desire your country for my home,
As he who would be your knight completely.

15   Just as the winter despoils the verdure
Of the beautiful garden, until eventually summer
Has reclothed it, thus in that degree
My heart languishes, but it is hopeful
That again it may come to you, joyous and glad;
20   I desire your country for my home,
As he who would be your knight completely.

Above all beauties the most beautiful born,
I would no longer desire paradise on earth,
If I no longer had your beloved presence,
25   As he who would be your knight completely.

VIII   From the committed heart, which changes not a jot,
At once the thought issues and flies
Much sooner than the falcon from his mew;
His wings are Delight and Desire:
5   In one moment he passes over the sea
To you, my lady, where he takes the straight path,
In place of me, until I see you again.

If my thought might know how to come
To you, my sweet lady, to tell
10   My will, and on its return
To relate your pleasure to me also,
Never in all the world would there be so good a messenger;
Because a hundred thousand times a day I send him
To your court, until I see you again.

15   But however much he speaks, he salutes you,
From him who is all yours entirely.
In order to serve you I have made my commitment,

Come vostre amant et vostre Chivaler:
Le pensement qe j'ai de vous plener,
20   C'est soulement qe mon las coer convoie
En bon espoir, tanque jeo vous revoie.

Ceste balade a vous fait envoier
Mon coer, mon corps, ma sovereine joie:
Tenetz certein qe jeo vous vuill amer
25   En bon espoir, tanque jeo vous revoie.

IX   Trop tart a ceo qe jeo desire et proie
Vient ma fortune au point, il m'est avis;
Mais nepourquant mon coer toutdis se ploie,
Parfit, verai, loial, entalentis
5   De vous veoir, qui sui tout vos amis
Si tresentier qe dire ne porroie:
Q'apres dieu et les saintz de Paradis
En vous remaint ma sovereine joie.

De mes deux oels ainçois qe jeo vous voie,
10   Millfoitz le jour mon coer y est tramis
En lieu de moi d'aler la droite voie
Pour visiter et vous et vo paiis:
Et tanqu'il s'est en vo presence mis,
Desir ades l'encoste et le convoie,
15   Com cil q'est tant de vostre amour suspris,
Qe nullement se poet partir en voie.

Descoverir a vous si jeo me doie,
En vous amer sui tielement ravys,
Q'au plus sovent mon sentement forsvoie,
20   Ne sai si chald ou froid, ou mors ou vifs
Ou halt ou bass, ou certains ou faillis,
Ou tempre ou tard, ou pres ou loings jeo soie:
Mais en pensant je sui tant esbaubis,
Q'il m'est avis sicom jeo songeroie.

25   Pour vous, ma dame, en peine m'esbanoie,
Jeo ris en plour et en santé languis,
Jeue en tristour et en seurté m'esfroie,
Ars en gelée et en chalour fremis,
D'amer puissant, d'amour povere et mendis,
30   Jeo sui tout vostre, et si vous fuissetz moie,
En tout le mond n'eust uns si rejoïs
De ses amours, sicom jeo lors serroie.

As your lover and your knight:
The thought that I have wholly for you —
20   That alone guides my wretched heart
In good hope, until I see you again.

This balade I make to send to you,
My heart, my body, my sovereign joy:
Hold certain that I wish to love you
25   In good hope, until I see you again.

IX   Altogether too late from her whom I desire and petition
Comes my reward, it seems to me;
But nevertheless my heart always yields itself,
Perfect, true, loyal, desirous
5   To see you, because I am entirely your friend,
So completely that I am unable to say:
Because after God and the saints of Paradise
In you remains my sovereign joy.

From my two eyes until I may see you,
10   A thousand times a day my heart sends itself
In my stead to travel the straight path
To visit both you and your country;
And until it sets itself in your presence,
Desire continually accompanies it and conveys it,
15   Like him who so greatly sighs for your love
That in no way is he able to depart.

Thus I must disclose myself to you —
By your love I am completely ravished,
You who most often lead my feelings astray,
20   So I know not hot or cold, or death or life,
High or low, or certainty or deception,
Or early or late, or how close or far I may be:
But in thought I am so confused,
That it seems to me just as if I were dreaming.

25   For you, my lady, in pain I take pleasure,
I laugh in tears and languish in good health,
Play in sadness and in surety am afraid,
Burn in frost and in heat shiver —
Powerful from love, from love poor and begging,
30   I am altogether yours, and if you were mine,
In all the world no one would rejoice
From his love, just as I would then.

O tresgentile dame, simple et coie,
Des graces et des vertus replenis,
35 Lessetz venir merci, jeo vous supploie,
Et demorir, tanqu'il m'avera guaris;
Car sanz vous vivre ne suis poestis.
Tout sont en vous li bien qe jeo voldroie,
En vostre aguard ma fortune est assis,
40 Ceo qe vous plest de bon grée jeo l'otroie.

La flour des flours plus belle au droit devis,
Ceste compleignte a vous directe envoie:
Croietz moi, dame, ensi com jeo vous dis,
En vous remaint ma sovereine joie.

X Mon tresdouls coer, mon coer avetz souleine,
Jeo n'en puiss autre, si jeo voir dirrai;
Q'en vous, ma dame, est toute grace pleine.
A bone houre est qe jeo vous aqueintai,
5 Maisqu'il vous pleust qe jeo vous amerai,
Au fin qe vo pité vers moi se plie,
Q'avoir porrai vostre ameisté complie.

Mais la fortune qui les amantz meine
Au plus sovent me met en grant esmai,
10 En si halt lieu qe jeo moun coer asseine,
Qe passe toutz les autres a l'essai:
Q'a mon avis n'est une qe jeo sai
Pareil a vous, par quoi moun coer s'allie,
Q'avoir porrai vostre ameisté complie.

15 S'amour me volt hoster de toute peine,
Et faire tant qe jeo m'esjoierai,
Vous estes mesmes celle sovereine,
Sanz qui jammais en ese viverai:
Et puis q'ensi moun coer doné vous ai,
20 Ne lerrai, dame, qe ne vous supplie,
Q'avoir porrai vostre ameisté complie.

A vo bealté semblable au Mois de Maii,
Qant le solail s'espant sur la florie,
Ceste balade escrite envoierai,
25 Q'avoir porrai vostre ameisté complie.

XI Mes sens foreins se pourront bien movoir,
Mais li coers maint en un soul point toutdis,

O most gentle lady, simple and coy,
With graces and with virtue replete,
35   Let mercy come, I implore you,
And remain, until I have healed myself;
Because without you I lack the strength to live.
All the good things that I desire are in you,
In your care my fortune is placed:
40   Those things that you enjoy I guarantee through good service.

Flower, by right the most beautiful of flowers,
This complaint to you I send directly:
Believe me, lady, just as I tell you,
In you remains my sovereign joy.

X   My sweetest heart, my heart remains single-minded,
I am unable to have it otherwise, if I say truly;
In you, my lady, is every complete grace.
It will be a joyous moment when I shall love you,
5   Provided that it might please you that I love you,
That at last your pity may turn toward me,
So that I may have your full amity.

But that Fortune that leads lovers
All too often gives me great dismay,
10   Because of the high place where I dispose my heart,
Which surpasses all the others, at a throw:
In my opinion no one whom I know
Equals you — therefore my heart binds itself [to you],
So that I may have your full amity.

15   If Love wishes to remove me from all pain
And cause me to rejoice,
You yourself are that very sovereign,
Without whom I never may live in ease:
And since that thus I have given my heart to you,
20   Do not permit yourself, lady, not to bend,
So that I may have your full amity.

To your beauty resembling the month of May,
When the sun spreads itself over the flowers,
I shall send this written balade,
25   So that I may have your full amity.

XI   My senses are able easily to move themselves far away,
But the heart remains in one place always,

Et c'est, ma dame, en vous, pour dire voir,
A qui jeo vuill servir en faitz et ditz:
5   Car pour sercher le monde, a moun avis
Vous estes la plus belle et graciouse,
Si vous fuissetz un poi plus amerouse.

Soubtz ciel n'est uns, maisqu'il vous poet veoir,
Qu'il ne serroit tantost d'amer suspris;
10   Q'en la bealté qe dieus t'ad fait avoir
Sont les vertus si pleinement compris,
Qe riens y falt; dont l'en doit doner pris
A vous, ma doulce dame gloriouse,
Si vous fuissetz un poi plus amerouse.

15   Jeo sui del tout, ma dame, en vo pooir,
Come cil qui sui par droit amour soubgis
De noet et jour pour faire vo voloir,
Et dieus le sciet qe ceo n'est pas envis:
Par quoi jeo quiers vos graces et mercis;
20   Car par reson vous me serretz pitouse,
Si vous fuissetz un poi plus amerouse.

A vous, ma dame, envoie cest escris,
Qe trop perestes belle et dangerouse:
Meilour de vous om sciet en null paiis,
25   Si vous fuissetz un poi plus amerouse.

XII   La dame a la Chalandre comparer
Porrai, la quelle en droit de sa nature
Desdeigne l'omme a tiel point reguarder,
Quant il serra de mort en aventure.
5   Et c'est le pis des griefs mals qe j'endure,
Vo tresgent corps, ma dame, quant jeo voie
Et le favour de vo reguard procure,
Danger ses oels destorne en autre voie.

Helas, quant pour le coer trestout entier,
10   Qe j'ai doné sanz point de forsfaiture,
Ne me deignetz en tant reguerdoner,
Q'avoir porrai la soule reguardure
De vous, q'avetz et l'oill et la feture
Dont jeo languis; car ce jeo me convoie,
15   Par devant vous quant jeo me plus assure,
Danger ses oels destorne en autre voie.

And it is, my lady, in you, to say truly,
Whom I wish to serve in deed and word:
5   Because — though one might search the world — in my opinion
You are the most beautiful and gracious,
If only you showed a bit more affection.

Under heaven there is no one, were he to see you,
Who would not be seized by the greatest love;
10   Because in the beauty that God gave you
So completely are your virtues so fully realized,
That nothing is at fault; thus one should give honor
To you, my sweet, glorious lady,
If only you showed a bit more affection.

15   I am, my lady, completely in your power,
As the one who himself is subject to true love
Night and day, in order to do your wishes,
And God knows that it is not done reluctantly:
By this I seek your grace and mercy;
20   Because reasonably you would take pity upon me,
If only you showed a bit more affection.

These words, my lady, I send to you,
Who appear very beautiful and disdainful:
No one knows your like in any country —
25   If only you showed a bit more affection!

XII   My lady I can compare to the plover,
She who according to her nature
Disdains to regard a man at that moment
When he will be overcome by death.
5   And it is the worst of the terrible hurt I endure,
[That] when I see your most beautiful person, my lady,
And the favor of your regard I procure,
Disdain turns your eyes in another direction.

Alas, when even my whole heart entire
10   I have given without any limit,
Nor thought myself worthy of any reward at all,
To be able to have a single look
From you, who have both the eye and the form
For which I languish; because when I steer myself
15   Into your presence, when I am most self-assured,
Disdain turns your eyes in another direction.

Si tresbeals oels sanz merci pour mirer
N'acorde pas, ma dame, a vo mesure:
De vo reguard hostetz pourceo danger,
20   Prenetz pité de vostre creature,
Monstrez moi l'oill de grace en sa figure,
Douls, vair, riant et plein de toute joie;
Car jesq'en cy, ou si jeo chante ou plure,
Danger ses oels destorne en autre voie.

25   En toute humilité sanz mesprisure
Jeo me compleigns, ensi come faire doie,
Q'a moi, qui sui del tout soubtz vostre cure,
Danger ses oels destorne en autre voie.

XIII   Au mois de Marsz, u tant y ad muance,
Puiss resembler les douls mals que j'endure:
Ore ai trové, ore ai perdu fiance,
Siq'en amer truis ma fortune dure;
5   Qu'elle est sanz point, sanz reule et sanz mesure,
N'ad pas egual le pois en sa balance,
Ore ai le coer en ease, ore en destance.

Qant jeo remire al oill sanz variance
La gentilesce et la doulce figure,
10   Le sens, l'onour, le port, la contenance
De ma tresnoble dame, en qui nature
Ad toutz biens mis, lors est ma joie pure,
Q'amour par sa tresdigne pourveance
M'ad fait amer u tant y ad plesance.

15   Mais quant me vient la droite sovenance,
Coment ma doulce dame est a dessure
En halt estat, et ma nounsuffisance
Compense a si tresnoble creature,
Lors en devient ma joie plus obscure
20   Par droit paour et par deseperance,
Qe lune quant eglips la desavance.

Pour vous, q'avetz ma vie en aventure,
Ceste balade ai fait en remembrance:
Si porte ades le jolif mal sanz cure,
25   Tanq'il vous plest de m'en faire allegance.

XIIII   Pour penser de ma dame sovereine,
En qui tout bien sont plainement assis,

For eyes so very beautiful to look without mercy
Does not accord, my lady, with your temper:
From your regard therefore remove disdain,
20   Take pity on your creature,
Show me the eye of grace in your person,
Sweet, gray, laughing, and full of all joy;
Because so far, whether I sing or cry,
Disdain turns your eyes in another direction.

25   In all humility without offense
I lament, just as I ought to do,
When from me, who himself is totally under your control,
Disdain turns your eyes in another direction.

XIII   The month of March, where there is so much change,
May resemble the sad evils that I endure:
Now I have found, now I have lost assurance,
Since I find my fortune in love hard;
5   It is without end, without rule and without measure,
It lacks any balancing point:
Now the heart has ease, now discord.

When again I cast my eye without wavering upon
The gentility and the sweet person,
10   The sensibility, the honor, the carriage, the countenance
Of my most noble lady, to whom Nature
Has given all goodness, then is my joy pure,
That Love through its very dignified purveyance
Caused me to love where there is so much pleasance.

15   But when I come to the true remembrance
How my sweet lady is above
In high estate, and my insufficiency
Weighs upon that very noble creature,
Then my joy becomes very obscure
20   Through real fear and through loss of hope,
Just as the moon diminishes in an eclipse.

For you, who have my life at hazard,
I have made this balade in remembrance:
Thus I bear continually the happy evil without cure,
25   Until you might please to give me relief.

XIIII   When I think about my sovereign lady,
In whom all good things are obviously present,

Qe riens y falt de ce dont corps humeine
Doit par reson avoir loenge et pris,
5   Lors sui d'amour si finement espris,
Dont maintenant m'estoet soeffrir la peine
Plus qe Paris ne soeffrist pour Heleine.

Tant plus de moi ma dame se desdeigne,
Come plus la prie; et si jeo mot ne dis,
10   Qe valt ce, lors qe jeo ma dolour meine
De ceo dont jeo ma dame n'ai requis?
Ensi de deux jeo sui tant entrepris,
Qe parler n'ose a dame si halteine,
Et si m'en tais, jeo voi la mort procheine.

15   Mais si pités, qui les douls coers enseine,
Pour moi ne parle et die son avis,
Et la fierté de son corage asseine,
Et plie au fin q'elle ait de moi mercis,
Jeo serrai mortz ou tant enmaladis,
20   Ne puiss faillir del un avoir estreine;
Ensi, ma doulce dame, a vous me pleigne.

Ceste balade a vous, ma dame, escris,
Q'a vous parler me falt du bouche aleine;
Par quoi soubtz vostre grace jeo languis,
25   Sanz vous avoir ne puiss ma joie pleine.

XV   Com l'esperver qe vole par creance
Et de son las ne poet partir envoie,
De mes amours ensi par resemblance
Jeo sui liez, sique par nulle voie
5   Ne puiss aler, s'amour ne me convoie:
Vous m'avetz, dame, estrait de tiele Mue,
Combien qe vo presence ades ne voie,
Mon coer remaint, que point ne se remue.

Soubtz vo constreignte et soubtz vo governance
10   Amour m'ad dit qe jeo me supple et ploie,
Sicome foial doit faire a sa liegance,
Et plus d'assetz, si faire le porroie:
Pour ce, ma doulce dame, a vous m'otroie,
Car a ce point j'ai fait ma retenue,
15   Qe si le corps de moi fuist ore a Troie,
Mon coer remaint, qe point ne se remue.

Who lacks nothing for which the human body
Ought by reason to have praise and honor,
5 Then I am by love so finely set afire,
Whereupon I must suffer pain
More than Paris ever suffered for Helen.

My lady disdains me all the more,
The more I entreat; and thus I say not a word,
10 Because what use is it, when I display my pain,
When I ask for that which my lady doesn't have?
So between the two I am so greatly dismayed,
Who dares not speak to a lady so haughty,
And if I remain silent, I foresee death soon.

15 But if pity, which instructs the downcast heart,
Speaks not for me and gives his counsel,
And strikes pride from the heart,
And bends her at last to have mercy on me,
I shall die or become sick,
20 I cannot fail to have one fortune or the other;
Thus, my sweet lady, I complain to you.

This balade for you, my lady, I write,
Because I cannot breathe a word to you;
Because under your grace I languish,
25 Without you I cannot have my heart's content.

XV Like the sparrow hawk that flies with a leash
And is unable to break loose from his cord,
So in just that fashion by my love
Am I bound, because in no way whatsoever
5 Is love capable, either to depart itself, or to carry me away:
You have me, lady, close in such a Cage,
That although you are not always present,
My heart remains, unable to tear itself away.

Under your constraint and under your governance
10 Love has told me that I should yield and submit,
Just as a vassal ought to perform his allegiance,
And copiously, if I am able to do it:
For that, my sweet lady, may you acquiesce to me,
Because now I have made my commitment,
15 Who, if my body were now in Troy,
My heart will remain, unable to tear itself away.

Sicome le Mois de Maii les prées avance,
Q'est tout flori quant l'erbe se verdoie,
Ensi par vous revient ma contienance,
20   De vo bealté si penser jeo le doie:
Et si merci me volt vestir de joie
Pour la bounté qe vous avetz vestue,
En tiel espoir, ma dame, uque jeo soie,
Mon coer remaint, qe point ne se remue.

25   A vostre ymage est tout ceo qe jeo proie,
Quant ceste lettre a vous serra venue;
Q'a vous servir, come cil q'est vostre proie,
Mon coer remaint, qe point ne se remue.

XVI   Camelion est une beste fiere,
Qui vit tansoulement de l'air sanz plus;
Ensi pour dire en mesme la maniere,
De soul espoir qe j'ai d'amour conçuz
5   Sont mes pensers en vie sustenuz:
Mais par gouster de chose qe jeo sente,
Combien qe jeo le serche sus et jus,
Ne puiss de grace trover celle sente.

N'est pas ma sustenance assetz pleniere
10   De vein espoir qe m'ad ensi repuz;
Ainz en devient ma faim tant plus amiere
D'ardant desir qe m'est d'amour accruz:
De mon repast jeo sui ensi deçuz,
Q'ove voide main espoir ses douns presente,
15   Qe quant jeo quide meux estre au dessus
En halt estat, jeo fais plus grief descente

Quiqu'est devant, souhaid n'est pas derere
Au feste quelle espoir avera tenuz;
A volenté sanz fait est chamberere:
20   Tiels officers sont ainçois retenuz,
Par ceux jeo vive et vuill ceo qe ne puiss,
Ma fortune est contraire a mon entente;
Ensi morrai, si jeo merci ne truis,
Q'en vein espoir ascun profit n'avente.

25   A vous, en qui sont toutz bien contenuz,
Q'es flour des autres la plus excellente,
Ceste balade avoec centmil salutz
Envoie, dame, maisq'il vous talente.

Just as the month of May propagates the meadows,
Which all flourish when the plants become green,
Just so you revive my countenance,
20 Whenever I think about your beauty:
Thus also mercy would deck me with joy,
For the bounty which you have donned.
In hope of that, my lady, wherever I may be,
My heart remains, unable to tear itself away.

25 All my prayers are to your image
When this letter shall come to you;
In order to serve you, like one that is your prey,
My heart remains, unable to tear itself away.

XVI The chameleon is a wild beast
Who lives on air alone;
Thus, so to say, is my manner also:
By the sole hope for love that I have conceived
5 Are my thoughts in life sustained:
But by feeding on this food of the mind,
However much I seek it up and down,
I am unable to find a path of grace for myself.

My sustenance is insufficiently provided
10 By the vain hope which so thrusts me away;
Rather my hunger becomes the more bitter
Even as ardent desire causes me to love all the more:
About my meal I am thus deceived,
With what empty hand hope presents its gifts,
15 So that when I expect to be better at the end —
In high estate — I make a much sadder descent.

Whosoever is in the front, Desire is not behind
At the feast that Hope has set out;
Desire — easily, willingly — is the serving-maid:
20 Such sort of officers are retained,
Through them I live and wish for what I can't achieve;
My fortune is contrary to my intent;
Thus I shall die, if I do not find mercy,
When some profit does not follow after vain hope.

25 To you, in whom are all good things contained,
Who is the most excellent flower of all,
This balade with a hundred thousand salutes
I send, lady, if only that it may please you.

XVII   Ne sai si de ma dame la durtée
               Salvant l'estat d'amour jeo blamerai;
               Bien sai qe par tresfine loialté
               De tout mon coer la serve et serviray,
5   Mais le guardon, s'ascun deservi ai,
               Ne sai coment, m'est toutdis eslongé:
               Dont jeo ma dame point n'escuseray;
               Tant meinz reprens, com plus l'averay doné.

               A moun avis ceo n'est pas egalté,
10   Solonc reson si jeo le voir dirrai,
               A doner tout, coer, corps et volenté,
               Quant pour tout ceo reprendre ne porray
               D'amour la meindre chose qe jeo sai.
               Om dist, poi valt service q'est sanz fée;
15   Mais ja pour tant ma dame ne lerray,
               Q'a lui servir m'ai tout abandoné.

               Ma dame, qui sciet langage a plentée,
               Rien me respont quant jeo la prierai;
               Et s'ensi soit q'elle ait a moi parlée,
20   D'un mot soulein lors sa response orrai,
               A basse vois tantost me dirra, "nay."
               C'est sur toutz autres ditz qe jeo plus hee;
               Le mot est brief, mais qant vient a l'essay,
               La sentence est de grant dolour parée.

25   Ceste balade a celle envoieray,
               En qui riens falt fors soulement pitée:
               Ne puis lesser, maisque jeo l'ameray,
               Q'a sa merci jeo m'ai recomandé.

XVIII   Les goutes d'eaue qe cheont menu
               L'en voit sovent percer la dure piere;
               Mais cest essample n'est pas avenu,
               Semblablement qe jeo de ma priere
5   La tendre oraille de ma dame chiere
               Percer porrai, ainz il m'est defendu:
               Com plus la prie, et meinz m'ad entendu.

               Tiel esperver crieis unqes ne fu,
               Qe jeo ne crie plus en ma maniere
10   As toutz les foitz qe jeo voi temps et lu;
               Et toutdis maint ma dame d'une chiere,
               Assetz plus dure qe n'est la rochiere.

XVII   I do not know if I blame the hardheartedness of my lady,
             Defending the stature of love;
             I know well that with exquisite loyalty
             With all my heart I serve her and shall serve,
5   But the reward that I have deserved —
             I do not know how — is always kept at a distance:
             Therefore I do not excuse my lady at all;
             The more I give, the greater is my rejection.

             In my opinion that is not parity —
10   According to reason, if I may speak the truth —
             To give all, heart, body and will,
             Then for all that not to be able to get back
             The least thing of love that I know.
             Men say, poor is the service that is without reward;
15   But never for so much will my lady make allowance,
             When in order to serve her I have abandoned myself.

             My lady, who has a full command of language,
             Makes no response to me when I entreat;
             But thus it is, should she speak to me,
20   Then I hear her response in one word alone,
             A worthless voice immediately will say to me, "No."
             It is the word above all others that I hate most;
             The word is brief, but when it comes into use,
             The sentence is draped with great sadness.

25   This balade to her I shall send,
             In which nothing is wanting except pity:
             I am unable to leave off from loving her;
             Unto her mercy I recommend myself.

XVIII   Little drops of water that fall
             Often are able to pierce the hard stone;
             But that case doesn't come to pass
             When likewise I, with my prayer,
5   The tender ear of my cheerful lady
             Try to pierce: rather, I am prevented.
             The more I pray, the less I am heeded.

             No sparrow hawk ever was so loud in crying
             That I, in my manner, do not cry more,
10   As often as I see time and place;
             And always my lady maintains the same demeanor,
             Altogether harder than rock.

Ne sai dont jeo ma dame ai offendu;
Com plus la prie, et meinz m'ad entendu.

15 Le ciel amont de la justice dieu
Trespercerai, si jeo les seintz requiere;
Mais a ce point c'est ma dame abstenu,
Qe toutdis clot s'oraille a ma matiere.
Om perce ainçois du marbre la quarere,
20 Q'elle ait a ma requeste un mot rendu;
Com plus la prie, et meinz m'ad entendu.

La dieurté de ma dame est ensi fiere
Com Diamant, qe n'est de riens fendu:
Ceo lettre en ceo me serra messagiere;
25 Com plus la prie, et meinz m'ad entendu.

XIX Om solt danter la beste plus salvage
Par les paroles dire soulement,
Et par parole changer le visage,
Et les semblances muer de la gent:
5 Mais jeo ne voie ascun experiment,
Qe de ma dame torne le corage;
Celle art n'est pas dessoubtz le firmament
Por atrapper un tiel oisel en cage.

Jeo parle et prie et serve et faitz hommage
10 De tout mon coer entier, mais nequedent
Ne puis troever d'amour celle avantage,
Dont ma tresdoulce dame ascunement
Me deigne un soul regard pitousement
Doner; mais plus qe Sibille le sage
15 S'estrange, ensi qe jeo ne sai coment
Pour atrapper un tiel oisel en cage.

Loigns de mon proeu et pres de mon damage,
Jeo trieus toutdis le fin du parlement;
Ne sai parler un mot de tiel estage,
20 Par quoi ma dame ne change son talent:
Sique jeo puiss veoir tout clierement
Qe ma parole est sanz vertu volage,
Et sanz exploit, sicom frivole au vent,
Pour atrapper un tiel oisel en cage.

25 Ma dame, en qui toute ma grace attent,
Vous m'avetz tant soubgit en vo servage,

I do not know whence I have offended my lady;
The more I pray, the less I am heeded.

15   The heaven of God the Judge above
I may pierce through, if I entreat the saints;
But upon this point my lady abstains,
Who always closes her ear to my argument.
One may pierce the marble stone-quarry but
20   She has returned a single word to my request;
The more I pray, the less I am heeded.

The hardness of my lady is as fierce
As diamond, which nothing splits:
This letter to her will be my messenger;
25   The more I pray, the less I am heeded.

XIX   Customarily one tames the most savage beast
Solely by speaking well-chosen words,
And by speaking the visage changes,
And transforms its looks to comely:
5   But I cannot see any device
That may turn the heart of my lady;
There is no art beneath the heavens
To trap such a bird in a cage.

I speak and pray and serve and do homage
10   With all my heart entire, but nevertheless
I am unable to find advantage in love
Because my very sweet lady disdains
To give me compassionately a single look
At all, but more than the sage Sibyl
15   Removes herself: thus I do not know how
To trap such a bird in a cage.

Far from my profit and near to my disadvantage,
Always I find the end of my conversation;
I do not know how to speak a word of that kind
20   By which my lady might change her inclination:
Thus I am able to see altogether clearly
That my speech is without power — worthless,
And without success, as if a trifle on the wind —
To trap such a bird in a cage.

25   My lady, in whom all of my grace belongs,
You have me so subject in your service,

Qe jeo n'ai sens, reson n'entendement,
Pour atrapper un tiel oisel en cage.

XX   Fortune, om dist, de sa Roe vire ades;
A mon avis mais il n'est pas ensi,
Car as toutz jours la troeve d'un reles,
Qe jeo sai nulle variance en li,
5   Ainz est en mes deseases establi,
En bass me tient, q'a lever ne me lesse:
De mes amours est tout ceo qe jeo di,
Ma dolour monte et ma joie descresce.

Apres la guerre om voit venir la pes,
10   Apres l'ivern est l'estée beal flori,
Mais mon estat ne voi changer jammes,
Qe jeo d'amour porrai troever merci.
He, noble dame, pour quoi est il ensi?
Soubtz vostre main gist ma fortune oppresse,
15   Tanq'il vous plest qe jeo serrai guari,
Ma dolour monte et ma joie descresce.

Celle infortune dont Palamedes
Chaoit, fist tant q'Agamenon chosi
Fuist a l'empire: auci Diomedes,
20   Par ceo qe Troilus estoit guerpi,
De ses amours la fortune ad saisi,
Du fille au Calcas mesna sa leesce:
Mais endroit moi la fortune est faili,
Ma dolour monte et ma joie descresce.

25   Le coer entier avoec ceo lettre ci
Envoie a vous, ma dame et ma dieuesce:
Prenetz pité de mon trespovere cri,
Ma dolour monte et ma joie descresce.

XXI   Au solail, qe les herbes eslumine
Et fait florir, jeo fai comparisoun
De celle q'ad dessoubtz sa discipline
Mon coer, mon corps, mes sens et ma resoun
5   Par fin amour trestout a sa bandoun:
Si menerai par tant joiouse vie,
Et servirai de bon entencioun,
Sanz mal penser d'ascune vilenie.

That I have no sense, reason nor understanding,
To trap such a bird in a cage.

XX   Fortune, they say, is always turning her wheel;
But in my opinion it is not so,
Because every day I seek release from it,
Yet I know no variance in place at all.
5   Thus it is established for my torment:
I remain at the bottom, from which I am not allowed to rise.
All that I speak is about my love;
My sadness rises and my joy descends.

After war one expects peace to come,
10   After winter is the beautiful foliage of spring;
But my state I am unable ever to change.
When I ought to find mercy from love,
Ah, noble lady, why is it thus?
Under your hand is my fortune oppressed;
15   Whenever you please I may be healed.
My sadness rises and my joy descends.

That misfortune that Palamedes
Endured was so that Agamemnon might be chosen
As the emperor: also Diomedes,
20   On account of whom Troilus was deserted —
Of his love Fortune had possession,
The daughter of Calchas rejoiced:
But in my case, Fortune is failing,
My sadness rises and my joy descends.

25   The whole heart with this letter here
I send you, my lady and my goddess:
Take pity on my most wretched cry,
My sadness rises and my joy descends.

XXI   To the sunshine that illumines the plants
And brings the flowers, I compare
That which has under its rule
My heart, my body, my sense and my reason.
5   Because of the pure love entirely in her absolute power —
By that I shall live a joyful life,
And serve with good intention,
Without bad thought of any vulgarity.

Si femme porroit estre celestine
10   De char humeine a la creacion,
Jeo croi bien qe ma dame soit devine;
Q'elle ad le port et la condicion
De si tressainte conversacioun,
Si plein d'onour, si plein de courtoisie,
15   Q'a lui servir j'ai fait ma veneisoun,
Sanz mal penser d'ascune vilenie.

Une autre tiele belle et femeline,
Trestout le mond pour sercher enviroun,
Ne truist om, car elle ad de sa covine
20   Honte et paour pour guarder sa mesoun,
N'i laist entrer ascun amant feloun:
Dont sui joious, car jeo de ma partie
La vuill amer d'oneste affeccioun,
Sanz mal penser d'ascune vilenie.

25   Mirour d'onour, essample de bon noun,
En bealté chaste et as vertus amie,
Ma dame, jeo vous aime et autre noun,
Sanz mal penser d'ascune vilenie.

XXII   J'ai bien sovent oï parler d'amour,
Mais ja devant n'esprovai la nature
De son estat, mais ore au present jour
Jeo sui cheeuz de soudeine aventure
5   En la sotie, u jeo languis sanz cure,
Ne sai coment j'en puiss avoir socour:
Car ma fortune est en ce cas si dure,
Q'ore est ma vie en ris, ore est en plour.

Pour bien penser jeo truiss assetz vigour,
10   Mais quant jeo doi parler en ascune hure,
Le coer me falt de si tresgrant paour,
Q'il hoste et tolt la vois et la parlure;
Q'au peine lors si jeo ma regardure
Porrai tenir a veoir la doulçour
15   De celle en qui j'ai mis toute ma cure,
Q'ore est ma vie en ris, ore est en plour.

Quant puiss mirer la face et la colour
De ma tresdoulce dame et sa feture,
Pour regarder en si tresbeal mirour
20   Jeo sui ravi de joie oultre mesure:
Mais tost apres, quant sui soulein, jeo plure,

If a woman is able to be celestial —
10 Of human flesh, at her creation —
I believe well that my lady should be divine;
Because she has the carriage and the state,
With conversation so very holy,
So full of honor, so full of courtesy,
15 That to serve her I have made my endeavor,
Without bad thought of any wickedness.

Another so beautiful and feminine,
Even if one were to search throughout the whole world,
A man cannot find, because she has in her company
20 Pride and Shame to guard her house;
No felonious lover is allowed to enter:
Thus I am joyous, because I in my part
Wish to love her with honest affection,
Without bad thought of any deceit.

25 Mirror of honor, example of good name,
And beauty chaste and friend of virtue,
My lady, I love you and no other,
Without bad thought of any degradation.

XXII   I have often heard good things said about love,
But I never before experienced the nature
Of his estate; however, now at the present day
I am fallen suddenly by chance
5 Into the madness, wherein I languish without cure.
I know not how I may be able to have succor;
Because my fortune is in this case so hard,
Now my life is in laughter, now in tears.

I find enough strength to think good things,
10 But when at any hour I ought to speak,
My heart casts me into such a very great fear,
That takes away and removes voice and speech;
I have such pain, then, unless I my gaze
Am able to hold in sight of the sweetness
15 Of her in whom I have placed all of my care.
Now my life is in laughter, now in tears.

When I am able to admire the face and the color
Of my very sweet lady, and her features,
Gazing into so very beautiful a mirror
20 I am ravished with joy beyond measure:
But immediately afterwards, when I am alone, I weep.

Ma joie ensi se melle de dolour,
Ne sai quant sui dessoubtz ne quant dessure,
Q'ore est ma vie en ris, ore est en plour.

25   A vous, tresbelle et bone creature,
Salvant toutdis l'estat de vostre honour,
Ceo lettre envoie: agardetz l'escripture,
Q'ore est ma vie en ris, ore est en plour.

XXIII   Pour un regard au primere acqueintance,
Quant jeo la bealté de ma dame vi,
Du coer, du corps trestoute m'obeissance
Lui ai doné, tant sui d'amour ravi:
5   Du destre main jeo l'ai ma foi plevi,
Sur quoi ma dame ad resceu moun hommage,
Com son servant et son loial ami;
A bon houre est qe jeo vi celle ymage.

Par lui veoir sanz autre sustenance,
10   Mais qe danger ne me soit anemi,
Il m'est avis de toute ma creance
Q'as toutz les jours jeo viveroie ensi:
Et c'est tout voir qe jeo lui aime si,
Qe mieulx voldroie morir en son servage,
15   Qe vivere ailours mill auns loigntain de li:
A bone houre est qe jeo vi celle ymage.

De son consail ceo me dist esperance,
Qe quant ma dame averai long temps servi
Et fait son gré d'onour et de plesance,
20   Lors solonc ceo qe j'averai deservi
Le reguerdoun me serra de merci;
Q'elle est plus noble et franche de corage
Qe Maii, quant ad la terre tout flori:
A bon houre est qe jeo vi celle ymage.

25   Ceo dit envoie a vous, ma dame, en qui
La gentilesce et le treshalt parage
Se monstront, dont espoir m'ad rejoï:
A bon houre est qe jeo vi celle ymage.

XXIIII   Jeo quide qe ma dame de sa mein
M'ad deinz le coer escript son pro pre noun;
Car quant jeo puiss oïr le chapellein
Sa letanie dire et sa leçoun,

My joy thus is mingled with sadness,
I do not know how much I am below and how much on high,
Now my life is in laughter, now in tears.

25   To you, most beautiful and good creature,
Saving always the estate of your honor,
I send this letter: regard the writing.
Now my life is in laughter, now in tears.

XXIII   Thinking back on the first meeting
When I saw the beauty of my lady,
My service — of the heart, of the body — altogether —
To her I gave, so greatly was I ravished by love.
5   With my right hand I have pledged her my faithfulness,
Through which my lady has received my homage,
As her servant and her loyal friend:
It was a happy hour when I saw her face.

Just to look on her, without other sustenance,
10   Provided that Danger might not be an enemy to me,
I believe with full conviction
That I should live thus every day:
And it is altogether true that I love her so,
That I would rather die in her service,
15   Than to live elsewhere a thousand years away from her.
It was a happy hour when I saw her face.

Hope gives me this advice,
That when I shall have served my lady a long time
And done her honorable service and pleasure,
20   Then according to that which I shall have deserved
Mercy will be my reward;
For she is more noble and free of heart
Than May, when the earth is in flower:
It was a happy hour when I saw her face.

25   This poem I send to you, my lady, in whom
Gentility and noblest birth
Display themselves, wherefore I gladden myself with hope:
It was a happy hour when I saw her face.

XXIIII   I think that with her hand my lady
Has written her proper name inside my heart;
Because when I am able to hear the chaplain
Say his litany and his lesson,

5   Jeo ne sai nomer autre, si le noun;
       Car j'ai le coer de fin amour si plein,
       Q'en lui gist toute ma devocioun:
       Dieus doignt qe jeo ne prie pas en vein!

       Pour penser les amours de temps longtein,
10   Com la priere de Pigmalion
       Faisoit miracle, et l'image au darrein
       De piere en char mua de s'oreisoun,
       J'ai graunt espoir de la comparisoun
       Qe par sovent prier serrai certein
15   De grace; et pour si noble reguerdoun
       Dieus doignt qe jeo ne prie pas en vein!

       Com cil qui songe et est en nouncertein,
       Ainz semble a lui qu'il vait tout environ
       Et fait et dit, ensi quant sui soulein,
20   A moi parlant jeo fais maint question,
       Despute et puis responde a ma resoun,
       Ne sai si jeo sui faie ou chose humein:
       Tiel est d'amour ma contemplacion;
       Dieus doignt qe jeo ne prie pas en vein!

25   A vous, qe m'avetz en subjeccion,
       Soul apres dieu si m'estes soverein,
       Envoie cette supplicacion:
       Dieus doignt qe jeo ne prie pas en vein!

XXV   Ma dame, si ceo fuist a vo plesir,
       Au plus sovent jeo vous visiteroie;
       Mais le fals jangle et le tresfals conspir
       De mesdisantz m'ont destorbé la voie,
5   Et vostre honour sur toute riens voldroie:
       Par quoi, ma dame, en droit de ma partie
       En lieu de moi mon coer a vous envoie;
       Car qui bien aime ses amours tard oblie.

       Ils sont assetz des tiels qui de mentir
10   Portont le clief pendant a lour curroie;
       Du quoi, ma dame, jeo ne puiss sentir
       Coment aler, ainçois me torne envoie:
       Mais sache dieus, par tout uque jeo soie,
       D'entier voloir sanz nulle departie
15   A vous me tiens, a vous mon coer se ploie;
       Car qui bien aime ses amours tard oblie.

5   I cannot pronounce another name, except hers;
Because I have a heart so full of pure love,
That all my devotion rests in her:
May God grant that I pray not in vain!

Calling to mind loves of long ago,
10   How the prayer of Pygmalion
Brought about a miracle, and the image at last
Transformed from stone to flesh by means of his prayer,
I have great hope of the comparison —
That through frequent prayer I may be certain
15   Of grace; and for so noble a reward
May God grant that I pray not in vain!

Like one who dreams and is in uncertainty —
First it seems to him that he goes all about
And acts and speaks — thus when I am alone,
20   Talking to myself, I form many a question,
I dispute, and then respond, with my reason;
I do not know if I am fay or a human creature:
Such is my contemplation of love;
May God grant that I pray not in vain!

25   To you, who have me in subjection —
Alone after God you are so much my sovereign —
I send this supplication:
May God grant that I pray not in vain!

XXV   My lady, if it might please you,
I would visit you more often;
But the false jangle and the too-false conspiracy
Of slanderers have disturbed my way,
5   And above all else I wish for your honor:
Therefore, my lady, as for my part,
In place of myself I send my heart to you;
Because he who loves well forgets his loves late.

There are enough of those who in order to deceive
10   Carry the key hanging from their belts;
For this reason, my lady, I am unable to know
How to go; rather, I turn myself away:
But God knows, fully, wherever I may be,
With complete desire without any parting
15   I hold firm to you, to you my heart itself inclines;
Because he who loves well forgets his loves late.

De vo presence a long temps abstenir
Grief m'est, en cas q'a force ensi feroie;
Et d'autrepart, si jeo voldrai venir,
20   Sanz vostre esgard ceo faire ne porroie:
Comandetz moi ceo qe jeo faire en doie,
Car vous avetz de moi la seignorie,
Tout est en vous, ma dolour et ma joie;
Car qui bien aime ses amours tard oblie.

25   As mesdisantz, dont bon amour s'esfroie,
De male langue dieus les motz maldie;
Q'en lour despit a vostre amour m'otroie;
Car qui bien aime ses amours tard oblie.

XXVI   Salutz honour et toute reverence,
Com cil d'amour q'est tout vostre soubgit,
Ma dame, a vous et a vostre excellence
Envoie, s'il vous plest, d'umble espirit,
5   Pour fare a vous plesance, honour, profit:
De tout mon coer entier jeo le desire,
Selonc le corps combien qe j'ai petit,
Sanz autre doun le coer doit bien suffire.

Qui donne soi, c'est une experience
10   Qe l'autre bien ne serront escondit:
Si plein com dieus m'ad de sa providence
Fait et formé, si plein sanz contredit
Soul apres lui, ma dame, en fait et dit
Vous donne; et si Rois fuisse d'un Empire,
15   Tout est a vous: mais en amour perfit
Sanz autre doun le coer doit bien suffire.

Primer quant vi l'estat de vo presence,
En vous mirer me vint si grant delit,
Q'unqes depuiss d'ascune negligence
20   Mon coer pensant vostre bealté n'oublit:
Par quoi toutdis me croist celle appetit
De vous amer, plus qe ne porrai dire;
Et pour descrire amour en son droit plit,
Sanz autre doun le coer doit bien suffire.

25   A vous, ma dame, envoie ceste escript,
Ne sai si vo danger le voet despire;
Mais, si reson soit en ce cas eslit,
Sanz autre doun le coer doit bien suffire.

To abstain from your presence a long time —
It is painful to me, in case it must needs be done;
And on the other hand, should I want to come,
20   To do so without your counsel would be impossible:
Command me what I ought to do,
Because you have lordship over me.
All is in you, my sadness and my joy —
Because he who loves well forgets his loves late.

25   As for slanderers, of whom good Love is frightened,
May God curse the words from a wicked tongue;
In despite of them I give myself to your love;
Because he who loves well forgets his loves late.

XXVI   Salutations, honor, and all reverence,
As one in love who is wholly your subject,
To you and to your excellence, my lady,
I send with a humble spirit, if you please,
5   To give you pleasure, honor, profit:
With all my whole heart I desire it.
Although I have but little besides my body,
Lacking another gift, the heart should well suffice.

If a man gives himself, it is a proof
10   That his other goods will not be refused:
As fully as God me by His providence
Made and formed, so fully without contradiction
Alone after to Him, my lady, in deed and word
I would give [it] to you; and if I might be a king of an empire,
15   All would be yours: but in perfect love
Lacking another gift, the heart should well suffice.

The first time when I saw the dignity of your presence,
To gaze on you gave me such great delight,
That ever since without any negligence
20   My heart, thinking about your beauty, forgets not:
Because always that appetite grows in me
For your love, more than I am able to say;
And to describe love in his true condition,
Lacking another gift, the heart should well suffice.

25   To you, my lady, I send this writing.
I do not know if your aversion to love may wish to despise it;
But if reason may be chosen in this case,
Lacking another gift, the heart should well suffice.

XXVII   Ma dame, quant jeo vi vostre oill [vair et] riant,
                Cupide m'ad ferru de tiele plaie
                Parmi le coer d'un dart d'amour ardant,
                Qe nulle medicine m'est verraie,
5   Si vous n'aidetz; mais certes jeo me paie,
                Car soubtz la cure de si bone mein
                Meulx vuil languir qe sanz vous estre sein.

                Amour de sa constreignte est un tirant,
                Mais sa banere quant merci desplaie,
10   Lors est il suef, courtois et confortant:
                Ceo poet savoir qui la fortune essaie;
                Mais combien qu'il sa grace me deslaie,
                Ma dame, jeo me tiens a vous certein;
                Mieulx vuill languir qe sanz vous estre sein.

15   Ensi ne tout guari ne languisant,
                Ma dame, soubtz l'espoir de vo manaie
                Je vive, et sui vos graces attendant.
                Tanque merci ses oignementz attraie,
                Et le destroit de ma dolour allaie:
20   Mais si guaris ne soie enquore au plein,
                Mieulx vuill languir qe sanz vous estre sein.

                Pour vous, q'avetz la bealté plus qe faie,
                Ceo lettre ai fait sanz null penser vilein:
                Parentre deus combien qe jeo m'esmaie,
25   Mieulx vuill languir qe sanz vous estre sein.

XXVIII   Dame, u est ore celle naturesce,
                Qe soloit estre en vous tiel temps jeo vi,
                Q'il ne vous plest de vostre gentilesce
                Un soul salutz mander a vostre ami?
5   Ne quier de vous forsque le coer demi,
                Et vous avetz le mien trestout entier:
                Om voit sovent de petit poi doner.

                Les vertus de franchise et de largesce
                Jeo sai, ma dame, en vous sont establi;
10   Et vous savetz ma peine et ma destresce,
                Dont par dolour jeo sui sempres faili
                En le defalte soul de vo merci,
                Q'il ne vous plest un mot a moi mander:
                Om voit sovent de petit poi doner.

XXVII

My lady, when I saw your eye blue-gray and laughing,
Cupid struck me such a wound
Through the heart with a burning dart of love,
That there is no true medicine for me
5   If you do not help; but certainly I am at peace,
Because under the care of your so estimable hand
I'd rather be sick than well without you.

Love in its compulsion is a tyrant,
But whenever its banner displays mercy,
10   Then is it gentle, courteous and comforting:
The one whom Fortune tests can know;
But as much as he dismisses his grace from me,
My lady, I bind myself to you certainly;
I'd rather be sick than well without you.

15   Thus neither entirely healed nor ill,
My lady, under hope of your care
I live, and I await your graces,
Until mercy may bring the ointments
And alleviate the difficulty of my sadness:
20   But if I may not heal again completely,
I'd rather be sick than well without you.

For you, who have more than a fairy beauty,
I have made this letter without any coarse thought:
As much as I am dismayed between the two,
25   I'd rather be sick than well without you.

XXVIII

Lady, where is now that gentle nature,
That many times I have seen to be customary in you,
That it does not please you from your gentility
To send a single greeting to your friend?
5   I seek from you but half a heart,
And you have all of mine entirely.
Often one sees little being given.

The virtues of liberality and largesse
I know, my lady, are established in you;
10   And you know my pain and my distress.
Thus I am always falling into sadness
In the lack alone of your mercy,
That it does not please you to send a word to me.
Often one sees little being given.

15   Tout qanque j'ai, ma dame, a vo noblesce
      De coer et corps jeo l'ai doné parmi;
      Par quoi ne vous desplese, en ma simplesce
      De vostre amour si jeo demande ensi;
      Car cil qui done il ad doun deservi,
20   Loial servant doit avoir son loer:
      Om voit sovent de petit poi doner.

      Ma doulce dame, qui m'avetz oubli,
      Prenetz ceo dit de moi pour remembrer,
      Et mandetz moi de vos beals ditz auci;
25   Q'om voit sovent de petit poi doner.

XXIX   Par droite cause et par necessité,
      Q'est sanz feintise honeste et resonable,
      M'ai par un temps de vous, dame, eslongé,
      Dont par reson jeo serroie excusable:
5   Mais fame, q'est par les paiis volable,
      De vo corous me dist novelle ades;
      Si m'ad apris, et jeo le croi sanz fable,
      Q'est d'amour loigns est de desease pres.

      Si vous, ma dame, scieussetz ma pensé,
10   Q'a vous servir remaint toutditz estable,
      Ne serrai point sanz cause refusé:
      Car jeo vous tiens si bone et merciable,
      Qe jeo, q'a vous sui toutditz serviçable,
      Et de mon grée ne vuill partir jammes,
15   Vo grace averai; et c'est tout veritable,
      Q'est d'amour loigns est de desease pres.

      Le fait de l'omme est en la volenté,
      Car qui bien voet par droit est commendable;
      Et pourcella, ma tresbelle honourée,
20   Hostetz corous et soietz amiable:
      Si riens ai fait q'a vous n'est pas greable,
      De vo merci m'en donetz un reles;
      Q'ore a l'essai la chose est bien provable,
      Q'est d'amour loigns est de desease pres.

25   Ma graciouse dame et honourable,
      Ceste balade a vous pour sercher pes
      Envoie; car jeo sui assetz creable,
      Q'est d'amour loigns est de desease pres.

15   Everything that I have, my lady, to your nobility
Of heart and body I have given utterly;
May it not displease you, in my simplicity
If I thus make request of your love;
Because he who gives deserves a gift,
20   A loyal servant, should have his reward.
Often one sees little being given.

My sweet lady, who has forgotten me,
Receive this poem from me as remembrance,
And send me also a beautiful poem of yours —
25   To one who often one sees little being given.

XXIX   For a just cause and by necessity,
That is without pretense honest and reasonable,
I have removed myself for a time from you, lady.
Therefore by reason I should be excusable;
5   But Rumor, that is ready to fly throughout the country,
Tells me news continually about your anger;
Thus have I learned, and I believe it without exaggeration,
Whoever is far away from love is near distress.

If you, my lady, knew my mind,
10   Which always remains stable to serve you,
I would not at all be refused without cause:
Because I hold you so good and merciful,
That I, who am unwaveringly in your service,
And wish never to part of my own free will,
15   Should have your grace; and it is entirely true,
Whoever is far away from love is near distress.

A man's deed is in his will,
Because whoso wishes well by right is commendable;
And for that reason, my very beautiful, honored one,
20   Take away anger and be amiable:
If I have done nothing that is disagreeable to you,
Of your mercy give me a release;
For now in the trial is the thing well provable,
Whoever is far away from love is near distress.

25   My gracious lady and honor-worthy,
This balade to you in search of peace
I send; because I am sufficiently ready to believe
Whoever is far away from love is near distress.

XXX   Si com la Nief, quant le fort vent tempeste,
                     Par halte mier se torne ci et la,
                     Ma dame, ensi moun coer maint en tempeste,
                     Quant le danger de vo parole orra;
5   Le Nief qe vostre bouche soufflera
                     Me fait sigler sur le peril de vie:
                     Q'est en danger, falt qu'il merci supplie.

                     Rois Uluxes, sicom nous dist la geste,
                     Vers son paiis de Troie qui sigla,
10   N'ot tiel paour du peril et moleste,
                     Quant les Sereines en la Mier passa,
                     Et le danger de Circes eschapa,
                     Qe le paour n'est plus de ma partie;
                     Q'est en danger, falt qu'il merci supplie.

15   Danger, qui tolt d'amour toute la feste,
                     Unqes un mot de confort ne sona;
                     Ainz plus cruel qe n'est la fiere beste,
                     Au point quant danger me respondera,
                     La chiere porte, et quant le nai dirra,
20   Plus que la mort m'estone celle oïe:
                     Q' est en danger, falt qu'il merci supplie.

                     Vers vous, ma bone dame, horspris cella
                     Qe danger maint en vostre compainie,
                     Ceste balade en mon message irra:
25   Q'est en danger, falt qu'il merci supplie.

XXXI   Ma belle dame, bone et graciouse,
                     Si pour bealté l'en doit amour doner,
                     La bealté, dame, avetz si plentevouse,
                     Qe vo bealté porra nulls coers passer,
5   Qe ne l'estoet par fine force amer,
                     Et obeïr d'amour la discipline
                     Par soulement vo bealté regarder:
                     Car bon amour a les vertus encline.

                     Et si bounté, q'est assetz vertuouse
10   De sa nature, amour porra causer,
                     Vous estes, dame, assetz plus bountevouse
                     Q'ascun amant le purra deviser:
                     Et ceo me fait vostre amour desirer
                     Secondement apres l'amour divine,
15   Pour chier tenir, servir et honourer;
                     Car bon amour a les vertus encline.

XXX
        Just as the ship, when the strong wind storms,
        Turns itself here and there, because of the high seas,
        Thus my heart remains in tempest, my lady,
        When it hears the reluctance to love in your speech;
5   The ship that your mouth blows upon
        Makes me navigate in peril of life:
        Whosoever is in danger, he must beg for mercy.

        King Ulysses, as the story tells us,
        Who sailed back to his country from Troy,
10   Had no such fear of peril or molestation,
        When he passed the Sirens in the sea,
        And escaped the danger of Circe,
        Because his fear is no more than on my part:
        Whosoever is in danger, he must beg for mercy.

15   Danger, who from love strips all celebration,
        Never utters a word of comfort;
        On the contrary, a fierce beast is not more cruel.
        At that moment whenever Danger responds to me,
        He takes away the dear harbor, and whenever he says "No,"
20   That sound paralyzes me more than death:
        Whosoever is in danger, he must beg for mercy.

        To you, my good lady (unless
        Danger remains in your company),
        This balade will bear my message:
25   Whosoever is in danger, he must beg for mercy.

XXXI
        My beautiful lady, good and gracious,
        If for beauty one ought to give love,
        Then the beauty, lady, you have is so abundant,
        That from your beauty no heart is able to escape,
5   But it must necessarily love completely,
        And obey the discipline of love
        Solely to look upon your beauty:
        Because good love draws toward the virtues.

        And if goodness, that is most virtuous
10   By its nature, can cause love —
        And you are, lady, the most excellent
        That any lover will be able to describe —
        Then that makes me desire your love
        Second only to the love divine,
15   To hold dear, to serve and honor;
        Because good love inclines toward the virtues.

Et si la sort de grace est amourouse,
Lors porrai bien, ma dame, tesmoigner,
Vo grace entre la gent est si famouse,
20   Q'a quelle part qe jeo me vuil torner,
Jeo puiss oïr vo grace proclamer:
Toutz en parlont et diont lour covine,
L'om est benoit qui vous purroit happer;
Car bon amour a les vertus encline.

25   Ma dame, en qui sont trestout bien plener,
Tresfressche flour, honeste et femeline,
Ceste balade a vous fais envoier;
Car bon amour a les vertus encline.

XXXII   Cest aun novell Janus, q'ad double face,
L'yvern passer et l'estée voit venant:
Comparison de moi si j'ensi face,
Contraire a luy mes oills sont regardant,
5   Je voi l'ivern venir froid et nuisant,
Et l'estée vait, ne sai sa revenue;
Q'amour me poignt et point ne me salue.

La cliere Estée, qui le solail embrace,
Devient obscure a moi, siq' au devant
10   L'yvern me tolt d'amour toute la grace:
Dont par dolour jeo sui mat et pesant,
Ne sai jeuer, ne sai chanter par tant,
Ainz sui covert dessoubtz la triste Nue;
Q'amour me poignt et point ne me salue.

15   Vo bealté croist, q'a null temps se desface;
Pourceo, ma dame, a vous est acordant
Qe vo bounté se monstre en toute place:
Mais jeo, pour quoi qe sui tout vo servant,
Ne puis veoir de grace ascun semblant,
20   C'est une dure et forte retenue;
Q'amour me poignt et point ne me salue.

XXXIII   Au comencer del aun present novell
Mon corps ove tout le coer a bone estreine
Jeo done a vous, ma dame, sanz repell,
Pour le tenir sicom vostre demeine:
5   Ne sai conter les joies que jeo meine
De vous servir, et pour moi guardoner,
Si plus n'y soit, donetz le regarder.

And if the lot of grace is love-worthy,
Then, my lady, I am well be able to bear witness,
That your grace is so famous among the people,
20 That wherever I want to turn,
I am able to hear your grace proclaimed:
Among themselves all in conversation, and talking.
That man is blessed who might be able to catch you:
Because good love inclines toward the virtues.

25 My lady, in whom completely are all good things,
Most fresh flower, honest and feminine,
I make this balade to send to you;
Because good love inclines toward the virtues.

XXXII It is a new Janus, who has a double face
To escape the winter and see the spring coming:
Thus a comparison I make to myself.
My eyes look contrarily to his,
5 I want the winter to come, cold and hurtful,
And the spring to go, and know no return;
Because love pierces me and saves me not at all.

The bright spring, which the sun embraces,
Becomes dark to me, since earlier
10 The winter took away from me all the grace of love:
Thus through grief I am dull and downcast,
I know no sport, in consequence, nor singing:
Instead I am roofed over beneath the sad cloud;
Because love pierces me and saves me not at all.

15 Your beauty grows, that time cannot efface;
Thus, my lady, for you it is appropriate
That your goodness displays itself everywhere:
But I, because I am entirely your servant,
Am unable to behold any semblance of grace;
20 It is a hard and difficult service,
Because love pierces me and saves me not at all.

XXXIII At the beginning of the present new year
My body along with all my heart, with good wishes
I give to you, my lady, without recall,
To hold as if it were your demesne:
5 I know not how to count the joys that I pursue
In your service, and as a reward to me,
If nothing else, consider the gift.

          Ne quier de vous avoir autre Juel

          Fors soulement vostre ameisté certeine;

10   Guardetz vo Nouche, guardetz le vostre anel,

          Vo beal semblant m'est joie sovereine,

          Q'a mon avis toute autre chose est veine:

          Et s'il vous plest, ma dame, sanz danger,

          Si plus n'y soit, donetz le regarder.

15   L'en solt toutditz au feste de Noël

          Reprendre joie et hoster toute peine

          Et doner douns; mais jeo ne demande el,

          De vo noblesce si noun q'il vois deigne

          Doner a moi d'amour ascune enseigne,

20   Dont jeo porrai ma fortune esperer:

          Si plus n'y soit, donetz le regarder.

          A vous, ma doulce dame treshalteine,

          Ceste balade vait pour desporter;

          Et pour le bounté dont vous estes pleine,

25   Si plus n'y soit, donetz le regarder.

XXXIIII   Saint Valentin l'amour et la nature

          De toutz oiseals ad en governement;

          Dont chascun d'eaux semblable a sa mesure

          Une compaigne honeste a son talent

5   Eslist tout d'un acord et d'un assent:

          Pour celle soule laist a covenir

          Toutes les autres, car nature aprent,

          U li coers est, le corps falt obeïr.

          Ma doulce dame, ensi jeo vous assure

10   Qe jeo vous ai eslieu semblablement;

          Sur toutes autres estes a dessure

          De mon amour si tresentierement,

          Qe riens y falt par quoi joiousement

          De coer et corps jeo vous voldrai servir:

15   Car de reson c'est une experiment,

          U li coers est, le corps falt obeïr.

          Pour remembrer jadis celle aventure

          De Alceone et Ceïx ensement,

          Com dieus muoit en oisel lour figure,

20   Ma volenté serroit tout tielement,

          Qe sanz envie et danger de la gent

          Nous porroions ensemble par loisir

I ask to have no other jewel from you
Except only your assured amity;
10   Keep your brooch, keep your ring,
Your beautiful appearance is sovereign joy to me,
In my view all other things are vain:
And if you please, my lady, without reluctance,
If nothing else, consider the gift.

15   One should always at Christmastime
Retain joy and reject all pain,
And give gifts; but I ask for nothing except,
Through your noblesse, that you deign
To give to me some sign of love,
20   From which I can hope for better fortune:
If nothing else, consider the gift.

To you, my sweet lady most high,
This balade is sent for entertainment:
And for the sake of the goodness of which you are full;
25   If nothing else, consider the gift.

XXXIIII   St. Valentine the love and the nature
Of all the birds has in governance;
Wherefore each bird its like, in its degree,
A companion honest in its inclination
5   Selects, all of one accord and one assent:
For that one alone it gladly leaves
All the others: because Nature teaches
Where the heart is, the body must follow.

My sweet lady, thus I assure you
10   That I have chosen you similarly;
Above all the others you are on high —
So supremely sacred to my love
That nothing is wanting because joyfully
With heart and body I wish to serve you:
15   Because by reason it is proven,
Where the heart is, the body must follow.

Always keep in mind the fate,
Moreover, of Alceone and Ceix,
How God transformed their bodies into birds:
20   My desire would be altogether the same,
That without envy and interference from people
We would be able together at leisure

Voler tout francs en nostre esbatement:
U li coers est, le corps falt obeïr.

25   Ma belle oisel, vers qui mon pensement
S'en vole ades sanz null contretenir,
Pren cest escript, car jeo sai voirement,
U li coers est, let corps falt obeïr.

XXXV   Saint Valentin plus qe null Emperour
Ad parlement et convocacion
Des toutz oiseals, qui vienont a son jour,
U la compaigne prent son compaignon
5   En droit amour; mais par comparison
D'ascune part ne puiss avoir la moie:
Qui soul remaint ne poet avoir grant joie.

Com la fenix souleine est au sojour
En Arabie celle regioun,
10   Ensi ma dame en droit de son amour
Souleine maint, ou si jeo vuill ou noun,
N'ad cure de ma supplicacion,
Sique d'amour ne sai troever la voie:
Qui soul remaint ne poet avoir grant joie.

15   O com nature est pleine de favour
A ceos oiseals q'ont lour eleccion!
O si jeo fuisse en droit de mon atour
En ceo soul cas de lour condicioun!
Plus poet nature qe ne poet resoun,
20   En mon estat tresbien le sente et voie:
Qui soul remaint ne poet avoir grant joie.

Chascun Tarcel gentil ad sa falcoun,
Mais j'ai faili de ceo q'avoir voldroie:
Ma dame, c'est le fin de mon chançoun,
25   Qui soul remaint ne poet avoir grant joie.

XXXVI   Pour comparer ce jolif temps de Maii,
Jeo le dirrai semblable a Paradis;
Car lors chantont et Merle et Papegai,
Les champs sont vert, les herbes sont floris,
5   Lors est nature dame du paiis;
Dont Venus poignt l'amant au tiel assai,
Q'encontre amour n'est qui poet dire Nai.

To fly wholly free for our diversion:
Where the heart is, the body must follow.

25   My beautiful bird, toward whom my thoughts
Fly themselves always, without any opposition,
Take this writing, because I know truthfully,
Where the heart is, the body must follow.

XXXV   St. Valentine, greater than any emperor,
Holds a parliament and assembly
Of all the birds, who come on his day,
Where the female takes her mate
5   In proper love; but by comparison
Of such a thing I am unable to have my own part:
Whosoever remains alone is unable to have great joy.

As the phoenix is alone in its home
In the region of Arabia,
10   Just so my lady in the place of her love
Remains alone, where whether I wish it or not,
She has no care about my supplication,
Because I know not how to find the pathway of love:
Whosoever remains alone is unable to have great joy.

15   Oh how Nature is full of favor
To those birds who have their choice!
Oh if, instead of my state, I might be
In just that same situation of theirs!
Nature is more capable than reason is,
20   And in my state it senses very well the path:
Whosoever remains alone is unable to have great joy.

Each gentle tercel has her falcon,
But I am lacking what I want to have:
My lady, it is the end of my song,
25   Whosoever remains alone is unable to have great joy.

XXXVI   To liken the happy time of May,
I will call it similar to Paradise;
Because then the blackbird and the parrot sing,
The fields are green, the plants are in flower,
5   Then Nature is lady of the country;
Whereupon Venus pierces the lover so sharply —
He who encounters love is unable to say no.

Qant tout ceo voi et qe jeo penserai
Coment nature ad tout le mond suspris,
10   Dont pour le temps se fait minote et gai,
Et jeo des autres sui soulein horpris,
Com cil qui sanz amie est vrais amis,
N'est pas mervaile lors si jeo m'esmai,
Q'encontre amour n'est qui poet dire Nai.

15   En lieu de Rose urtie cuillerai,
Dont mes chapeals ferrai par tiel devis,
Qe toute joie et confort jeo lerrai,
Si celle soule, en qui j'ai mon coer mis,
Selonc le point qe j'ai sovent requis,
20   Ne deigne alegger les griefs mals qe j'ai;
Q'encontre amour n'est qui poet dire Nai.

Pour pité querre et pourchacer mercis,
Va t'en, balade, u jeo t'envoierai;
Q'ore en certein jeo l'ai tresbien apris,
25   Q'encontre amour n'est qui poet dire Nai.

XXXVII   El Mois de Maii la plus joiouse chose
C'est fin amour, mais vous, ma dame chiere,
Prenetz a vous plustost la ruge Rose
Pour vo desport, et plus la faites chiere
5   Qe mon amour ove toute la priere
Qe vous ai fait maint jour y ad passé:
Vous estes franche et jeo sui fort lié.

Jeo voi toutplein des flours deinz vo parclose,
Privé de vous mais jeo sui mis derere,
10   N'y puiss entrer, qe l'entrée m'est forclose.
Jeo prens tesmoign de vostre chamberere,
Qe sciet et voit trestoute la matiere,
De si long temps qe jeo vous ai amé:
Vous estes franche et jeo sui fort lié.

15   Qant l'erbe croist et la flour se desclose,
Maii m'ad hosté de sa blanche banere,
Dont pense assetz plus qe jeo dire n'ose
De vous, ma dame, qui m'estes si fiere;
A vo merci car si jeo me refiere,
20   Vostre danger tantost m'ad deslaié:
Vous estes franche et jeo sui fort lié.

When I see all that and I think about it,
How Nature has affected all the world with love,
10   Whence for the time it makes itself gracious and gay,
And I alone am excepted from the others,
As the one true lover who is without a beloved,
It is no wonder therefore if I upset myself:
He who encounters love is unable to say no.

15   In place of the Rose I cultivate nettles,
Wherefore I make my chaplets in such a manner
That I shall abandon all joy and comfort
If she alone, in whom I place my heart,
In accord with what I have often begged,
20   Deigns not to lighten the evil griefs that I have;
He who encounters love is unable to say no.

To ask for pity and to procure mercy,
Go, balade, where I shall send you;
Because now for certain I have learned,
25   He who encounters love is unable to say no.

XXXVII   In the month of May the most joyous thing
Is pure love, but you, my dear lady,
Take the red rose to yourself sooner
For your pleasure, and make it more welcome
5   Than my love, with all the entreaty
That I have made to you many a day:
You are free and I am tightly bound.

I see very plainly the flowers within your enclosure —
Open for you, but I am put back,
10   I am unable to enter it, because the entry is foreclosed to me.
I cling nevertheless to your chamberlain,
Who knows and sees all the matter,
For how long a time I have loved you:
You are free and I am tightly bound.

15   When the plant grows and the flower opens itself,
May has excluded me from her white banner,
Wherefore I think rather more what I dare not say
About you, my lady, who are so fierce to me;
Because if I make appeal to your mercy
20   Your Danger immediately would put me off:
You are free and I am tightly bound.

En le douls temps ma fortune est amiere,
Le Mois de Maii s'est en yvern mué,
L'urtie truis, si jeo la Rose quiere:
25 Vous estes franche et jeo sui fort lié.

XXXVIII Sicom la fine piere Daiamand
De sa nature attrait le ferr au soi,
Ma dame, ensi vo douls regard plesant
Par fine force attrait le coer de moi:
5 N'est pas en mon poair, qant jeo vous voi,
Qe ne vous aime oultre mesure ensi,
Qe j'ai pour vous toute autre chose oubli.

Soubtz ciel n'est oill, maisq'il vous soit voiant,
Qu'il n'ait le coer tantost deinz son recoi
10 Suspris de vostre amour et suspirant:
De tout le monde si jeo fuisse Roi,
Trop fuist petit, me semble en bone foi,
Pour vous amer, car jeo sui tant ravi,
Qe j'ai pour vous toute autre chose oubli.

15 Toutes vertus en vous sont apparant,
Qe nature poet doner de sa loi,
Et dieus vous ad doné le remenant
Des bones mours; par quoi tresbien le croi
Qe jeo ne puiss amer meilour de toi:
20 Vostre bealté m'ad tielement saisi,
Qe j'ai pour vous toute autre chose oubli.

D'omble esperit, sicom jeo faire doi,
U toute grace son hostell ad basti
Ceo lettre envoie ove si tresfin otroi,
25 Qe j'ai pour vous toute autre chose oubli.

XXXIX En vous, ma doulce dame sovereine,
Pour remembrer et sercher les vertus,
Si bounté quier, et vous en estes pleine,
Si bealté quier, vous estes au dessus,
5 Si grace quier, vous avetz le surplus;
Qe riens y falt de ceo dont char humeine
Doit avoir pris, car c'est tresbien conuz,
Molt est benoit q'ove vous sa vie meine.

In the sweet times my fortune is bitter,
The month of May transforms itself into winter,
I find the nettle, if I ask for the Rose:
25   You are free and I am tightly bound.

XXXVIII   Just as the pure lodestone
By its nature attracts the iron to itself,
So your sweet and pleasant appearance, my lady,
By pure force attracts my heart:
5   It is not in my power, when I see you,
Not to love you beyond measure so,
That for you I have forgotten all other things.

Under heaven there is no man's eye but, should it look at you,
(Unless his heart forthwith is hidden away)
10   He will be seized by your love, and sigh:
If I might be king of all the world,
All would be worth little, it seems to me in good faith,
For want of your love, because I am so completely carried away,
That for you I have forgotten all other things.

15   In you all virtues are apparent
That Nature is able to give, according to her law,
And God has given you all the remaining
Good habits; for which reason I very well believe it,
That I am unable to love better than you:
20   Your beauty has seized me so,
That for you I have forgotten all other things.

With humble spirit, just as I ought to do,
Where all grace his home has built
This letter I send now with such complete surrender
25   That for you I have forgotten all other things.

XXXIX   To call you to mind, my sweet, sovereign lady,
And to make the rounds of your virtues —
I seek goodness, and you are fully of it,
I seek beauty, and you are on high,
5   I seek grace, and you have more than enough.
Because nothing is lacking for which human flesh
Ought to have honor — thus it is very well known,
He is greatly blessed who may lead his life with you.

Qui vo persone en son corage asseine,
10 Trop ad dur coer s'il ne soit retenuz
Pour vous servir come a sa capiteine:
Pour moi le di, q'a ceo me sui renduz,
Et si vous ai de rien, dame, offenduz,
Vous me poetz sicom vostre demeine
15 Bien chastier; q'en vostre amour jeo trieus,
Molt est benoit q'ove vous sa vie meine.

N'est un soul jour de toute la semeine,
El quell deinz soi mon coer milfoitz et pluis
De vous ne pense: ascune foitz me pleigne,
20 Et c'est quant jeo sui loign; mais quant venuz
Sui en presence, uque vous ai veeuz,
Lors est sur tout ma joie plus certeine:
Ensi de vous ma reson ai concluz,
Molt est benoit q'ove vous sa vie meine.

25 Ma dame, en qui tout bien sont contenuz,
Ceo lettre envoie a vo noblesce halteine
Ove Mil et Mil et Mil et Mil salutz:
Molt est benoit q'ove vous sa vie meine.

XL Om dist, promesses ne sont pas estables;
Ceo piert en vous, ma dame, au tiele enseigne,
Qe les paroles avetz amiables,
Mais en vos faitz vous n'estes pas certeine.
5 Vous m'avetz fait com jadis fist Heleine,
Quant prist Paris et laissa Menelai;
Ne puiss hoster, maisque de vous me pleigne:
Loials amours se provont a l'essai.

Si vos promesses fuissent veritables,
10 Sur vo parole q'estoit primereine
Vous ne serretz, ma dame, si changables,
Pour lesser qe vous avetz en demeine
Et prendre ailours la chose q'est foreine.
Vous savetz bien, ma dame, et jeo le sai,
15 Selonc qe le proverbe nous enseine,
Loials amours se provont a l'essai.

Qant verité d'amour se tome en fables,
Et qe vergoigne pas ne le restreigne
Parmi les voies qe sont honourables,
20 N'est un vertu qe la fortune meine.
Vostre ameisté vers un n'est pas souleine,

	Whoever addresses himself to your person in his heart,
10	Very hard is his heart who might hold himself back
	From serving you as his captain;
	I say for myself, I have surrendered myself to it,
	And if I have offended you in anything, lady,
	You are able to punish me well,
15	As your own, since in your love I find myself.
	He is greatly blessed who may lead his life with you.

There is not a single day in the whole week
In which my heart might a thousand times and more
Not think on you: I complained sometimes,
20 But it is when I was far away. Yet when I came
Into your presence, where I saw you,
Then my joy is absolutely very certain:
Therefore for you I have reduced my reason to silence.
He is greatly blessed who leads his life with you.

25 My lady, in whom all good things are contained,
This letter I send to your high nobility
With a thousand and a thousand and a thousand and a thousand greetings:
He is greatly blessed who leads his life with you.

XL Promises are not stable, it is said;
That appears in you, my lady, from many a sign,
Because you have speech worthy of love
But in your deeds you are not reliable.
5 You have treated me as Helen once did,
When she took Paris and left Menelaus;
I am unable to refrain, but I complain to you:
Loyal lovers are proven at the test.

If your promises were reliable,
10 It would be in your speech first of all —
You would not be, my lady, so changeable,
As to leave what you have in your possession
And take elsewhere something foreign.
You know well, my lady, and I know it,
15 According as the proverb teaches us,
Loyal lovers are proven at the test.

When love's truth transforms itself into fable,
And shame does not restrain it
Along paths that are honorable,
20 There is no power that may stay Fortune.
Your affection is not solely to one alone,

Ainz est a deux: c'est un chaunçon verrai,
Dont chanterai sovent a basse aleine,
Loials amours se provont a l'essai.

25   A dieu, ma joie, a dieu, ma triste peine,
Ore est yvern, qe soloit estre Maii;
Ne sai pour quoi Cupide me desdeigne:
Loials amours se provont a l'essai.

XLI   Des fals amantz tantz sont au jour present,
Dont les amies porront bien doloir:
Cil qui plus jure et fait son serement
De bien amer, plus pense a decevoir.
5   Jeo sui de celles une, a dire voir,
Qui me compleigns d'amour et sa feintise;
Par quoi, de fals amantz pour peas avoir,
Bon est qe bone dame bien s'avise.

Ascuns y ad qui voet bien amer sent,
10   Et a chascune il fait bien assavoir
Qu'il l'aime sanz nulle autre soulement:
Par tiel engin destorne le savoir
De l'innocent, qe quide recevoir
De ses amours la loialté promise:
15   Mais pour guarder s'onour et son devoir,
Bon est qe bone dame bien s'avise.

Les lievres de la bouche q'ensi ment
Cil tricheour tant beal les sciet movoir,
Q'a peine est nulle qe parfitement
20   Sache en ceo point le mal aparcevoir:
Mais cil q'ensi d'amour son estovoir
Pourchace, ad bien deservi la Juise;
Si dis pource q'a tiel mal removoir
Bon est qe bone dame bien s'avise.

25   Tu q'es au matin un et autre au soir,
Ceste balade envoie a ta reprise,
Pour toi guerpir et mettre a nonchaloir:
Bon est qe bone dame bien s'avise.

XLII   Semblables sont la fortune et les dées
Au fals amant, quant il d'amour s'aqueinte;
Sa loialté pleine est des falsetés,
Plustost deçoit, quant il se fait plus queinte:

But rather to two: that is a true song,
That I shall sing often, softly —
Loyal lovers are proven at the test.

25   Good-bye, my joy, good-bye, my sorrowful pain,
Now it is winter, where once it was May;
I know not why Cupid disdains me:
Loyal lovers are proven at the test.

XLI   There are so many false lovers today —
Whose ladies can well grieve:
He who promises most and makes his sworn oath
Of virtuous love, he thinks more of deceiving.
5   I am one of those, to speak truth,
Who myself complain about love and his deceit;
Because, in order to have peace from a false lover,
It is good that a virtuous lady reflects carefully.

Anyone who wishes to love a hundred well,
10   To each one he makes it well known
That he will love her alone, without any other:
By such a device he turns aside the understanding
Of the innocent, who thinks to receive
The loyalty of his loves guaranteed:
15   But in order to guard her honor and her duty,
It is good that a virtuous lady reflects carefully.

The lips of the mouth that lies in such a way,
The deceiver well knows to move them gently —
Which is no trouble for one who perfectly
20   Understands in a moment to perceive the evil:
But he who his needs from love thus
Procures, he well deserves condemnation;
I speak thus because, to avoid such evil,
It is good that a virtuous lady reflects carefully.

25   You who are one person in the morning and another at night,
This balade I send for your reproach,
To renounce you and to send contempt:
It is good that a virtuous lady reflects carefully.

XLII   Fortune and dice are similar
To a false lover, when he is involved with love:
His loyalty is full of deceptions —
When he makes himself very agreeable, the sooner he deceives.

5   A toi le di, q'as trahi femme meinte,
     Ceo q'as mespris restorer ne poetz,
     Et pourcella, de ta falsine atteinte
     Si tu voldras briser l'estrein, brisetz.

     Trop tard conu m'est ceo qe fait avetz,
10   Qe m'as hosté de toi par tiele empeinte,
     Qe jammais jour ne serrai retournetz
     Pour obeïr n'a toi n'a ta constreignte.
     He, fals amis, com ta parole est feinte!
     Les viels promesses toutes sont quassetz,
15   Trop as en toi la gentilesce exteinte:
     Si tu voldras briser l'estrein, brisetz.

     O tu, mirour des mutabilitées,
     Des fals amantz en toi l'image est peinte,
     Tes sens se muent en subtilitées,
20   Sil q'ensi fait n'ad pas la vie seinte.
     Tu as derrour la conscience enceinte,
     Dont fraude et malengin sont engendrez;
     Tu as vers moi ta loialté si freinte,
     Si tu voldras briser l'estrein, brisetz.

25   En les malvois malice n'est restreignte,
     Tu n'en serras de ta part escusez;
     As toutz amantz jeo fais ceste compleignte:
     Si tu voldras briser l'estrein, brisetz.

XLIII   Plus tricherous qe Jason a Medée,
     A Deianire ou q'Ercules estoit,
     Plus q'Eneas, q'avoit Dido lessée,
     Plus qe Theseüs, q'Adriagne amoit,
5   Ou Demephon, quant Phillis oublioit,
     Je trieus, helas, q'amer jadis soloie:
     Dont chanterai desore en mon endroit,
     C'est ma dolour, qe fuist ainçois ma joie.

     Unqes Ector, q'ama Pantasilée,
10   En tiele haste a Troie ne s'armoit,
     Qe tu tout nud n'es deinz le lit couché,
     Amis as toutes, quelqe venir doit,
     Ne poet chaloir, mais q'une femne y soit;
     Si es comun plus qe la halte voie.
15   Helas, qe la fortune me deçoit,
     C'est ma dolour, qe fuist ainçois ma joie.

5   To you I say it, who have betrayed women very often,
     That you have committed an offense you are unable to restore,
     And for that, convicted by your falsehood,
     If you wish to break the bond, break it.

     I recognized too late what you had done —
10   Thus you have cut me off from yourself with such an assault,
     That never, ever shall I turn again,
     To be disposed either toward you or your constraints.
     Ho, false friend, how your talk is false!
     The vile promises all are shattered,
15   You have extinguished all the gentility in yourself:
     If you wish to break the bond, break it.

     Oh you, mirror of mutabilities,
     In you is painted the image of false lovers;
     Your thoughts transform themselves into subtleties.
20   He who does so has no holy life.
     You have underhandedly made Conscience pregnant:
     Therefore Fraud and Deceit are engendered.
     You have broken your loyalty to me indeed —
     If you wish to break the bond, break it.

25   Malice among the evil is not restrained;
     You will not be excused for your part.
     To all lovers I make this complaint.
     If you wish to break the bond, break it.

XLIII   More treacherous than Jason to Medea,
     Or than Hercules was to Deianira,
     More than Aeneas, who left Dido,
     More than Theseus, who made love to Ariadne,
5   Or Demophon, when he forgot Phillis —
     So I find him, alas, whom I was wont to love:
     Thus henceforth for my part I shall sing,
     It is my grief, that once was my joy.

     Never did Hector, whom Penthesilea loved,
10   In such haste arm himself at Troy,
     As you fully naked have lain down in bed —
     You take every lover, whoever might come
     It matters not at all, so long as it might be a woman;
     Thus you are more common than the highway.
15   Alas, that Fortune has deceived me,
     It is my grief, that once was my joy.

De Lancelot si fuissetz remembré,
Et de Tristrans, com il se contenoit,
Generides, Florent, Partonopé,
20   Chascun de ceaux sa loialté guardoit.
Mais tu, helas, q'est ceo qe te forsvoit
De moi, q'a toi jammais null jour falsoie?
Tu es a large et jeo sui en destroit,
C'est ma dolour, qe fuist ainçois ma joie.

25   Des toutz les mals tu q'es le plus maloit,
Ceste compleignte a ton oraille envoie;
Santé me laist et langour me reçoit,
C'est ma dolour, qe fuist ainçois ma joie.

XLIIII   Vailant, courtois, gentil et renomée,
Loial, verrai, certain de vo promesse,
Vous m'avetz vostre corps et coer donné,
Qe jeo resçoive et prens a grant leesce.
5   Si jeo de Rome fuisse l'emperesse,
Vostre ameisté refuserai jeo mie,
Q'au tiel ami jeo vuill bien estre amie.

La halte fame qe l'en m'ad recontée
De vo valour et de vo grant prouesse
10   De joie m'ad l'oreille trespercée,
Et conforté le coer, siq'en destresce
Ne puiss languir, ainz de vo gentilesce
Pour remembrer sui des toutz mals guarie;
Q'au tiel ami jeo vuil bien estre amie.

15   Et puisq'il est ensi de verité,
Qe l'ameisté de vous vers moi se dresce,
Le coer de moi vers vous s'est adrescée
De bien amer par droite naturesce.
Tresdouls amis, tenetz ma foi expresse,
20   Ceo point d'acord tendrai toute ma vie,
Q'au tiel ami jeo vuill bien estre amie.

Par loialté, confort, chierté, tendresce,
Ceste ma lettre, quoique nulls en die,
Ove tout le coer envoie a vo noblesce;
25   Q'au tiel ami jeo vuill bien estre amie.

XLV   Ma dame, jeo vous doi bien comparer
Au cristall, qe les autres eslumine;

Let it be remembered thus about Lancelot,
And about Tristan, how he behaved himself,
Generides, Florent, Partonope —
20   Each of them maintained his loyalty.
But you, alas, what is that which led you astray
From me, who has never been false to you a single day?
You are at large and I am in dire straits,
It is my grief, that once was my joy.

25   Of all evil things you are the most wicked.
I send this complaint for your ear:
Health leaves me and sickness seizes me,
It is my grief, that once was my joy.

XLIIII   Valiant, courteous, honorable and renowned,
Loyal, true, unwavering in your promise,
You have given me your body and your heart,
Which I receive and accept with great delight.
5   If I were the empress of Rome,
Your friendship I would never refuse,
Because to such a friend I wish to be a good friend.

The high fame which has been recounted to me
About your valor and great prowess
10   Has pierced my ear through with joy,
And comforted the heart, which in distress
I was not able to let languish; but — by your worthiness
Remembered — I am healed of all sickness;
Because to such a friend I wish to be a good friend.

15   And since it is thus the truth,
That your friendship directs itself to me,
My heart addresses itself to you
With honorable love, by natural right.
Very sweet love, retain my expressed faith.
20   At this moment of accord I offer all of my life,
Because to such a friend I wish to be a good friend.

In loyalty, comfort, affection, tenderness,
Here is my letter, whatsoever any may say of it,
Now all my heart I send to your nobleness;
25   Because to such a friend I wish to be a good friend.

XLV   My lady, I well ought to compare you
To crystal, that illumines the others;

Car celle piere qui la poet toucher
De sa vertu reçoit sa medicine,
5   Si en devient plus preciouse et fine:
Ensi pour vo bounté considerer
Toutz les amantz se porront amender.

Vostre figure auci pour deviser,
La chiere avetz et belle et femeline,
10   Du quelle, qant jeo me puiss aviser,
Jeo sui constreint, ensi com de famine,
Pour vous amer de tiele discipline,
Dont m'est avis qe pour vous essampler
Toutz les amantz se porront amender.

15   El Cristall dame om porra bien noter
Deux propretés semblable a vo covine:
Le Cristall est de soi et blanc et clier;
Dieus et nature ensi par double line
Vous ont de l'un et l'autre fait saisine:
20   Par quoi des biens qe vous avetz pleiner
Toutz les amantz se porront amender.

Ceste balade, dame, a vous encline
Envoie pour vos graces commender:
De vostre essample et de vostre doctrine
25   Toutz les amantz se porront amender.

XLVI   En resemblance d'aigle, qui surmonte
Toute autre oisel pour voler au dessure,
Tresdouls amis, vostre amour tant amonte
Sur toutz amantz, par quoi jeo vous assure
5   De bien amer, sauf toutdis la mesure
De mon honour, le quell jeo guarderai:
Si parler n'ose, ades jeo penserai.

Par les paiis la fame vole et conte
Coment prouesce est toute en vostre cure,
10   Et quant jeo puiss oïr si noble conte
De vo valour, jeo met toute ma cure,
A mon poair dont vostre honour procure:
Mais pour les gentz tresbien m'aviserai;
Si parler n'ose, ades jeo penserai.

15   Entre nous dames, quant mettons a la compte
Vo noble port et vo fiere estature,
Lors en deviens un poi rugge pour honte,

Because whatever is able to touch that stone
Through its power receives a cure,
5   So it becomes more precious and fine:
Thus by meditating on your goodness,
All lovers will be able to amend themselves.

To describe your appearance, as well:
You have a face both beautiful and feminine,
10   Of such a kind, when I consider it,
I am compelled, exactly as by famine,
To love you in such a manner,
In such a way that, with you as an example
All lovers will be able to amend themselves.

15   In the crystal, lady, one is able to note well
Two properties likenable to your disposition:
The crystal is in itself both white and clear;
God and Nature thus by a double lineage
Have of the one and the other given you possession:
20   Because by the good things that you have in full,
All lovers will be able to amend themselves.

This balade, lady, addressed to you,
I send to commend your graces:
By your example and by your teaching,
25   All lovers will be able to amend themselves.

XLVI   In resemblance to the eagle, who surmounts
All other birds for flying up above,
Very sweet friend, your love so great mounts
Above all lovers, for which I assure you
5   Of true love, saving always the measure
Of my honor, which I shall protect:
If I dare not speak, I shall think unceasingly.

Throughout the land the story flies, and tells
How prowess is altogether your concern,
10   And when I am able to hear so noble a tale
About your valor, I put aside all my care,
With my power thus to obtain your honor:
But because of the people I take very great care;
If I dare not speak, I shall think unceasingly.

15   Between us ladies, when we take reckoning of
Your noble bearing and your fierce stature,
Then from that I become a little red with shame,

Mais jeo le torne ensi par envoisure,
Q'aparcevoir null poet la coverture:
20   Par tiel colour en joie jeo m'esmai;
Si parler n'ose, ades jeo penserai.

A vous, q'avetz d'onour celle aventure,
Qe vos valours toutz passont a l'essai,
Droitz est q'amour vous rende sa droiture:
25   Si parler n'ose, ades jeo penserai.

XLVII   Li corps se tient par manger et par boire,
Et fin amour le coer fait sustenir,
Mais plus d'assetz est digne la memoire
De vrai amour, qui le sciet maintenir:
5   Pourceo, ma dame, a vous me vuill tenir,
De tiel amour qe ja ne falsera:
N'est pas oiceus sil qui bien amera.

Des tiels y ad qui sont d'amour en gloire,
Par quoi li coers se poet bien rejoïr;
10   Des tiels y ad qui sont en purgatoire,
Qe mieulx lour fuist assetz de mort morir;
Ascuns d'espoir ont pris le vein desir,
Dont sanz esploit l'amant souhaidera:
N'est pas oiceus sil qui bien amera.

15   De fin amour qui voet savoir l'istoire,
Il falt q'il sache et bien et mal suffrir;
Plus est divers qe l'en ne porra croire:
Et nepourquant ne m'en puiss abstenir,
Ainz me covient amer, servir, cherir
20   La belle en qui moun coer sojournera:
N'est pas oiceus sil qui bien amera.

Demi parti de joie et de suspir
Ceste balade a vous, ma dame, irra;
Q'en la santé d'amour m'estoet languir:
25   N'est pas oiceus sil qui bien amera.

XLVIII   Amour est une chose merveilouse,
Dont nulls porra savoir le droit certein;
Amour de soi est la foi tricherouse,
Qe plus promette et meinz apporte au mein;
5   Le riche est povere et le courtois vilein,

20

But I transform it then by jesting,
So that no one is able to recognize the pretense:
By such color with joy I frighten myself;
If I dare not speak, I shall think unceasingly.

25

To you, who with honor have such adventure,
That your valor surpasses all others at the trial,
Right it is that for love you render your just claim:
If I dare not speak, I shall think unceasingly.

XLVII

The body maintains itself by eating and drinking,
And noble love sustains the heart,
But more worthy, by much, is the memory
Of true love, if a man knows to preserve it.

5

Because of that, my lady, I wish to be loyal to you,
To such love that I shall never falsify:
He is not lazy, whoever will love well.

Some there are in love's glory,
For which the body is able to rejoice;

10

Some there are in purgatory,
Who would much rather die their deaths;
Some have seized upon the vain desire of hope,
For which the lover wishes without success:
He is not lazy, whoever will love well.

15

Whoever is able to know the history of noble love,
He must know to endure both the good and the bad;
It is so very diverse that he will not be able to believe it:
And nevertheless I myself am not able to abstain,
But I am obliged to love, to serve, to cherish

20

The beautiful one in whom my heart will dwell:
He is not lazy, whoever will love well.

Divided half in joy and in sighs
This balade to you, my lady, will go;
Because in the health of love I must languish:

25

He is not lazy, whoever will love well.

XLVIII

Love is a marvelous thing
Of which no one is able to know the true certainty;
Love itself is a treacherous faith,
That promises much and delivers less in the end;

5

The rich man is poor and the courteous is a boor,

L'espine est molle et la rose est urtie:
En toutz errours amour se justefie.

L'amier est douls et la doulçour merdouse,
Labour est ease et le repos grievein,
10   Le doel plesant, la seurté perilouse,
Le halt est bass, si est le bass haltein,
Qant l'en mieulx quide avoir, tout est en vein,
Le ris en plour, le sens torne en folie
En toutz errours amour se justefie.

15   Amour est une voie dangerouse,
Le pres est loign, et loign remaint proschein;
Amour est chose odible et graciouse,
Orguil est humble et service est desdeign,
L'aignelle est fiere et le leon humein,
20   L'oue est en cage, la merle est forsbanie:
En toutz errours amour se justifie.

Ore est amour salvage, ore est soulein,
N'est qui d'amour poet dire la sotie;
Amour est serf, amour est soverein;
25   En toutz errours amour se justifie.

XLIX   As bons est bon et a les mals malvois
Amour, qui des natures est regent;
Mais l'omme qui de reson ad le pois,
Cil par reson doit amer bonement:
5   Car qui deinz soi sanz mal penser comprent,
De bon amour la verité pleinere,
Lors est amour d'onour la droite miere.

Bon amour doit son dieu amer ainçois,
Qui son dieu aime il aime verraiment,
10   Si ad de trois amours le primer chois;
Et apres dieu il doit secondement
Amer son proesme a soi semblablement;
Car cil q'ensi voet guarder la maniere,
Lors est amour d'onour la droite miere.

15   Le tierce point dont amour ad la vois,
Amour en son endroit ceo nous aprent
Soubtz matrimoine de les seintes lois,
Par vie honeste et nonpas autrement.
En ces trois pointz gist tout l'experiment

The thorn is soft and the rose is a nettle:
In all errors love justifies itself.

The bitter is sweet and sweetness foul,
Labor is ease and repose work,
10   Grief pleasant, security perilous,
The high is low, just as the low is high,
When one expects to have better, everything is in vain,
Laughter in tears, the sense turns to folly
In all errors love justifies itself.

15   Love is a dangerous path,
The near is far, and far away remains near;
Love is a thing hateful and gracious,
Pride is humble and service is disdain,
The lamb is fierce and the lion tolerant,
20   The goose is caged, the blackbird is ousted:
In all errors love justifies itself.

Now love is savage, now is it lonesome,
There is no one who is able to describe the folly of love:
Love is a serf, love is a sovereign;
25   In all errors love justifies itself.

XLIX   Good to the good and to the evil, evil
Is Love, who is ruler of all natures;
But the man who has a measure of reason,
He, on account of that reason, should love willingly:
5   Because when a man serves without evil within himself he understands
Fully the truth about right love:
Then Love is the rightful mother to Honor.

Good Love should love his God first:
Whoever loves his God, he loves in truth:
10   Thus He has the first choice of three loves.
And, after God, one should secondly
Love his neighbor as himself;
Because if he is thus able to maintain this manner,
Then Love is the rightful mother to Honor.

15   The third point of which Love has the title —
This Love in his way teaches us
Under the holy law of matrimony,
By honest life and not any other.
In these three points lies all the experience

20   De boun amour, et si j'ensi le quiere,
        Lors est amour d'onour la droite miere.

        De bon amour, pour prendre avisement,
        Jeo vous ai dit la forme et la matiere;
        Car quique voet amer honestement,
25   Lors est amour d'onour la droite miere.

L   De vrai honour est amour tout le chief,
        Qui le corage et le memorial
        Des bones mours fait guarder sanz meschief:
        De l'averous il fait franc et loial,
5   Et de vilein courtois et liberal,
        Et de couard plus fiers qe n'est leoun;
        De l'envious il hoste tout le mal:
        Amour s'acorde a nature et resoun.

        Ceo q'ainz fuist aspre, amour le tempre suef,
10   Si fait du guerre pes, et est causal
        Dont toute vie honeste ad soun relief.
        Sibien les choses qe sont natural,
        Com celles qe sont d'omme resonal,
        Amour par tout sa jurediccioun
15   Claime a tenir, et par especial
        Amour s'acorde a nature et resoun.

        Au droit amant riens est pesant ne grief,
        Dont conscience en soun judicial
        Forsvoit, mais li malvois plus qe la Nief
20   Est en tempeste, et ad son governal
        D'onour perdu; sique du pois egual
        La fortune est et la condicioun
        De l'omme, et sur tout le plus cordial
        Amour s'acorde a nature et resoun.

25   N'est qui d'amour poet dire le final;
        Mais en droit moi c'est la conclusioun,
        Qui voet d'onour sercher l'original,
        Amour s'acorde a nature et reson.

LI   Amour de soi est bon en toute guise,
        Si resoun le governe et justifie;
        Mais autrement, s'il naist de fole emprise,
        N'est pas amour, ainz serra dit sotie.
5   Avise soi chascuns de sa partie,

20 Of good love, and if I seek after it thus,
Then Love is the rightful mother to Honor.

Of proper love, for consideration,
I have told you the form and the matter;
Because for whoever wishes to love honestly,
25 Then Love is the rightful mother to Honor.

L Of true honor wholly the chief is Love,
Who keeps the spirit and the memory
Of good morals safe from misfortune:
He makes the avaricious free and loyal,
5 And the boor courteous and liberal,
And the coward more fierce than the lion;
He drives away evil from the envious:
Love accords himself with Nature and Reason.

That which once was bitter, Love makes gentle,
10 Just so he makes peace of war, and is the cause
By which all honest life has his help.
Both to the things that are natural,
And to those that are rational to man,
Love throughout his jurisdiction
15 Holds claim and, in particular,
Love accords himself with Nature and Reason.

To a proper lover nothing is burdensome or grievous,
When conscience in his judgment
Goes astray; but a wicked one, more than any ship,
20 Is tempest-tossed, and loses his rudder
Of honor. Thus of equal weights
Are Fortune and the condition
Of man — and of his heart most, above all,
Love accords himself with Nature and Reason.

25 There is no one who is able to recount the end of love;
But for my part, this is the conclusion:
Whoever wishes to discover the origin of Honor,
Love accords himself with Nature and Reason.

LI Love in itself is good in every guise,
If reason governs and justifies it;
But otherwise, it is but a foolish enterprise,
It is not love, but will be called madness.
5 Let each one for his part deliberate for himself,

Car ma resoun de novell acqueintance
M'ad fait amer d'amour la plus cherie
Virgine et miere, en qui gist ma creance.

As toutes dames jeo doi moun servise
10   Abandoner par droite courtasie
Mais a ma dame pleine de franchise
Pour comparer n'est une en ceste vie.
Qui voet amer ne poet faillir d'amie,
Car perdurable amour sanz variance
15   Remaint en luy, com celle q'est florie
De bien, d'onour, de joie et de plesance.

De tout mon coer jeo l'aime et serve et prise,
Et amerai sanz nulle departie;
Par quoi j'espoir d'avoir ma rewardise,
20   Pour quelle jeo ma dame ades supplie:
C'est, qant mon corps lerra la compaignie
De m'alme, lors lui deigne en remembrance
D'amour doner a moi le pourpartie,
Dont puiss avoir le ciel en heritance.

25   O gentile Engleterre, a toi j'escrits,
Pour remembrer ta joie q'est novelle,
Qe te survient du noble Roi Henri,
Par qui dieus ad redrescé ta querele:
A dieu purceo prient et cil et celle,
30   Q'il de sa grace au fort Roi coroné
Doignt peas, honour, joie et prosperité.

Because my reason through new friendship
Has made me love one most cherished by love —
Virgin and mother, in whom lies my belief.

I ought my service to all ladies

10   Abandon, by rightful courtesy,
Except to my Lady full of liberality —
There is no one comparable in this life.
Whoever desires love cannot fall short with this ladylove,
Because lasting love without variance

15   Abides in Her, as the one who is adorned
With goodness, honor, joy and pleasure.

With all my heart I love Her, and serve and praise,
And I shall love without cessation;
Because I hope to have my reward

20   For which I have asked my Lady unceasingly:
It is, when my body parts company
From my soul, then She may deign, remembering
My love, to give to me a share,
So that I shall be able to have heaven as inheritance.

25   Oh gentle England, I write for you,
For remembrance of your new joy,
Which comes to you from the noble King Henry,
By whom God has redressed your quarrel:
Let one and all therefore pray to God,

30   That He who with His grace crowned the King indeed
May give peace, honor, joy and prosperity.

EXPLANATORY NOTES TO THE *CINKANTE BALADES*

ABBREVIATIONS: Boethius: Boethius, *Consolation of Philosophy;* **BD**: Chaucer, *Book of the Duchess*; **CA**: Gower, *Confessio Amantis*, ed. Peck; **F**: Oxford, Bodleian Library, MS Fairfax 3; **G**: Glasgow, University of Glasgow Library, MS Hunter 59 (T.2.17); **Mac**: Macaulay, ed., *The Complete Works of John Gower*; **MO**: Gower, *Mirour de l'Omme*, trans. Wilson; **OF**: Old French; **PF**: Chaucer, *Parliament of Fowls*; **RR**: Chaucer, *Romaunt of the Rose*; **Roman de la Rose**: Guillaume de Lorris and Jean de Meun, *Le Roman de la Rose*; **Whiting**: Whiting, *Chaucer's Use of Proverbs*.

A note on capitalization: in these translations capitalization usually adheres to Macaulay's practice, which, in general, replicates forms in the manuscript. Wherever capitalization may help the modern reader better comprehend Gower's intention — as for example, in the case of theological concepts (e.g., "Providence," *Cinkante Balades*, Dedication I.3) or allegorical figures (e.g., "Danger," *Cinkante Balades*, XXIII.10) — capitalization is added here.

DEDICATION I

1   *Pité* is translated as "mercy," but diphthongs typically reduce in Anglo-Norman, thus "piety" is an alternative. It would not be out of poetic character for Gower to have desired, and so engineered, the dual resonance.

5   *Par vous.* Lit. "Through you."

9–14   See Textual Notes, p. 148, for Macaulay's reconstruction of the missing lines.

DEDICATION II

20   *reçoit.* Indicative present tense, third person, but following "vendra" a subjunctive or optative seems intended.

21   *estre.* From "esse" and "stare"; hence, "existed."

24   *d'ascune.* "Of any[one]" but possibly also simply "any villainy."

I (CINKANTE BALADES)

1–14   Part of fol. 12 is torn out, thus both recto and verso portions are missing.

8   *en vostre grace.* "In your grace"; see *MO* lines 6645, 11436, and 27536, where "grace" is paired with "mercy"; also *MO* line 15215, paired with "pité"; *MO* line 18926, paired with "pardoun." "In your grace" is common in *CA*, with the same sense, e.g., 1.732, "I put me therof in your grace"; and see further Chaucer's *Troilus and Criseyde*, e.g., III.472, Troilus "so ful stood in his lady grace"; and *Canterbury Tales*, e.g., of the Squire, General Prologue I(A)88, "in hope to stonden in his lady grace."

13   *-ssetz.* Probably "[a]ssetz"; hence "enough," "well enough."

14   *en autre place.* Lit. "in another place."

17   *plesance.* "Pleasures, happiness"; in context, perhaps ironic.

22   *fortune.* I.e., Fortuna; see Boethius, 2.pr.1.

II L'IVERN S'EN VAIT ET L'ESTÉE VIENT FLORI

4   *renovelle.* Lit. "renews," "restores."

5   *De mes amours.* Lit. "In accord with my affections."

8   *pres.* ["soon after."] Compare Modern French *près*, "near."

21   *que bon vous semblera.* Lit. "whatever seems good to you."

22   *se poet tenir.* Lit. "is able to maintain itself," but Gower often uses present tense for future — as is clearly the sense here.

27   *il vous remembrera.* An impersonal construction normally, but here "il" seems meant to highlight the letter, since three lines earlier Gower — surprisingly, against his common practice throughout the balades and *MO* — makes "ce lettre" masculine.

III D'ARDANT DESIR CELLE AMOROUSE PEIGNE

4   *Pour vous.* Causal, i.e., "Because of you."

6   *De sa justice amour moun coer enhorte.* I.e., "My heart exhorts Love to establish, bring about, or enforce justice"; alternatively, with "amour" as the subject, "Love exhorts my heart with its justice."

16   *A toutz les jours sanz departir me ploie.* Lit. "Every day without [separating, taking leave] I fold [bend] (<*ploier*) myself"; but clearly both "me ploie" and "sanz departir" here are used figuratively, the former implying a contortionist's effort, the latter in the sense of "unremittingly, without yielding or changing course."

N.b., the reappearance of "sanz departir" in the following two balades, IIII and IIII*, suggests purposive interconnection there, and with III here.

IIII D'ENTIER VOLOIR SANZ JAMMES DEPARTIR

17   *Q'en mon pensant*. Lit. "In my thought, recollection."

V POUR UNE SOULE AVOIR ET REJOÏR

2   *a noun chaloir*. Impersonal: "to be of no importance" (compare Modern English "nonchalant").

16   *la.* "her"; alternatively, "it."

18   *Benoite soit*. Present subjunctive, hence perhaps conditional: "might be."

19   *porra tenir*. Lit. "is able to."

25 ff.   ☞ **Marginalia** in F: *Les balades d'amont jesqes enci sont fait especialement pour ceaux q'attendont lours amours par droite mariage.* ["The balades from the beginning up to this point are made especially for those who wait on their loves in expectation of marriage."] *q'attendont.* Lit. "wait on."

VI LA FAME ET LA TRESHALTE RENOMÉE

2 ff.   ☞ **Marginalia** in F: *Les balades d'ici jesqes au fin du livere sont universeles a tout le monde, selonc les propretés et les condicions des Amantz, qui sont diversement travailez en la fortune d'amour.* ["The balades from here until the end of the book are universal, for everyone, according to the properties and conditions of Lovers who are diversely suffering the fortunes of Love."] *la fortune d'amour.* Lit. singular, "fortune of Love"; idiomatically plural in English, i.e., "ups and downs." Hence Fortuna as a personification is not intended.

5   *M'ad trespercié l'oreille et est impresse*. Lit. requires a singular subject, but Gower's evident intention hearkens back to plural nouns in lines 1–2.

6–7   *par quoi mon oill desire, / Vostre presence au fin qe jeo remire*. N.b., Gower here extends the usual one-line refrain by a half a line.

7   *Vostre presence*. Lit. "your [physical] presence," so perhaps with pointedly high courtly intent (compare "noblesce," "grant valour," and "haltesse" in stanza 2), and thus to be taken less idiomatically than "in person."

         remire. "look on" with additional senses of "admire," "contemplate"; "remirer" also carries a reflexive sense of "look at one's self" (in a mirror).

20   *Le bon amour*. Lit. "good love," by courtly tradition "loyal."

VII DE FIN AMOUR C'EST LE DROIT ET NATURE

1	*fin amour.* I.e., "amour courtoise," love as idealized in the courtly tradition: refined, pure, noble, ennobling, loyal, gentle, unwavering.
5	*honourée.* Both "honorable one" and (implied) "the one [I] honor."
23–24	*Plus . . . plus.* "More" (quantity) as well as "more" (time): Gower plays upon the elasticity of the word for punning effect.

VIII D'ESTABLE COER, QUI NULLEMENT SE MUE

2	*le penser.* Lit. an infinitive, here presented as masculine: hence, e.g., "Ses Eles" (line 4), and throughout, indicating the wings of thought, not of the falcon.
4	*souhaid et desirer.* Allegorical personifications.
17	*retenue.* Macaulay (Mac, 1:463, note VIII.17) translates "engagement"; the central idea, however, seems to be a vow of loyalty, even of vassalage. Compare XV.14 and *Traitié* III.20.
22	*Ceste balade a vous fait envoier.* Lit. "This balade is made to send to you."

IX TROP TART A CEO QE JEO DESIRE ET PROIE

5	*amis.* Lit. "friend" but in the courtly sense much larger: "one who loves you," "lover."
8	*En vous remaint ma sovereine joie.* N.b., Gower twice breaks patterns in this poem by a) adding a fourth and fifth stanza to the usual three, and b) closing only the first and final stanzas with this refrain line, rather than repeating throughout.
9–10	*De mes deux oels ainçois qe jeo vous voie, / Millfoitz le jour mon coer y est tramis.* I.e., the eye as the window to the soul/heart; see *Roman de la Rose*, e.g., lines 1692, 1741, etc.
14	*Desir.* Personification.
25	*m'esbanoie.* Lit. "I divert myself."
28	*fremis.* Lit. "shake, quiver."
37	*ne suis poestis.* Lit. "I am not powerful [enough]."

X MON TRESDOULS COER, MON COER AVETZ SOULEINE

6	*plie.* Lit. "bow, bend," so perhaps here with a sense of the lover's lowliness and the lady's exaltation; compare "si halt lieu" (line 10) and "supplie" (line 20).

7   *ameisté.* "Amity" is a weak English substitute for a broader and more passionate courtly term; see "amis" (IX.5).

8   *la fortune.* Here taken as Fortuna, since it "leads" ("meine").

10   *si halt lieu.* Lit. "so high a place," e.g., "honored," "exalted."

13   *s'allie.* Lit. "binds itself" ("to you" implicit).

15   *S'amour.* Personification, since it "wishes" ("volt").

16   *Et faire tant qe jeo m'esjoierai.* Lit. "And to act so that I may rejoice."

20   *supplie.* Lit. "bend" but with broader resonances: "bend the knee," i.e., "humbly beg" (feudal); "supplicate"; and compare as a reflexive, "prostrate one's self"; see also "plie," above (line 6).

24   *balade escrite.* "Written balade," perhaps recalling the earlier, exclusively sung form (?) or to emphasize the lover's originality ("this balade I have made").

XI MES SENS FOREINS SE POURRONT BIEN MOVOIR

7   *Si vous fuissetz un poi plus amerouse.* Lit. "If you were a little bit more amorous"; so, perhaps, "more inclined to love."

20   *par reson.* Lit. "by reason," "according to reason."

22   *cest escris.* Lit. "this writing."

23   *dangerouse.* "Disdainful," "rebuffing," "blunt," "uncourteous"; for Gower's usage, see the personification "Danger" in *Roman de la Rose* and *CA.*

24   *Meilour de vous om sciet en null paiis.* Lit. "Better than you one knows in no country."

XII LA DAME A LA CHALANDRE COMPARER

1   *la Chalandre.* "Plover": compare *MO* lines 10707–17. Wilson translates "lark," apparently following Chaucer's usage, *RR* lines 663 and 914, where "chelaundre/ chalaundres/chalaundre" appear, respectively, in lists of singing birds; hence Skeat's glossary, s.v. "chalaundre," "a species of lark (*Alauda calandra*)." But that the lark is Gower's bird is doubtful. In *MO,* lines 10708–10, the chalandre is used to represent "Contemplacioun" and "au mye nuyt tout coy / Devers le ciel prent son voloy / Si halt comme puet en sa mesure" ("at midnight very quietly takes flight toward heaven, as high as it can possibly go," trans. Wilson). Larks, rightly known for their singing, not their meditative example, are not night fliers, and *Alaudra calandra,* while common in France (whence *Roman de la Rose,* which Chaucer translates), did not inhabit fourteenth-century England. More likely Gower had in mind the "charadrius," which in Deuteronomy 14:16–18 (at 18) and Leviticus 11:19 is listed among unclean birds of the shore and marsh

(e.g., heron, swan, stork, cormorant, "porphirion" [sultana-hen, *Fulica porphyrio*], night heron, bittern, hoopoe); but his direct source was a version of *Physiologus*, which notes

> If someone is ill, whether he will live or die can be known from the charadrius. The bird turns his face away from the man whose illness will bring death . . . if the disease is not fatal, the charadrius stares the sick man in the face and the sick man stares back at the charadrius, who releases him from his illness. Then, flying up to the atmosphere of the sun, the charadrius burns away the sick man's illness and scatters it abroad. (trans. Curley, 7–8)

Plovers — properly birds of the order *Charadriiformes*, which includes the genus *Charadrius* (as well as the genus *Vanellus*, the lapwing) — are small waders common in England. Of particular interest to the Kentishman Gower might have been *Charadrius alexandrinus*, the Kentish or Snowy Plover, which until recently bred in England and gets its name from its all-white appearance when viewed in flight, from below. Perhaps not insignificantly, *Physiologus* describes the charadrius as "entirely white with no black part at all" (trans. Curley, p. 7). See also *Bestiary*, trans. White (a translation of Cambridge University Library MS II.4.26, a twelfth-century Latin prose bestiary possibly from Revesby Abbey in Lincolnshire), which argues (p. 115n1) for the "white wagtail (*Motacilla alba Linn.*) for wagtails are still regarded in Ireland with a superstitious dread. The markings of their heads are skull-like." The most extensive study is G. C. Druce, "The Chalandrios and Its Legend, Sculpted upon the Twelfth Century Doorway of the Alne Church, Yorkshire," *Yorkshire Archaeological Journal* 69 (1912–13), 381–416.

13   *la feture.* "Form" but also "face," "features," "bodily shape."

22   *vair.* "Varius," "variegated," "mottled," "parti-colored," but also "various," "changeable." This is the standard eye-description for damsels of romance (see Oiseuse [Idleness], *Roman de la Rose,* line 521 [*RR*, line 546: "Hir yen grey as is a faucoun"]); for example, Guinevere, Iseult, and other beautiful women in romances are often praised for their "gray" eyes. "Gray" is usually translated as a color, blue and/or gray, sometimes as "bright, shining" (see Greimas, *Dictionnaire*, "clair"); but perhaps "changeable" is an intended part of the mix as well. See XXVII.1.

XIII AU MOIS DE MARSZ, U TANT Y AD MUANCE

7   *Ore ai le coer en ease, ore en destance.* N.b., predictably a line from this position would repeat throughout, but Gower avoids a refrain in this balade. See poems XIIII, XVI, and XVII below.

11   *nature.* Nature, personification; compare Alain of Lille, *De planctu Naturae*; *PF*.

21   *desavance.* "Diminishes," or perhaps "dims."

22   *en aventure.* Implies both randomness and risk.

XIIII POUR PENSER DE MA DAME SOVEREINE

7   *Plus qe Paris ne soeffrist pour Heleine.* N.b., predictably a line from this position would repeat throughout, but Gower avoids a refrain in this balade. See XIII, above, and XVI and XVII, below.

20   *Ne puiss faillir del un avoir estreine.* I follow Macaulay's translation of this line; see Mac, 1:464, note 20.

23   *Q'a vous parler me falt du bouche aleine.* Lit. "Because to speak to you breath of/from the mouth fails me."

XV COM L'ESPERVER QE VOLE PAR CREANCE

14   *retenue.* See VIII.17, above; compare *Traitié* III.20.

XVI CAMELION EST UNE BESTE FIERE

1   *Camelion.* That chameleons lived on air was common belief; see Dan Michel, *Ayenbite of Inwyt,* 1:62. This classical notion was carried into the Renaissance; see Shakespeare, *Hamlet,* III.ii.93.

8   *Ne puiss de grace trover celle sente.* N.b., predictably a line from this position would repeat throughout, but Gower avoids a refrain in this balade. See XIII and XIV, above, and XVII, below.

18   *espoir.* Here, allegorical personification; but compare "De vein espoir," XVI.10.

19   *A volenté sanz fait est chamberere.* The subject must be "souhaid" above (XVI.17).

XVII NE SAI SI DE MA DAME LA DURTÉE

8   *Tant meinz reprens, com plus l'averay doné* ["The more I give, the greater is my rejection"]. N.b., predictably a line from this position would repeat throughout, but Gower avoids a refrain in this balade. See XIII, XIV, and XVI, above.

14   *Om dist, poi valt service q'est sanz fée.* ["Men say, poor is the service that is without reward."] Cited as a proverb in Whiting (p. 296).

XVIII LES GOUTES D'EAUE QE CHEONT MENU

8   *Tiel esperver crieis unqes ne fu.* "Esperver" is (technically) the Eurasian sparrow hawk (*Accipter nisus*), the most common hawk native to England; often, however, members of the families *Accipitridae* and *Falconidae*, true falcons, have been

casually blended (e.g., the North American sparrow "hawk," *Falco sparverius*; John Hill, *History of Animals* [1752], the sparrow hawk, a "yellow-legged falcon," p. 341). *Accipter nisus* is not unusual in its cry; Gower is probably using the term generally, with reference to the piercing cry of all raptors. See *MO* lines 25285–87; Chaucer, The Squire's Tale, *Canterbury Tales* V(F) 411–13: "Ther sat a faucon over hire heed ful hye, / That with a pitous voys so gan to crye / That all the wode resouned of hire crye."

23 *Diamant*. "Diamond" in most lapidaries, e.g., Peterborough: "Diamand" [LIX]; North Midland: "Dyamaunde"; London: "Diamaunde" [XVII]; Sloane: "Diamonde" [I]; however, see Peterborough: "adamas" [V] for "diamond" (and the directive "Require ulterius in diamonde") and its proximity there to "adamant" [VI] for "adamant"; see Sloane: "adamand" [IV] for "adamant." Complicating the case further is that both share several characteristics, the most important one for determining Gower's meaning here being impenetrable hardness. Thus, an alternative translation here must be "adamant," "lodestone," the iron-based, magnetic stone from India. See XXXVIII, stanza 1.

XIX OM SOLT DANTER LA BESTE PLUS SALVAGE

1–2 *Om solt danter . . . soulement*. Compare Arion, *CA* Prol.1057–65; compare also Orpheus, in Boethius, III.met.12.

14–15 *Sibille le sage / S'estrange*. Virgil's Sybil inhabits a cave in Cumae opening into Hades (*Aeneid* VI) but she neither retreats there nor is difficult for Aeneas to find. Gower's reference is probably to Ovid's retelling of Aeneas' encounter, *Metamorphoses* XIV.130–53, in which the Sybil explains that while Apollo granted her a thousand years of life, she did not think also to ask for continuing youth. When she discovered her error, he sought to exchange youth for her virginity. Refusing, she doomed herself to "shrivel / . . . from [her] full form to but a tiny thing, and [her] limbs, / consumed by age, [to] shrink to a feather's weight" (lines 147–49, trans. Miller). Obviously to "remove herself" in that way has significant implications for the balade as a whole.

XX FORTUNE, OM DIST, DE SA ROE VIRE ADES

1   *Fortune, om dist, de sa Roe vire ades*. Lit. "Fortune, one says, about her wheel has to turn." See Boethius, II.pr.1.

11 *estat*. "State," or perhaps "place, position."

17–18 *Palamedes . . . Agamenon*. "The clever one" helped Agamemnon by exposing Odysseus' feigned madness; Gower's source is Hyginus' *Fabulae*, 95.2.

19–20 *Diomedes . . . Troilus*. See Chaucer, *Troilus and Criseyde*, Book V.

22 *Du fille au Calcas*. I.e., Criseyde.

XXI AU SOLAIL, QE LES HERBES ESLUMINE

6   *menerai.* Lit. "pursue" (as in a hunt); "conduct," "administer." The choice of a verb with disparate nuances — all appropriate to and enriching the context — is common Gowerian practice.

8   *vilenie.* Lit. "churlishness, discourtesy, vulgarity" but in the "celestial" context of the subsequent stanza, perhaps also to be understood contrastingly in a modern sense, i.e., as "wickedness, evil." In contrast with "honest affection" (line 23), the sense is lecherous deception. See also *CA* 8.1431, where "vileinie" describes the attempts by multiple young men to deflower Thaise in Leonin's brothel, where the term equates with "lechery" and "villainous behavior."

9–13   *Si femme . . . conversacioun.* The language of deification is noteworthy here and throughout. See especially XXIIII and XXXI.

19   *Ne truist.* Subjunctive third person singular.

20   *Honte et paour.* See *Roman de la Rose*, lines 3011–16.

XXII J'AI BIEN SOVENT OÏ PARLER D'AMOUR

8   *en ris . . . en plour.* "In laughter . . . in tears," or perhaps "joyful . . . in lament."

12   *hoste et tolt.* Both mean "remove"; pairs of synonyms are stylistic embellishments.

XXIII POUR UN REGARD AU PRIMERE ACQUEINTANCE

5   *Du destre main jeo l'ai ma foi plevi.* See *Traitié* XVII.2.

8   *ymage.* Lit. "image," "likeness," "figure."

9   *lui.* One expects the feminine "la," but Gower treats masculine and feminine forms interchangeably, guided by metrical need. Perhaps he has in mind something like Bel Aceuil (Fair Welcome) in *Roman de la Rose*, who, though grammatically masculine, is the quality of the woman most ardently sought by her suitors who would hope to discover him revealed through her countenance, uninhibited by Danger (line 10).

17   *esperance.* Personification, "Hope"; see *Roman de la Rose*, e.g., lines 2615–25.

XXIIII JEO QUIDE QE MA DAME DE SA MEIN

7   *Q'en lui gist toute ma devocioun.* See XXI, stanza 2, and XXXI, stanza 3, for other examples of the Lover worshipping the Lady.

22   *faie.* "Enchanted," or perhaps "a faerie"; compare XXVII.22.

26   *Soul apres dieu si m'estes soverein.* Compare XXI, stanza 2.

XXV MA DAME, SI CEO FUIST A VO PLESIR

8   *Car qui bien aime ses amours tard oblie.* ["Because he who loves well forgets his loves
            late."] Fisher, *John Gower: Moral Philosoper* (p. 76), notes — incorrectly — this
            line as "used by Chaucer in the rondel at the end of the *Parliament of Fowls*"
            (actually a note in the margin in several *PF* manuscripts, at line 680: "Qui bien
            aime a tard oublie"); similar (albeit octosyllabic) lines have been noted (e.g., in
            Machaut's "Le lay de plour" [*Oeuvres*, I, 283] and Moniot d'Arras' hymn to the
            Virgin; Deschamps uses the line exactly in Balade 1345 [*Oeuvres*, VII, 124–25]);
            cited in Whiting (p. 40) as a French proverb.

9–10   *Ils sont . . . curroie.* Compare perhaps Exeter Book Riddle 44.

25   *bon amour.* Personification, the God of Love; see *Roman de la Rose*, lines 863 ff.

26   *De male langue.* Compare Malebouche, *Roman de la Rose*, lines 2823 and 3871–92;
            see also Dedication I.22–25.

XXVI SALUTZ HONOUR ET TOUTE REVERENCE

14   *Vous donne.* There is no expressed object (one expects "myself").

XXVII MA DAME, QUANT JEO VI VOSTRE OILL [VAIR ET] RIANT

1   *vostre oill [vair et] riant.* Macaulay notes (Mac, 1:466, note XXVII.1) "The first
            line is too long, but the mistake may be that of the author. Similarly in *MO*, lines
            3116 and 14568, we have lines which are each a foot too long for the metre. In
            all cases it would be easy to correct: here, for example, by reading 'Ma dame,
            quant jeo vi vostre oill riant.'" Compare XII.8.

8–9   *Amour . . . desplaie.* Compare Petrarch, Sonnet 140.

12   *deslaie.* Lit. "releases, lets go."

16   *manaie.* "Care"; also "pity, mercy, protection."

22   *la bealté plus qe faie.* Compare XXIIII.22, and *CA* 4.1321.

23   *vilein.* Compare XXI: "Sanz mal penser d'ascune vilenie" (lines 8, 16, 24, and 28).

XXVIII DAME, U EST ORE CELLE NATURESCE

7   *Om voit sovent de petit poi doner.* ["Often one sees little being given."] Cited as a proverb in Whiting (p. 296).

11   *Dont par dolour jeo sui sempres faili.* Lit. "Thus through sadness I am always lacking."

16   *parmi.* Lit. "throughout," so perhaps "always"?

XXIX PAR DROITE CAUSE ET PAR NECESSITÉ

5   *Mais fame, q'est par les paiis volable.* Fame in its avatar of Rumor; see Shakespeare, *Henry IV Part 2*, Induction.

7   *fable.* Lit. "(untrue) story," "falsehood."

8   *Q'est d'amour loigns est de desease pres.* ["Whoever is far away from love is near distress."] Cited as a proverb in Whiting (p. 296).

XXX SI COM LA NIEF, QUANT LE FORT VENT TEMPESTE

4   *orra.* Lit. future third person singular "will hear."

10–13   *N'ot tiel paour . . . de ma partie.* I.e., "Ulysses' fear of the Sirens or Circe was no greater than mine of you now."

19   *La chiere porte.* Lit. "The dear door/gate" (*porte*=feminine); but masculine "port" ("harbor/port"), given both Gower's general lack of concern about gender and the nautical imagery here, seems more likely. See also "port" (masculine)= "pass, narrow passage" in context of Ulysses' voyage (and perhaps with a bawdy undertone as well).

XXXI MA BELLE DAME, BONE ET GRACIOUSE

8   *bon amour.* That is, "virtuous love." Compare "fin amour" in XXI.5 and XXIIII.6.

XXXII CEST AUN NOVELL JANUS, Q'AD DOUBLE FACE

1   *Janus.* The two-faced Roman god of portals; hence Latin "Januarius," the first month of the Roman calendar.

7   *salue.* "Saves"; possibly "greets," but "point" suggests "saves."

XXXIII AU COMENCER DEL AUN PRESENT NOVELL

4   *Pour le tenir sicom vostre demeine.* ["To hold as if it were your demesne."] I.e., a feudal lordship, land solely owned by the lord and worked by peasant tenants. As a lawyer with demonstrable experience buying and selling property, Gower would have been familiar with the legal distinctions implicit in the term.

XXXIIII SAINT VALENTIN L'AMOUR ET LA NATURE

1–8   *Saint Valentin . . . obeïr.* See *PF* line 309 ff.; Nature here clearly is to be taken as the goddess. See also Chaucer, *Legend of Good Women* F line 145, G line 131; Alain of Lille, *De planctu Naturae* Prose 1.

8   *U li coers est, le corps falt obeïr.* ["Where the heart is, the body must follow."] Cited as a proverb in Whiting (p. 296).

18–19   *Alceone et Ceïx . . . figure.* See Ovid, *Metamorphoses* XI.410 ff.; see also *BD* lines 62–220.

XXXV SAINT VALENTIN PLUS QE NULL EMPEROUR

8–9   *Com la fenix . . . regioun.* ["As the phoenix . . . region of Arabia."] On the regeneration of phoenix in fire, see *Physiologus* (trans. Curley, p. 13) where, however, the bird is said to originate in India, and is apparently a species, not a unique bird; Ovid, *Metamorphoses* XV.391 ff., includes its singularity, but locates its habitat as Assyria; Isidore, *Etymologies* XII.vii.22, and *Bestiary* (trans. White, pp. 125–28) list all the elements: uniqueness, fiery reproduction, Arabia. Assuming Cambridge University Library MS II.4.26 is of English origin, Gower would seem to be following an English tradition. See the Black Knight's praise of the "goode Faire White" as "the soleyn fenix of Arabye, / For ther livyth never but oon" (*BD* lines 982–83).

22   *Chascun Tarcel . . . falcoun.* See *PF* lines 393 ff.

XXXVI POUR COMPARER CE JOLIF TEMPS DE MAII

3   *Car lors chantont et Merle et Papegai.* The British blackbird (*Turdus merula*) is the most tuneful of the three major indigenous thrushes, singing from January to June; the parrot (or perhaps a woodpecker) has a song only in poetry (see Chaucer's Sir Thopas, *Canterbury Tales* VII[B²]767, although probably a joke). Gower seems to have considered the "papegai" a generally exotic — and sinless? — bird; see *MO* line 26781.

15   *Rose.* See *Roman de la Rose* lines 1613 ff., especially 1652–87.

16   *chapeals.* Chaplet-making in May is traditional for lovers; see also *Roman de la Rose* line 1651.

18   *j'ai mon coer mis.* Lit. "I have placed my heart."

XXXVII El Mois de Maii la plus joiouse chose

15   *se desclose.* Lit. "discloses itself."

16   *Maii m'ad hosté de sa blanche banere.* Or perhaps "bright banner," i.e., with color, flowers, etc.?

XXXVIII Sicom la fine piere Daiamand

1–2   *Daiamand.* Not "diamond" here (as in XVIII.23) but "lodestone, magnet"; compare OF "aimant"=both "diamond" or "lodestone" (Greimas, *Dictionnaire*); compare also lapidaries, e.g., Sloane: "adamand" [IV]; Peterborough: "adamant" (VI), an entry ending "Require ulterius in magnetes," and which follows "adamas" [V], an entry ending "Require ulterius in diamonde"; compare also Peterborough: "magnes" [CVII]), Old English: "magneten," London: "magnete" (XXI), North Midland: "magnete" (XX). The common denominator appears to be ferrous metals — iron and steel — which the hardness of diamond breaks or cuts through, and the lodestone attracts, or vice versa: see, e.g., the preference of the "piere dyamant tresfine" for an iron over a gold setting in *MO* line 12463 ff.

13   *ravi.* "Carried away," or perhaps "ravished."

15–18   *Toutes vertus . . . mours.* Gower has in mind the cardinal virtues (Prudence, Justice, Temperance, and Fortitude) and the theological or divine virtues (Faith, Hope, and Charity; see 1 Corinthians 13:13). The former are products of nature, the latter gifts of God; see Aquinas, *Summa Theologica* Q.61.1–2, Q.62.1–4, and Q.63.1–4.

18   *mours.* "Mores, morals," or perhaps "customs" in the sense of "habits," as Aquinas' "mos" is often translated (e.g., by Pegis).

XL Om dist, promesses ne sont pas estables

5–6   *Heleine . . . Menelai.* See XIIII and *Traitié* X.

13   *Et prendre ailours la chose q'est foreine.* See lines 5–6 above; Helen and Menelaus are Greeks, Paris a Trojan.

XLI Des fals amantz tantz sont au jour present

1–2   *Des fals amantz . . . doloir.* N.b., XLI–XLIV and LXVI are in the voice of the lady.

8   *bien s'avise.* Lit. "advises herself well."

25   *Tu.* N.b., in her contempt, the lady adopts the familiar pronoun (second person singular) when addressing the rejected suitor throughout XLI–XLIII.

XLII Semblables sont la fortune et les dées

1   *la fortune.* Clearly the goddess Fortune, who "pretends to be friendly to those she intends to cheat" (Boethius, II.pr.1).

12   *constreignte.* Lit. "constraint, binding" but also with the sense of "compulsion," as is perhaps intended here.

21–22   *la conscience . . . fraude et malengin.* Clearly allegorically imagined, as figures capable of pregnancy and being born.

XLIII Plus tricherous qe Jason a Medée

1–5   *Jason . . . Phillis.* See Jason and Medea, *CA* 5.3247 ff., *Traitié* VIII; Deianira and Hercules, *CA* 2.2258 ff., *Traitié* VII; Aeneas and Dido, *CA* 4.77 ff.; Theseus and Ariadne, *CA* 5.5231 ff.; Demophon and Phyllis, *CA* 4.731 ff.; see also Ovid, *Heroides* XII, IX, VII, X, and II; see also note 9 below. Fisher, *John Gower: Moral Philosopher* (p. 76), compares this opening list to Oton de Graunson's "Ho! Doulce Yseult, qui fus a la fontaine / Avec Tristan, Jason et Medea" (as cited by Fisher, p. 344n21); see also Yeager, *Gower's Poetic*, pp. 109–10.

8   *C'est ma dolour, qe fuist ainçois ma joie.* Fisher, *John Gower: Moral Philosopher* (p. 76), notes the echo of the refrain in Machaut XXIV: "C'est ma dolour et la fin de ma joie"; see also Yeager, *Gower's Poetic*, pp. 110–11.

9   *Ector . . . Pantasilée.* See *CA* 4.2138 ff., 5.2547 ff.; and Benoît de Ste.-More, *Roman de Troie* lines 23283 ff. (also a main source for Jason and Medea, *CA* 5.3247 ff. and perhaps for note 1–5, above).

17–19   *Lancelot . . . Partonopé.* All eponymous knights of romances; Lancelot and Tristran, see *CA* 8.2500 ff., *Traitié* XV; Florent, see *CA* 1.1407 ff. Generides and Partonopé (of Blois) appear here uniquely; for manuscripts and early editions, see Loomis and Loomis, *Medieval Romances*.

XLIIII VAILANT, COURTOIS, GENTIL ET RENOMÉE

2   *de vo promesse.* N.b., addressing her new, loyal suitor, the lady uses the formal
           pronoun (third person singular).

5   *Si jeo de Rome fuisse l'emperesse.* Fisher, *John Gower: Moral Philosopher* (p. 76):
           echoes Deschamps balade CCCCVII (3.20) "Telle dame estre emperies de
           Romme"; see also Yeager, *Gower's Poetic*, pp. 110–11.

7   *ami . . . amie.* "Your friendship . . . good friend." Or perhaps "lover . . . lover" (or
           even "boyfriend . . . girlfriend," noting gender distinction available in French).

XLV MA DAME, JEO VOUS DOI BIEN COMPARER

1   *Ma dame.* N.b., XLV and XLVII are spoken by the new lover.

2–4   *cristall . . . medicine.* Not universally cited in the lapidaries; properties include
           focusing the sun's rays to start fires and increasing the milk of nursing women:
           see London XXXVI; also, probably more pertinent: "Touch ye Christall with ye
           stone that hath lost his vertue through ye sine of him / that bereth him uppon
           him, so yt he amend him of his sinne he shall returne his strength as in his kind
           through ye vertue of ye Christall stone" (Sloane XXVI); and see also Peterborough
           XXXIX.

17   *Le Cristall est de soi et blanc et clier.* "Christall is cleare and white," Sloane XXVI;
           "Manye trowen that snowe or yesse is mad hard in spas of many yers,"
           Peterborough XXXIX, describing the origin of crystal.

XLVI EN RESEMBLANCE D'AIGLE, QUI SURMONTE

1–2   *d'aigle . . . dessure.* Eagles, when they age, are said to fly to the sun to restore
           youth. See *Physiologus* (trans. Curley, p. 12) and *Bestiary* (trans. White, p. 105).

20   *m'esmai.* "frighten myself," or perhaps "I am troubled."

XLVIII AMOUR EST UNE CHOSE MERVEILOUSE

20   *la merle est forsbanie.* Lit. "the blackbird is banished" (i.e., the bird kept for its
           melodious song is replaced by a goose).

XLIX AS BONS EST BON ET A LES MALS MALVOIS

9–12   *Qui son dieu . . . semblablement.* See Matthew 22:37–39, Mark 12:29–31.

L DE VRAI HONOUR EST AMOUR TOUT LE CHIEF

1   *De vrai honour est amour tout le chief* ["Of true honor wholly the chief is Love"].
           Cited as a proverb in Whiting (p. 296).

4   *franc et loial.* "Free and loyal"; or perhaps "openhanded and trustworthy,
           honorable."

8   *Amour s'acorde a nature et resoun.* By "Love" here Gower means the god of Love;
           yet probably also the universal God who is Love: see Dante, *Paradiso* XXXIII.145:
           "l'amor che move il sole e l'altre stele"; and Boethius, II.met.8.

12–13   *Sibien les choses . . . resonal.* ["Both to the things . . . rational to man."] Broadly,
           the two parts of human nature: see Aquinas, *Summa Theologica* Q.75.a.6. See also
           Traitié I.

26   *Mais en droit moi c'est la conclusioun.* Very likely marks the original end of the
           Cinkante Balades. Along with the two dedicatory balades to Henry IV at the
           beginning, LI and the seven-line prayer for England under Henry's rule are best
           taken — as Macaulay suggested (see below) — as original to British Library, MS
           Additional 59495 and occasionally composed. Absent these poems, no reference
           restricts what can be called the *Cinkante Balades* proper to an origin after the
           accession of Henry in 1399.

LI AMOUR DE SOI EST BON EN TOUTE GUISE

Macaulay (Mac, 1:470, note LI) notes: "This balade is not numbered [i.e., in the manuscript]
and does not form one of the 'Cinkante Balades' of which the title speaks. It is a kind of
devotional conclusion to the series. The envoy which follows, 'O gentile Engleterre,' does
not belong to this balade, being divided from it by a space in the MS. and having a different
system of rhymes. It is in fact the envoy of the whole book of balades."

25–31   *O gentile Engleterre . . . prosperité.* Compare with envoys to Dedicatory balades I
           and II, with which this stanza must be contemporaneous, and logically part of
           the same project, i.e., to collect and reshape work previously and independently
           composed into a presentation manuscript for Henry IV, one assumes not long
           after his coronation. Compare too with the controversial Latin explicit dedicating
           the *Confessio Amantis* to "Derbeie Comiti" ("the Count of Derby," i.e., Henry
           Bolingbroke) in F (Mac, 3:478; *CA* I.226) and similar manuscripts, seemingly
           also an attempt after the fact (whether in 1392 or 1400) to adapt earlier work to
           suit new and possibly urgent political circumstances.

TEXTUAL NOTES TO THE *CINKANTE BALADES*

ABBREVIATIONS: G: Glasgow, University of Glasgow Library, MS Hunter 59 (T.2.17); **Mac**: Macaulay, ed., *The Complete Works of John Gower*; **MS**: London, British Library, MS Additional 59495 (Trentham).

DEDICATION I

9–14   *H. aquile pullus . . . non apponet nocere ei.* Macaulay notes: "Owing to the loss of a part of the leaf (f. 12) on which the Latin occurs, the text of ll. 9–12 and of the first prose quotation which follows is imperfect. It runs thus:

> . . . . . pullus quo nunquam gracior vllus
> . . . . regit que tirannica colla subegit
> . . . ile cepit oleum quo regna recepit
> . . . ri iuncta stipiti noua stirps redit vncta.
> . . il proficiet inimicus in eo et filius iniqui
> . . . non apponet nocere ei.

The missing words are supplied from other copies of the same lines, which are found in a somewhat different arrangement in the All Souls' and Glasgow MSS. of the 'Vox Clamantis' (the prose quotations in the latter only)" (Mac, 1:336).

14   *faciat.* So G. MS: *faciet.*

DEDICATION II

Macaulay notes: "The damage to f. 12 of the MS. has caused the loss of a part of this Balade and of the next" (Mac, 1:336).

26–28   Mac: "The ends of these lines are somewhat damaged and have been conjecturally restored."

27   *Court.* MS: *Courte.*

CINKANTE BALADES

II L'IVERN S'EN VAIT ET L'ESTÉE VIENT FLORI

17   *novelle.* MS: *noue*[. . .].

III D'ARDANT DESIR CELLE AMOROUSE PEIGNE

10   *tielement.* MS: *tielment.*

IIII* SANZ DEPARTIR J'AI TOUT MON COER ASSIS

1   Mac: "In the MS. this and the preceding Balade are both numbered *IIII.*"

VII DE FIN AMOUR C'EST LE DROIT ET NATURE

5   *Pourceo.* MS: *Pouceo.*

IX TROP TART A CEO QE JEO DESIRE ET PROIE

37   *poestis.* MS: *poestes.*

XI MES SENS FOREINS SE POURRONT BIEN MOVOIR

15   *Jeo.* MS: *Iieo.*

XIII AU MOIS DE MARSZ, U TANT Y AD MUANCE

8   *al oill.* MS: *al loill.*

XIIII POUR PENSER DE MA DAME SOVEREINE

2   *En.* MS: *Een.*
15   *douls.* MS: *doules.*

XIX OM SOLT DANTER LA BESTE PLUS SALVAGE

24   *cage.* MS: *Cage.VII.*

XXI AU SOLAIL, QE LES HERBES ESLUMINE

18   *Trestout.* MS: *Terstout.*

XXV MA DAME, SI CEO FUIST A VO PLESIR

4　　　　　　*m'ont.* MS: *mout (?).*

XXX SI COM LA NIEF, QUANT LE FORT VENT TEMPESTE

5　　　　　　*Le Nief.* MS: *Perhaps rather "Le vent."*
12　　　　　*Circes.* MS: *circes.*

XXXII CEST AUN NOVELL JANUS, Q'AD DOUBLE FACE

5　　　　　　*nuisant.* MS: *nuisand.*
9　　　　　　*siq' au devant.* MS: *si siqau devant.*

XXXVI POUR COMPARER CE JOLIF TEMPS DE MAII

14, 25　　　*Nai.* MS: *nai.*

XXXVII EL MOIS DE MAII LA PLUS JOIOUSE CHOSE

3　　　　　　*ruge.* MS: *Ruge.*
19　　　　　*refiere.* MS: *refiers.*

XXXVIII SICOM LA FINE PIERE DAIAMAND

23　　　　　*hostell.* MS: *hoste*[. . .].

XLI DES FALS AMANTZ TANTZ SONT AU JOUR PRESENT

18　　　　　*les sciet.* MS: *le sciet.*

XLII SEMBLABLES SONT LA FORTUNE ET LES DÉES

12　　　　　*constreignte.* MS: *constregnte.*

XLIII PLUS TRICHEROUS QE JASON A MEDÉE

19　　　　　*Partonopé.* MS: *par Tonope.*

XLVIII AMOUR EST UNE CHOSE MERVEILOUSE

4　　　　　　*et.* MS: *e.*
8　　　　　　*L'amier.* MS: *La mier.*
11　　　　　*Le halt.* MS: *La halt.*

25   *toutz*. MS: *touz*.

XLIX AS BONS EST BON ET A LES MALS MALVOIS

19   *ces*. MS: *cest*.

LI AMOUR DE SOI EST BON EN TOUTE GUISE

15   *celle*. MS: *ce*[. . .].

Latin prose following text: *Expliciunt carmina Iohannis Gower, que Gallice composita Balades dicuntur.*

APPENDIX 1: A TRANSLATION OF THE *TRAITIÉ* (QUIXLEY)

"Quixley's ballades royal," as they were termed by their first and only previous modern editor, occupy folios 313–322 of London, British Library MS Stowe 951, and are the final of three works contained therein.[1] Described in a rubric in the manuscript as "Exhortacio contra vicium adulterii," they number nineteen balades plus an extra stanza that serves as an introduction of sorts to the translation proper. Of these poems, one (XIX) is wholly original to "Quixley," as is the prefatory stanza, where the translator/poet names himself; the others are his translations into Middle English from the eighteen French balades that comprise John Gower's *Traitié* — hence one reason for the inclusion of "Quixley's" work in the present volume. (Another reason — one more worthy, perhaps — is that the uniqueness of these poems as an early example of French-to-English translation deserves wider recognition.) In his introductory stanza, the translator/poet "Quixley" hides nothing, but he packs a good deal of information into a few lines. He makes explicit what he's done, and pointedly claims credit: "þis litel tretice" (translating, one supposes, Gower's "Traitié"), he says,

> Gower it made in frenshe with grete studie
> In balades ryale whos sentence here
> Translated hath Quixley in this manere.

A number of things are interesting here. Gower's name, the lines imply, was sufficiently well known as to require no further identification for the translator's projected Yorkshire readership — a telling reflection, one can infer, of the spread of the poet's reputation beyond London in the early fifteenth century. The point would seem strengthened by "Quixley's" apparent care at the outset to specify his work as translation, rather than original composition. Clearly, he knew and respected the difference, and he projects that sophistication onto his audience as well. Similarly, when he names the verse form as "balades ryale" — i.e., balades in rime royal stanza — "Quixley" demonstrates a technical knowledge of poetics and suggests, again, that this level of information would also matter to his readers.

Yet for all that, it is Gower's "sentence" — his moral instruction, or perhaps just his literal meaning — that here in these opening lines "Quixley" says he makes his focus. This decision is not without implications for the translation he produced. It isn't possible to identify "Quixley's" translation principles with anything like precision, since he left no known description of them. Placed side by side, however, "Quixley's" versions of Gower's originals divulge an assortment of priorities. As he suggests himself in the lines quoted above, getting

---

[1] Henry Noble MacCracken edited them under the title "Quixley's Ballades Royal (? 1402)" for the *Yorkshire Archaelogical Journal* in 1909.

across Gower's "sentence" must have held the top of "Quixley's" list, followed closely by sticking to the form of his original as faithfully as he could. Or at least to some elements of Gower's form: what he could see, "Quixley" copied; but as will be discussed in due course, his ear and Gower's were hearing different drums.

As much as possible, "Quixley" translates line by line, each of his own replicating in English the form and sense of Gower's corresponding line in French. Thus, like Gower's, "Quixley's" balades are three stanzas of rime royal (ABABBCC), with the seventh line of the first stanza repeating as the final line of the second and third, providing a refrain.[2] Where his English vocabulary and Gower's French corresponded, "Quixley" appears to have elected transliteration. His version of balade V is a prime example: in stanza 1, Gower's rhymes are "**reson**/eslire/**eleccion**/desdire/desire/**beste**/**honeste**" while "Quixley" has "**reson**/wyve/ **eleccion**/believe/alive/**beste**/**honeste**"; in stanza 2, Gower has "**profession**/*descrire*/**incarnacion**/ Sire/remire/**geste**/**honeste**" and "Quixley" "**profession**/*descryve*/**incarnacion**/arrive/dryve/ **geste**/**honeste**"; and in stanza 3, Gower has "**beneiçoun**/enspire/dissolucioun/lisre/dire/ moleste/**honeste**" and "Quixley" "**beneison**/mysselve/devocion/lyve/active/arreste/ **honeste**."

Not all cases are this close, of course. "Quixley" has it easier when Gower's rhymes are not, for example, on French infinitives (although he tries, as in the match of "descrire/ descryve," above) or on words which for "Quixley" offered only equivalents derived from Anglo-Saxon: "pour quoi" ("why," XIII.15) or "ghemir" ("groaning," XIV.18), to name two. But it is surprising, on close examination, how readily so many of Gower's French rhymes could be turned, with a shift of letter here or there, into recognizable English — an observation as valuable linguistically, perhaps, about Gower's Anglo-French as it is about the state of "Quixley's" vernacular. Indeed as a result, where "Quixley's" rhymes most stray from Gower's, his sense does, too — as in stanza 2 of balade I. First Gower (with a literal translation), then "Quixley":

> En dieu amer celle alme ad sa droiture,
> Tant soulement pour fermer le corage
> En tiel amour u nulle mesprisure
> De foldelit la poet mettre en servage
> De frele char, q'est toutdis en passage:
> Mais la bone alme est seinte et permanable;
> Dont sur le corps raison ert conestable.

[This soul in its rectitude loves God, / Exclusively to firm the heart / In such love that no misdeed / Of foul delight is able to put it in service / Of the weak flesh, which is always passing away: / But the good soul is holy and eternal; / Therefore reason is constable over the body.]

>   *   *   *   *

> For to þe soule þat is so clene & pure
> Parteneth to loue god in stedfastnesse;
> And nat encline to foule delite vnsure,

---

[2] There is one exception: the third stanza of Quixley's balade IV has eight lines, rhyming ABABAACC.

> Be which it myght deserue peynful duresse;
> Thassent is perilleus, as þat I gesse,
> Therfore schuld be þe soules mocion
> The flesche to holde vnder be reson.

Guessing at "Quixley's" motives for the changes he inserts is futile, of course, and — even were it possible to know — unlikely to repay the effort. The main point to be taken, probably, is that while "Quixley" for the most part renders Gower closely, he also goes his own way from time to time, enough to require a caveat: accept "Quixley" with caution, if perceiving Gower accurately is one's brief.

As noted above, however, "Quixley's" labors to replicate the *look* of Gower's balades did not extend to echoing their sound — an observation that might at first seem superfluous, given Gower's Anglo-French and "Quixley's" English as starting points. Metrical regularity, it seems fair to say, was one of Gower's poetical strengths, even in French — but it was not among "Quixley's." (Either that, or he invented a system of his own that eludes us still.) Too often "Quixley's" product resembles the first stanza of balade III:

> God bonde vs nat to þe moost parfitenesse,
> But wolde þat we euer parfite schuld be.
> Who þat to god voweth withoute excesse
> His body for to lyve in chastite,
> Myche is his mede; Who list nat this degree,
> Bot take a wyf to haue lawful issue; —
> God it plesyth al suche matrimoyne due.

Gower, in contrast, in the words of G. C. Macaulay, "is extremely regular. He does not allow himself any of those grosser licences of suppression or addition of syllables which have been noticed in Anglo-Norman verse of the later period."[3] Here is Gower's stanza that "Quixley" translated:

> Au plus parfit dieus ne nous obligea,
> Mais il voet bien qe nous soions parfitz.
> Cist homme a dieu sa chasteté dona,
> Et cist en dieu voet estre bons maritz:
> S'il quiert avoir espouse a son avis,
> Il plest a dieu de faire honeste issue
> Selonc la loi de seinte eglise due.

It would seem that Gower intended a symbiotic metricality, combining French syllabic counting (ten per line) with English measures based on stress. The lines above scan readily as iambic pentameter, with general suppression or elision of the final "–e" (a likely exception being "eglise" in the refrain). "Quixley," however, again appears to have approached his poetry visually: he counted his syllables, aiming at ten per line (although he often allows himself nine),[4] but seemingly paid scant heed to stress placement. Nor did "Quixley"

---

[3] Gower, *Complete Works*, 1:xvi.

[4] E.g., IV.1, IV.12, V.13, VI.12, and VII.3.

pronounce, or at least regularly pay attention to, final "–e."[5] The result, in any event, is a metrical rough-and-tumble, when read aloud.

In one respect "Quixley" may have altered his practice of replicating in his translations what he saw in Gower's original — but then again, perhaps not. Throughout the *Confessio Amantis*, Gower added Latin prose commentaries to his tales, and in the *Traitié* he did the same. (Indeed, because most known copies of the *Traitié* are found preceded in their manuscripts by the *Confessio*, Gower at one time may have come to consider these balades a kind of coda to his English poem.) All eighteen of Gower's balades have at least one Latin prose commentary; some have two — and in one case (X) there are three, one attached to each stanza. In the manuscripts of the *Confessio*, these Latin commentaries appear variously: some are in black ink, some in red, some are in the margin, and some are incorporated into the column of text.[6] Similar variation occurs with the commentaries in versions of the *Traitié*. Because Macaulay elected to use as the base manuscript for his definitive edition of both the *Confessio* and the *Traitié* London, British Library, MS Fairfax 3, which locates the Latin commentaries in the margins, in black, this has seemed the norm for generations of readers. British Library, MS Stowe 951, our only extant copy of "Quixley's" translation, rubricizes the Latin prose commentaries and installs them in line with the balades. Perhaps this was "Quixley's" preference — but it might easily have been what he saw in his working copy. (London, British Library, MS Harley 7184 presents the Latin of the *Confessio* like this, for example.) With what we know presently, we cannot be certain. In any case, "Quixley" copied Gower's original Latin commentaries faithfully: there are only four minor variations between what appears in British Library, MS Stowe 951 and British Library, MS Fairfax 3, and all are of the kind that could — again — reflect not "Quixley" but an exemplar differing in these instances from British Library, MS Fairfax 3, or even simple scribal error.[7] More important, perhaps, is that "Quixley" continued the practice by adding a prose Latin commentary to his own balade XIX, the final poem he seems not to have translated, but rather written himself, in conscious imitation of Gower. This suggests that "Quixley" considered the Latin prose commentaries at the very least stylistically integral to the *Traitié* as a whole work. Even more interesting perhaps is that, while translating the French, "Quixley" apparently saw no urgency also to make English of Gower's Latin commentaries — a clue, conceivably, to the language skills of "Quixley's" intended readership and, as will be addressed below, perhaps to his own identity as well.

THE MANUSCRIPT

London, British Library, MS Stowe 951 is a product of the first half of the fifteenth century; judging from its single hand, probably first quarter. From its language its copyist hailed from north-central Yorkshire, an area including the village of Quixley (modern

---

[5] Also noted by MacCracken, "Quixley's Ballades Royal," p. 36.

[6] *Mise en page*, with special attention to Latin in Gower manuscripts, has been studied fruitfully by Yeager, "English, Latin, and the Text"; Echard, "Designs for Reading"; and Coleman, "Lay Readers and Hard Latin."

[7] I.e., I: F3: possidebit, S951: debiat possidere; II: F3: castitatem affectat et corpus, S951: omits (likely scribal); III: F3: consistent, S951: subsistent; and VII: F3: Achelontis, S951: Acheloi.

Whixley).[8] It approximates quarto size (14 x 20.3 cm), and contains 322 folios, employing the same paper throughout, save the first and final leaf of each quire, which are vellum. The backing is leather and a later addition (ca. 1700s), but the boards, originally fastened by straps now lost, are of rough oak, .6 cm at their thickest, tapering toward the edges, and are clearly contemporary with the manuscript. Boards and leaves are cut flush. In overall appearance British Library, MS Stowe 951 is "squarish,"[9] rustic, homespun: not of professional manufacture.

In addition to Quixley's translations, the manuscript contains (folios 1–29r) an abridged *Three Kings of Cologne* — an English prose version of John of Hildesheim's (d. 1375) *Historia trium regum* by an anonymous translator — and (folios 32–312) the *Speculum vitae* (*Mirror of Life*), in English verse, sometimes attributed to William of Nassington (d. 1359).[10] There is no indication of other works having been included, or intended, although blank pages exist from the top third of folio 29r , where the *Historia trium regum* concludes, through folio 32r, where the *Speculum vitae* begins.[11] Three inks were used throughout the manuscript: a dark brown-black for all entries, red for the Latin commentaries in the translation, and a blue for enlarged capitals (randomly) in all three works. MS Stowe 951 thus appears to have been executed as a single piece, by a single copyist.[12] "Quixley's" translation is rendered in a large script in a single column, each page holding on average three stanzas plus a Latin commentary — that is, about a poem per page.

THE TRANSLATION: ITS DATE AND AUTHOR

Until now, the sole appearance of "Quixley's ballades royal" in print was the 1909 edition of Henry Noble MacCracken. MacCracken argued for a composition year of 1402, on the grounds that, for him, the best candidate for the identity of "Quixley" was one "John Quixley of Quixley, lord of the manor of Quixley, armiger, whose daughter Alice, on the 18th of September in 3 Henry IV (1402) married Thomas Banke, attorney of the Duchy of Lancaster."[13] Quixley manor stood "twelve miles away from . . . the manor of Stitenham, the home of the Gowers of Yorkshire," MacCracken wrote, and "it is probable that they took pride in the distinguished poet of their name" — enough perhaps to obtain a copy of "the

---

[8] See McIntosh, Samuels, and Bensken, *Linguistic Atlas of Late Mediaeval English*, p. 646 (LP 526), although n.b.: the entry analyzes only *Speculum vitae*, locating its origin near Liverpool; *Historia trium regum* and "Quixley's" translation, however, are noted simply as "not NM." A comparison of word-forms with LALME-mapped items (vol. 2), however, places the dialect of the balades in the region of Quixley (now Whixley), Yorkshire.

[9] The term is adapted from Ralph Hanna's description of British Library, MS Additional 59495, the Trentham MS; see *London Literature*, pp. 223–24.

[10] The main proponent of Nassington's authorship is Peterson, *William of Nassington*.

[11] It is possible the blank pages were left by a scribe aware of the abridgement, in anticipation of later additions to the *Historia trium regum* text.

[12] Interestingly, a hand that seems to be the scribe's proofed his work, and made corrections in the margins of both *Historia trium regum* and *Speculum vitae*. No such corrections are present in the translation.

[13] MacCracken, "Quixley's Ballades Royal," p. 38.

latest poem of John Gower's from London."[14] This copy was loaned to neighbor Quixley, who Englished it for his daughter's nuptials. It was Alice's marriage that clinched both date and identity for MacCracken, who followed Macaulay's belief that Gower wrote the *Traitié* as a wedding gift for his own wife, Agnes Groundolf, on the occasion of their marriage in 1398, and John Quixley — in MacCracken's view — "prepared this poem for his children, daughter, and son-in-law."[15] Were this true, it would have a host of significant implications, as MacCracken pointed out, not the least of them being that "Quixley's" identification of Gower's *Traitié* as "balades ryale" in his introductory verse would make it the earliest known application of the term, one usually connected (however incorrectly) to James I's employing the stanza in his *Kingis Quair*, ca. 1424.[16] It would be a significant indication, too, of how far and how quickly Gower's reputation and work already had spread, six years before his death. Yet as John Fisher proved decisively (and even MacCracken suspected), John Gower was no near relation of the Stittenham family; and while this distant consanguinity does not altogether obviate any possible interest by the Yorkshire Gowers in a London writer of their name, it does dampen the theory a bit.[17] Nor does it help that dating the translation so early, in 1402, demands major revisions of both accepted literary history and handwriting dating practices.

An explanation that likely suits the circumstances better can be found, however, if a different "Quixley" were the translator. A Robert de Quixley became prior of Nostell Priory and prebend of Bramham in 1393, posts he held until his death in 1427.[18] Nostell was an Augustinian house, dedicated to St. Oswald. Although no building remains visible today, it was situated some twenty-five miles southwest of York, and eight from the great Lancastrian stronghold of Pontefract Castle — hence well within the dialectal province of MS Stowe 951.[19] Beyond this long tenure — Robert de Quixley spent 34 years at his post, the longest service in Nostell's history — about the prior himself little is known. Nonetheless, a good deal may reasonably be inferred from the few facts we possess, beginning, perhaps, with that longevity itself. Prior Robert must, obviously, have been robust, and a steady, efficient administrator, one energetically dedicated to both the fiscal and (more importantly, perhaps) moral refurbishment of his house, battered earlier in the century by insolvency and "disobediences" of various brethren.[20] One fact we do have is that de Quixley either wrote, or at the very least closely directed the production of, an act book of Nostell's priors, *De*

---

[14] MacCracken, "Quixley's Ballades Royal," p. 39.

[15] Gower, *Complete Works*, 1:lxxiii–lxxiv; MacCracken, "Quixley's Ballades Royal," p. 39.

[16] MacCracken, "Quixley's Ballades Royal," p. 39n3; and see further Stevens, "Royal Stanza," pp. 62–76.

[17] Fisher, *John Gower: Moral Philosopher*, pp. 39–41. MacCracken remarks "While no relationship has been proved between these Gowers [i.e., of Stitenham] and John Gower of Kent and Suffolk . . ." ("Quixley's Ballades Royal," p. 39).

[18] York Archiepis Reg Arundel, folio 43.

[19] After the Dissolution, Nostell was sold, in 1547, to Sir Thomas Gargrave (d. 1579), speaker of the House of Commons (1558–59) and vice-president of the council of the North under Elizabeth I. (*Dictionary of National Biography* 8:875–76). Nothing remains of the original priory: on the property today is "Nostell Priory," an eighteenth–century house built by Sir Rowland Winn.

[20] See Allison, *History of the County of York*, pp. 231–35. See also Burrows, "Geography of Monastic Property."

gestis et actibus priorum monasterii sancti Oswaldi.[21] Pointedly, in a prefatory statement the author justifies this writing, not simply as an attempt to keep Nostell's history from being lost, but rather on moral grounds:

> By way of example for the servants of God, it is necessary to recount the deeds of illustrious men, inasmuch as virtues may be acquired by imitating the acts of good men, and vices avoided by very diligently forsaking the evil. For this reason I myself propose to commemorate in writing the means and the manner of founding the priory of St. Oswald of Nostell, and as well the acts of the priors of this same place, God willing.[22]

Implicit here is the writer's belief in the power of the book to effect moral rectitude.[23] The unusually emphatic underscoring of the authorial "I" ("ad presens . . . dispono") strongly suggests *De gestis et actibus priorum* to have been the achievement of Robert de Quixley himself; or if not, then that of a designated surrogate over whose shoulder Nostell's prior must have looked, as his orders were carried out and his vision of the salubrious power of the text made actual.

Unfortunately, no volume once belonging to the library of Nostell has been identified as extant today. Not even the remaining copy of *De gestis et actibus priorum* can be placed there with certainty. Thus it is difficult to test the theory that, as the preface to *De gestis et actibus priorum* implies, Prior Robert de Quixley assembled books as edifying bulwarks against an unfortunate repetition of his institution's errant past. Nonetheless, as a candidate for the "Quixley" behind British Library, MS Stowe 951, he fits rather better than does John Quixley of Quixley manor. This is especially true if, as seems likely, Prior Robert was also the author of *De gestis et actibus priorum*, with its expressed affirmation of the book as a salvific instrument. For on closer consideration of its contents, British Library, MS Stowe 951 was apparently assembled to be just such an instrument. The *Speculum vitae*, like Gower's *Traitié*, is a patently didactic work composed with moral reform in sight; but so is

---

[21] Leeds District Archives MS NP/C1, copied ca. 1489–1505.

[22] "Ad exemplum servorum dei, illustrium gesta virorum recitare constat necessarium, quatinus de factis bonorum virtutes imitando colligant, et malorum vitia diligentius deserendo devitent. Quamobrem modum et formam fundationis prioratus sancti Oswaldi de Nostell necnon gesta priorum eiusdem loci in scriptis deo volente ad presens commendare dispono." Leeds District Archives MS NP/C1, folio 84.

[23] Such an attitude toward the positive efficacy of books would not have been unique to Robert de Quixley; rather, it was the standard Augustinian position, as stated in the order's Rule, to promote reading both at meals and in private; see, e.g., Lawless, *Augustine of Hippo*, pp. 74–118; and further Robert of Bridlington, *Bridlington Dialogue*: "Proinde quoniam oratio et lectio potiora sunt quam quelibet exterior actio, ipsa quoque lectio sagina quedam est orationis, potioribus propensiorem curam modo clam, modo palam impendamus. Cum enim oramus, cum Deo lquimur. Cum autem legimus, nobiscum Deus loquitur" [Further, since prayer and reading are to be preferred to any outward activity, and reading is, moreover, the sustenance of prayer, we should devote ourselves more earnestly to those more desirable pursuits, sometimes in private, and sometimes in public. For when we pray, we speak to God; and when we read, God speaks to us], pp. 162, 163a. It was a lasting position in the order: "Codices," stated Robert Richardson (ca. 1530), "sunt religiosorum armature, contra diaboli tentationem" [Books are the armor of the religious against the temptation of the devil]; see Richardson, *Commentary on the Rule of St. Augustine*, p. 146. And see further Dickinson's description of the "strong studious tendency within the order," *Origins of the Austin Canons*, pp. 186–92.

— albeit to a less obvious degree — John of Hildesheim's *Historia trium regum*. Through its narrative of the double reward, both on earth via sanctification and above, with their heavenly ascent, of the three oriental kings who offered, along with their rich material gifts, the first public obeisance to Christ's divinity, the *Historia trium regum* powerfully directs its readers toward the meaning and value of unshakable faith and sustained, unrelenting perseverance in life's journey toward the bright light of God. It also tells the story of the nativity in a manner no doubt useful to Nostell canons who regularly served duty as parish priests — a pastoral task for which the pithy material of the *Traitié* condemning adultery could have come in handy as well.[24] Clearly, "Quixley" added his translation of Gower's *Traitié* to the *Speculum vitae* and the *Historia trium regum* because he thought it of a piece with these two works for a reason.[25] The way it is headed in the manuscript ("Exhortacio contra Vicium Adulterii") displays a moralizing utility, as do the first four lines of the prefatory stanza "Quixley" penned:

> Who þat liste loke in þis litel tretice
> May fynde what meschief is of auoutrie
> Wherfore he þat will eschewe þat vice
> He may see here to beware of folie.

Also pointing toward Robert de Quixley is the Augustinian affiliation of his house. Two of the three texts in MS Stowe 951 — the *Speculum vitae* and "Quixley's" *Traitié* translation — have Austin coloring of various kinds, both internal and external. Precise identification of William of Nassington, widely believed to have composed the *Speculum*, remains something of a vexed issue — as does, indeed, the *Speculum*'s authorship. He was perhaps a follower of the Rule of St. Augustine, although the evidence is slight and circumstantial.[26] In two of some forty–five whole and fragmentary manuscripts of the *Speculum* currently known, a prayer is offered for "Willm saule of Nassyngton" who "made þis tale in ynglys tonge" and one as well for a "Freere Johan . . . of Waldby" who "made þis tale in Latyn right."[27] Waldby (or Waldeby) was ruled out as a serious claimant of the *Speculum vitae* some time ago;[28] he was, nevertheless, an English provincial of the Austin friars (d. 1393?), a Yorkshireman and possibly the brother of Robert Waldby (d. 1398), archbishop of York and an Austin friar also.[29] The most likely candidate for the William of Nassington named with Waldby from

---

[24] When parish churches fell vacant, priories were often granted the right to take over their revenues in exchange for adopting requisite pastoral duties; see Burton, *Monastic Order*, pp. 238–40.

[25] Boffey would seem to be in agreement about Gower's project: see "'Cy ensuent trois chaunceons': Groups and Sequences of Middle English Lyrics," pp. 86–87.

[26] Peterson, *William of Nassington*, summarizes the difficulties, pp. 22–27.

[27] ". . . pray specialy / For Freere Johan saule of Waldby, / That fast studyd day and nyght, / And made this tale in Latyne right . . . Prayes also wt deuocion / For William saule of Nassyngtone, / That gaf hym als fulle besyly / Night and day to grete study / And made this tale in Inglys tonge." For the verses, see London, British Library, MS Royal 17 C.viii and London, British Library, MS Hatton 19.

[28] The connection, as well as spurious claims for Richard Rolle's authorship, was disproved by Hope Emily Allen; see "Authorship of the *Prick of Conscience*," pp. 163–70 and "*Speculum vitae*: Addendum," p. 136; also *Writings Ascribed to Richard Rolle*, pp. 371–72.

[29] On Waldeby, see especially Morrin, *John Waldeby*.

several possibilities ("of Nassington" being merely a toponymic identification, and common practice for religious) died in 1359, apparently after serving, among many posts, as chancellor first to John Grandisson, bishop of Exeter (d. 1369), and subsequently to William Zouche, archbishop of York (d. 1352).[30] Neither prelate was an Augustinian, but Grandisson, William of Nassington's earliest and continuous supporter, elected to be buried in the chapel of St. Radegund at Exeter, she being a patron saint of the Premonstratensians, who also followed the Rule of St. Augustine.[31] It is thus possible that the bishop and his chancellor grew close via a shared Austin practice, and that the scribal author of the *Speculum vitae*'s versified prayer for the Augustinian Waldby and William of Nassington was prompted to write these original verses by a mutual affiliation with the order.

More substantial indications of an Augustinian background for "Quixley," however, are the allusions he himself makes in the longest bit of writing we can be certain was his. Two of the three stanzas of his balade XIX, the original poem "Quixley" wrote to conclude his translation, evince a familiarity with Augustine's life and works. The first stanza of XIX thus recalls Augustine's self-portrayal in the *Confessions*:[32]

> A philosophre of a grete citee
> Whilom þer was, and of ful grete honour;
> Which after yhouth thoght þat ryght wele myght he
> His body stroonge emploie, as a lichour
> In fool delyte, so prykked hym þat stour;
> But grace of crist made hym soon repentyng,
> God of heuen, our blys without endyng.

The stanza following reflects Augustine's *De nuptiis et concupiscentia* (*On Marriage and Concupiscence*), albeit in a fashion more garbled than one might perhaps hope from an Austin prior.[33]

---

[30] See Peterson, *William of Nassington*, p. 19.

[31] On the Premonstratensians, see Colvin, *White Canons in England*.

[32] See especially *Confessions* IV.ii and VI.xv.

[33] Balade XIX.2 reads: "He wrote þat auoutier punysht shal be / To leese a lym, or prisonned ful soure, / Or schame shall hym falle of dishoneste, / Or elles pouert withoute eny socour, / Or sodeyn deeth to his grete dishonour; / Whoo enspyred thus hym to teche suche thyng? / God of heuen, our blys without endyng." Line 2 apparently takes literally Augustine's metaphors of the soul imprisoned by lust (variously, but see, e.g., *De nuptiis et concupiscentia*, I.xxvi, xxx, and xxxi); line 3, see *De nuptiis* I.vi. and vii; line 5, see *De nuptiis* I.i, xxx and xxxi; the refrain seems based on *De nuptiis* I.iii. For line 4 I find no close equivalent. Interestingly, the Latin commentary, which must be "Quixley's" product as well, differs considerably from the balade: "Philosophus quidam carnis de labe remorsus Plebis in exemplum verba refert unam de variis penam fortiter adulter eius ut amplexus omnis in orbe luat aut membrum perdet aut carceris antea subibit aut cadet infamis non reputandus homo aut sibi pauperies infortunata resistit. Aut moriens subito transit ab orbe reus." [A certain philosopher, vexed about the fleshly sin of the people, recounts in an exemplum that an adulterer who, having boldly embraced every manner of sexual sin in the world, must choose one punishment from among various: either lose his member, or go down into prison, or die in infamy, not to be considered a man of repute, or withstand dire poverty. Or, dying swiftly, the sinner passes from the world.] Such disparities between Latin commentary and English verse are not uncommon in Gower's own work, however, as historically scholars have noted. The ill-constructed Latin of the commentary to XIX may also provide a clue to

Of course, the works of Augustine were hardly the exclusive property of those pledged to his rule. But books did circulate between Austin houses to be read and copied, and St. Mary Overey in Southwark, notably where Gower lived and wrote the *Traitié*, was another Augustinian priory.[34] On balance it is many times easier to accept Gower's balades traveling north in the saddlebag of a Nostell canon up from London to be copied in the priory in the 1420s than to envision them reaching Quixley manor courtesy a scarcely related Gower of Stittenham, and finding their way fortuitously into the hands of John Quixley, in the nick of time for his daughter's wedding in 1402.[35] And, with the overbearing *terminus ad quem* of the Quixley nuptials set aside, placing a copy of the *Traitié* in Yorkshire for translation in the 1420s brings together received scholarly opinion of the hand, the linguistic features, and the use of "balades ryale" in British Library, MS Stowe 951 into single accord. This is a narrative only enhanced by Prior Robert de Quixley's concern to provide moral texts for his canons' reading — something his possible authorship of *De gestis et actibus priorum monasterii sancti Oswaldi* seems to suggest. And it helps explain as well both the puzzling retention of the Latin commentaries, and "Quixley's" original composition of another such for the added balade XIX, when Gower's French apparently required translation. For what Yorkshire audience was French fading, while Latin (ragged though "Quixley's" is) maintained currency, except perhaps among those in orders? Certainly that number included Austin friars and canons, who were taught preaching in both languages, and who regularly received sermons in both at triennial Chapter meetings.[36] Ultimately, British Library, MS Stowe 951 may very well be a holograph, at least as far as "Quixley's" rendering of Gower's

---

the awkward references to *De nuptiis*: "Quixley" may have had a problem construing Augustine's elegant style. Nor can we be certain of the state of his source text.

[34] On the founding of St. Mary Overey and Nostell as Austin priories, see Dickinson, *Origins of the Austin Canons*, pp. 119–21.

[35] Triennial Chapters were required of all English Austin abbots and priors after 1215, and could easily have provided occasion for book exchange. Extant Chapter Acts are incomplete, especially for those held in the south, but Acts from Chapters hosted by northern houses have Nostell several times as a gathering-place. While no known record survives of St. Mary Overey as host, the Acts of the Chapter at Newstead in 1371 have the priors of Southwark and Nostell together in attendance; at the Northampton Chapter in 1404, Southwark is unlisted. But Nostell is present, alongside the priors of Twynham and Southwick; both houses are from the see of Winchester, that of St. Mary Overey. See Salter, *Chapters of the Augustinian Canons*, pp. 69, 80. Another institutionalized conduit of exchange was through the three-member teams of visitors who annually circulated among houses, to report on their physical and spiritual condition. Visitors were appointed at the Chapter, and the position rotated among houses: e.g., Henry, prior of Southwark, was to oversee throughout the dioceses of Winchester and Salisbury, but gave up the position in 1392 due to failing health (Salter, p. xxix).

[36] Again, the testimony of the Chapter Acts is not irrelevant here, by way of illustrating the changing fortunes of French in Austin houses by the mid-fifteenth century: at Northampton in 1325, a statute was passed enjoining canons needing to speak during the hours of silence to use only Latin or French; but by 1443 sermons were delivered at the Oseney Chapter only in English and Latin (Salter, *Chapters of the Augustinian Canons*, p. 14; xxxi–xxxii). In this, Austin practice mirrors the chronology of the general shift away from French usage in England established by Baugh and Cable; see "Re-Establishment of English," in *History of the English Language*, and further Fisher, *Emergence of Standard English*, especially "Transition from Latin and French to English," pp. 43–46; but see also Machan, *English in the Middle Ages*, pp. 71–110, who presents a somewhat more nuanced sociolinguistic process.

balades is concerned, and the copying of the *Historia trium regum* and *Speculum vitae* the work of their translator-poet as well. That that poet-translator was Robert de Quixley, Yorkshireman, canon and prior, of the Augustinian house of Nostell, seems a credible, if not indeed a likely, possibility.

[PROLOGUE][37]

Who þat liste loke in þis litel tretice
May fynde what meschief is of auoutrie
Wherfore he þat will eschewe þat vice
He may see here to beware of folie
5　Gower it made in frenshe with grete studie
In balades ryale whos sentence here
Translated hath Quixley in this manere.

I.[38]

The hye maker of euery creature,
That sowle of man made vn to his liknesse,
10　To whiche as by reson of hir nature
God hath yeuen temperate sobrenesse,
The body to rewle and [for] more fulnesse,
Endowed hit hath of discrecion,
The flesche to holde vnder by reson

15　For to þe soule þat is so clene & pure
Parteneth to loue god in stedfastnesse;
And nat encline to foule delite vnsure,
Be which it myght deserue peynful duresse;
Thassent is perilleus, as þat I gesse,
20　Therfore schuld be þe soules mocion
The flesche to holde vnder be reson.

In a gode soule is reson and mesure,
Whoos heritage is heuenesse blesse;
The body is ordeyned for engendrure,
25　As hir gode spouse wedded in sikernesse;
And booth been oon withouten doubilnesse,
So þat mesure take his lawfull seson
The flesche to holde vnder be reson.

---

[37] This edition was prepared by MacCracken (see p. 153n1). He describes his editorial practices: "Words in brackets [ ] are inserted by me; words in parentheses ( ) are in the text, but are considered to be additions by the scribe, and superfluous." Italics indicate an abbvreviation that MacCracken has expanded.

[38] [*Heading:* Exhortacio Contra Vicium Adulterii.]

II.

The soule in loue desires continence,
30   And to lyue chaste, euer in goddes syght:
The body by kyndely experience
Desirs a wife, to multiplie aryght:
Blessed soules! *þat* oon stuffeth heuen bright,
That other erthe, such is goddys auys;
35   If oon be good, þat othre is more of prys.

For the soule þat maketh prouidence
May nat of goddes rewarde fayle, be ryght;
For in it is mych more intelligence,
And more vnderstondyng of felyng myght
40   Then in þe body, for his issue bright.
No, forthy! god made all to his seruys;
If oon be good þat othre is more of prys.

To the soule, god hath yheuen science
Of gode and ill, to chese and haue in sight
45   That þe body haue nat al reuerence,
But for to beye þe soule bothe day & nyght.
Thilk god, þat all nat*u*re hath wroght & dyght,
Hath sette booth twoo in state at his devys;
If oon be good þat othre is more of prys.

III.

50   God bonde vs nat to *þe* moost parfitenesse,
But wolde þat we euer parfite schuld be.
Who þat to god voweth withoute excesse
His body for to lyve in chastite,
Myche is his mede; Who list nat this degree,
55   Bot take a wyf to haue lawful issue;—
God it plesyth al suche matrimoyne due.

So first, whan god made of his hye godenesse
Adam and Eue, in paradyse made he
Mariage of hem two in all clennesse;
60   That of thai*re* seede al erth schuld haue plentee.
There vndertaken was spousalitee
Of þe oolde lawe first; so to continue,
God it pleseth al suche mat*r*imoyne due.

And sith þat god by his lawe ful exp*re*sse
65   Two p*er*sons hath ordeyned in vnitee,
Ryght is *þer*fore (þat) boothe in oon herte compresse
Thei*r*e loue, withouten chaunge or sotiltee,
In welthe to lyue and in aduersitee,

Schee his goode leef, & he hir spous ful trewe;
70   God it pleseth at suche matrimoyne due.

IV.

With loue whan trowth hath his aqueyntance,
Joyful then beon suche mariages alle!
But who þat purposeth by Deceiuance
Or fals semblant, to schewe his loue at alle
75   To syght, and vnderneth hydeth his galle,
That is as who of hardes maath a corde,
When þe hert to þe semblant list discorde.

Thilk mariage is goode, ful of plesance,
That of a vertuous loue hath his calle,
80   But who for Auarice, taketh his chance
Of mariage or luste, his loue is thralle;
Neuere schal that gracieusly befalle,
For consciens schal hym euere remorde;
Whan þe hert to þe semblant list descorde.

85   Honeste loue, þat to trowth dooth obeissance,
Maketh mariages goode and ryalle,
And who his hert in suche a gouernance
Dooth set, nat nedeth from his gode loue falle,
No of perillous chaunge to haue doutance;
90   For sayde it is, "auenturous balance
Is mariage," bot loue then is no lorde
When þe hert to þe semblant list discorde.

V.

Grete merueille is, and myche ayhein reson,
That when a man hath taken vnto wyue
95   A woman, at his owne eleccion;
And after that his trouth breketh belyue,
And dayly, as longe as he is alyue,
Newe loue seketh, as þat he were a beste;
A mans trowth to breke it is not honeste.

100   Of wedloke þe hooly profession
Myche more worthe is, þen I here can descryue.
Vnder which Criste to incarnacion
And in þe virginel wombe did arriue:
Who this matere lyst ferther for to dryue,
105   Let hym loke this ordre of holy geste,—
A mans trouth to breke it is not honeste.

Of wedloke þat hye and gode beneison
Of god & of þe holy goost myssyue,
By holy chirche, doon with deuocion
110 Enspireth þe sacrament terme of lyue;
Nat to be dissolued bot lyf actiue
Tobserue, and ay clennesse in hert arreste;
A mans trouth to breke it is not honeste.

VI.

Nectanabus, which of Egipt was kyng,
115 To defoule Olimpias þat was queene
Of Macedoyn, Philip hir lorde beyng
Absent, did suche labour as þat was seene
That Alisandre was goot hem betweene.
Bot what of ioye thay fonde in þaire errure?
120 The ende scheweth al the sore auenture.

If synne be nye, grace away gooth rennyng;
That preued wele, for þat synne was so keene
The son þe fadre slowgh withoute knowyng;
Therfore take hede, wittyng, & nothyng weene
125 That suche auoutrie with grief and teene
Venged wil be, of so grete forfeture;
The ende scheweth all the sore auenture.

Kyng Vlixes, to plese flesshly likyng,
Fro Penelopee dide hym fast to fleene;
130 Brak hir his trowth, & toke another yhyng,
Circes, to loue and gat of hir so scheene
Thelegonus, which, as þat storyes meene,
His fader slewe, loo! suche an engendrure
The ende scheweth al the sore auenture.

VII.

135 In þe desert of the hye & grete Inde,
He þat two pylers of brasse did ordeyne,
Hercules, toke his wyf, as I fynde,
The faire Deyanire, þat is to seyne
Of Calidoyne þe kynges doughter soleyne;
140 Conquerd hir of Achelois by bataille,—
Grete peril is to breke a mans spousaille.

Anoon lewdly after chaunged his mynde
For Eolen, þat he his spouse souuereyne
Hated, that other made hym so foole blynde
145 That what of hym sche list haue or atteyne
Was his plesir; no thynge wolde he restreyne,

The begynnyng and eende can not euenly faille:
Grete peril is to breke a mans spousaille.

Hit neuer was ne be schal in man kynde,
150 Bot of suche synne vengeance mot nede be pleyne.
For hercules þat fals was and vn kynde
Of a venymed schert was foul deseyne,
And brent hym self; parched euery veyne,
Of his mysdede he bare þe countre taylle.
155 Grete peril is to breke a mans spousaille.

VIII.

The noble knyght Jason, þat fro Colchos
The flees of golde by the helpe of Medee
Conquerd, wherof he (he) had ful mychel loos,—
Thurgh oute þe worlde he gate renommee,
160 The yhonge lady then praysed of beautee
With hym he toke, and wedded at deuyse;
Brokyn wedloke god will venge & dispise.

When Medee beste truste to haue hir lord cloos
In hir loue, and tweyne childre borne had sche,
165 Then hir forsoke Jason, and toke purpos
An other to loue, & breke his seuretee:—
That was Creusa kyng Creons doghter free—
Wher of vengance befell of due Justise;
Broken wedloke god will venge & despise.

170 When Medea this knewe, aanone sche roos
With angry hert, and ayens al pitee
Hir yhonge two sons, as thai had been hire foos,
In a grete raage sche slowgh, þat he myght see
How fals he was to hir, and thus was he
175 Despised, & his schame gan for tarise.
Broken wedloke god will venge & despise.

IX.

That Auoutier þat dooth continuance
In his foule synne, & hath therof delite,
Full litel can he drede goddes vengeance;
180 Wherof I fynde a Cronyque thus I-write
For ensample, gode is it to recite;
A man may note what it dooth signifie.
Horrible is þe synne of auoutrie.

Agamenon, þat had in gouuernance
185 Of grekes all þe chosyn floure soubgite

At troye, whan þat he was moost of puissance,
Climestre his wyfe was mychel to wyte;
For Egistus sche loued nat a lite,
And brake wedloke, to hir grete vilenye,
190   Horrible is þe synne of auoutrie.

Agamenon of deeth suffred penance,
And be treson was slayn, withoute respite,
Of his owne wyfe, þat had no repentance.
What fell þerof? Orestes had despit,
195   And with [his] hand he slewe hir in *þat* plite:
And Egist was hanged on galowes hye;
Horrible is þe synne of auoutrie.

X.

Loo, þe fairest worldly creature,
Þe wyfe of kyng of grece Menelay,
200   Whiche was þe fool synnere ou*er* mesure,
Helayne, for whom Parys made hym full gay,
After all her lust thoght it was no play,
Whan troye destroyed was, and brent to grounde;
So hye a synne god will of ryght confounde.

205   Tarquinius þe proude myght not endure
In his synne longe, for he foul did assay
To breke wedloke, be force of his luxure,
Chaste Lucresse Collatyns wyf bylay,
And he *þer*fore exiled was for ay;
210   Sche for sorowe slewe hir selfe in *þat* stounde;
So hye a synne god will of ryght confounde.

A Prince, Mundus, *þat* Rome had in his cure,
In Ysis Temple, þe moneth of May
Belay Pauline, of chastitee tresure,
215   By two prestes assent to *þat* foule play,
Wherof he banysht was withoute delay,—
Hanged were þe prestes as lawe then founde;
So hye a synne god will of ryght confounde.

XI.

Albyns, þat was a prince ful batailleus,
220   And þat first was kyng of all lumbardie,
Slewe his enmye as kyng victorieus,
Gurmund, which *þat* afore held chiualrie,
His doughter Rosamunde, þe beale cherie,
He weddyd after þat, but what may last?
225   Who euil doth, he mon be vnderthrast.

A wedloke suche was neuer gracieuse,
Where god lyst not it to senitifie.
The lady, whiche was wroth & yrous
That he hir fader slewe, anoon in hye
230 Hir owne husband to loue she gan denye,
And to Elmege, straunger, hir hert sche cast.
Who euyl dooth, he mon be vnderthrast.

Of synne spryngeth an ende malicieus,
For by poyson, made by grete sotelee,
235 Albins was dede, & sche, þat lichereus,
With hir Elmege, was brent for felonye
By þe duc of Rauenne in þe baillye
Of his palays, juggement was past,
Who euill dooth, he mon be vnderthrast.

XII.

240 The noble kyng of Athenes, Pandion,
Twoo doghters begat, Progne & Philomene;
Which bothe were vnder the proteccion
Of kyng Tereus, of Trace where he þe scheen
Lady Progne hath wedded, and made hir queene.
245 Bot þat other sister loued he myche more;
Wykked lyfe maath a man tabye ful sore.

Of foole delyte, contrarie to reson,
This Tereus kyng, by falshede ther foresene,
The virginite rauysht be treson
250 Of Philomene, þat no falshede couthe wene;
And brak his wedlok, for whiche son was seene
That fro wele was turned all his lore.
Wykked lyfe maath a man tabye ful sore.

Over cruele was vengeance þerof doon,
255 For his yhonge son his wyfe there slewe for tene,
And put his flesshe to sere decoccion,
And gafe þe fader to eete all bedeene,—
Therfore anone was he forschapen cleene
To a lapwynk, lo þe vengeance perfore!
260 Wykked lyfe maath a man tabye ful sore.

XIII.

Seint Abraham, chief of þe lawe oolde,
Froom Canaan fledde for a grete famine,
And toke with hym his wyfe, and what he wolde,
Vnto Egipte where he dredde of couyne,
265 When Pharao toke to concubyne

His wyfe Sarrai, he made ful grete murnyng.
Lordes of estate schuld tempre thair lykyng.

This Abraham dred myche þe kyng so bolde,
That he nat durst gaynstande þe said rauyne,
270 For to haue þees, þerof compleyne he nolde,
Therfore dyd hym þe kyngs fauour encline;
Bot yhit þe synne most haue his discipline,
For god chastiside hit, to be tokynyng,—
Lordes of estate schuld tempre ther lykyng.

275 Sodeynly or men wyst what befalle scholde
Thurghoute Egipt ther fell such a moryne
That Pharao, when his men hym þat tolde,
And what meschief, noon other medicyne
So astonyed couthe he then ymagyne,
280 But restored Sarray, with forthynkyng;
Lordes of estat schuld tempre ther lykyng.

XIV.
Myche is man[ne]s flesshe frele and vileyne;
Withouten grace may no man here do wele.
Therof scheweth þe bible, in certeyne,
285 Whan kyng Dauid did morther his knyght lele,
Vry, in þe bataille for Bersabee la bele;
A wyfe sche was, bot for þat he ne spared.
Noon is siker þat god hath not in warde.

The beautee þat he see in hir soleyne
290 Made hym of na poair his lustes frele
For to abstene, so þat of lufe þe peyne
Made hym to fall ayhenis god as rebelle.
Oon syn with another will entermelle.
Manslaght and auoutry had of hym garde.
295 Noon is siker þat god hath not in warde.

Bot he of his pitee souuereyne
Gafe grace vn to Dauid his prophet lele,
Tamende his gylt, saue þat betwix hem tweyne
The childe getyn deyed, thus did god dele;
300 For swete a soure; yhit by his prayers fele
Mercy asht he, mercy fande he rewarde.
Noon is siker þat god hath not in warde.

XV.
Open been bothe Cronyk and historie
Of Lancelote and of Tristram also,—

305   And yhit their foly is in þe memorye
        For ensampil, yheuyng vn to all tho
        That been alyue, nat for to lyuen so.
        Beware! I rede, of other mens folye:
        O brid by a nother can hym chastie.

310   Al tyme of yhere þe faire of loue sotie
        Is open to all þat lyst choese of two
        Cupides tonnes, to which þe peple flye,
        That oon is swete, & such is *þer* no moo;
        That other bitter is of peyne & woo;
315   Betwix hem two god is to modifie.
        Oon brid by a nother can hym chastie.

        To som pat in fortune will hem affie,
        Sche is bothe white and blak, now frend, now foo:
        Now lyue in ioye, now in purgatorie,
320   Withouten rest, withouten rewle: se, lo!
        How sche tourneth þe face hir sutoure fro.
        Therfore fole is þat in lust wol affie.
        Oon brid by a nother can hym chastie.

                    XVI.
        Men fyndes oft in diuers scripture
325   Many worthi, þat in armes had renoun;
        But few þere were þ*at* of chaste loue were sure,
        Ne þat clenly kept thaire condicioun,—
        As Valentinian made his sermoun
        To þe Romayns, alle be syche auys;
330   "Who þat his flessh venqueth most haue þe prys."

        For he þat ouercoms al auenture
        Of þe worlde, schuld haue a grete guerdoun.
        More owe he then, whome pryks þe flesshly cure,
        If he holde hit sugit vnder his abandoun,
335   Heuen to deserue, se this comparisoun,
        Whether the world is bet or paradise?
        Who þat his flessh venqueth most haue þe prys.

        And loue þat hath armes in his tenure,
        Ful stronge it is, bot þe *pro*fessioun
340   Of verray loue surmonteth al nature,
        And maath a man lyve in lawe of resoun.
        In mariage is the parfeccioun,
        Kepe he his trowth, þat in þis ordre lys.
        Who þat his flessh venqueth most haue þe pays.

XVII.

345   Trewe loue is betwix twoo þe holy bonde
      That all her lyfe stant, withoute dep*ar*tyng,
      As was þe trouth yplyght in þe ryght honde
      At þe chirche dore; but when other lykyng
      From twoo to three maketh a newe changyng
350   Then loue is non: what is þat auantage?
      To oon is oone ynogh in mariage.

      No loue þat is comune wil not longe stonde;
      A man to haue oone wyfe,—it is plesyng,
      But he þat ay chaunges fro londe to loonde
355   And in oon place, can nat haue his bydyng:
      Vnto Gawayn may he be resemblyng,
      Curteys of loue, bot he was ouer volage;
      To oon is oone ynogh in mariage.

      He may be lyke to þe moone nerehond,
360   That first gode loue schewith in apperyng,
      When he a wyfe to haue taketh on honde,
      Thof white or broune sche be; & maath changyng
      To a newe by morne, trust wele þ*at* suche thyng
      Shal he abye ryght sore at his passage;
365   To oon is oone ynough in mariage.

XVIII.

      Whoo þat of goolde hath [gret] aboundance
      Grete wroong he dooth þ*at* from a nother wight
      His money steeleth, ryght so [þe] meschaunce
      Will fall to hym þat preeseth day & nyght,
370   A nother mans wyfe, to defoule by myght,
      And his owene forsaketh for a newe;
      Such loue was neu*er* gode ne may be trewe.

      Of three blessed estats of gouuernance,
      Wedloke is þe second rewled aryght:
375   Whoo þat ordre setteth in fool plesance
      Miche may be doute, for peyne þat is hym dyght.
      Therefore gud is, wedloke in cristes syght
      To keþe honeste, waare auoutier untrewe!
      Suche loue was neu*er* goode ne may be trewe.

380   The conscience schuld weye al in balance,
      That when he of his fool delyte hath syght
      To haue remors & weue al such foul chance,
      For els no doute he shall lake heuens lyght.
      O gode wedloke! thi lyfe is faire and bryght;

385   O avoutier! beware to continewe!
       Suche loue was neuer gode ne may be trewe.

XIX.[39]

       A philosophre of a grete citee
       Whilom þer was, and of ful grete honour;
       Which after yhouth thoght þat ryght wele myght he
390   His body stroonge emploie, as a lichour
       In fool delyte, so prykked hym þat stour;
       But grace of crist made hym soon repentyng,
       God of heuen, our blys without endyng.

       He wrote þat auoutier punysht shal be
395   To leese a lym, or prisonned ful soure,
       Or schame shall hym falle of dishoneste,
       Or elles pouert withoute eny socour,
       Or sodeyn deeth to his grete dishonour;
       Whoo enspyred thus hym to teche suche thyng?
400   God of heuen, our blys without endyng.

       To all þe worldes vniversitee
       This balade be ensample and myrrour:
       And whoo lyst nat to stonde in this degree,
       Rather or þat he fall into errour
405   Of (flesshly) lust, I reede he chese þat peramour
       That is, was, and euer schall be lastyng,—
       God of heuen, our blys without endyng.
Amen.
Explicit.

---

[39] The rubric to this triple ballade (not in Gower's original version, which limits the whole matter of the philosopher) reads as follows:—
    "Philosophus quidam carnis de labe remorsus Plebis in exemplum verba refert unam de variis penam fortiter adulter eius ut amplexus omnis in orbe luat aut membrum perdet aut carceris antea subibit aut cadet infamis non reputandus homo aut sibi pauperies infortunata resistit. Aut moriens subito transit ab orbe reus."

APPENDIX 2: A NOTE ON GOWER'S FRENCH BY BRIAN MERRILEES

The form of French spoken and written in England following the Conquest is usually called Anglo-Norman (AN) but this term is not always applied to the period of the late fourteenth and fifteenth centuries for which Anglo-French (AF) is sometimes preferred. Anglo-French is a very broad term nonetheless and covers a variety of kinds of insular French, depending on the nature of the text and the training of the writer. Many administrative, legal, and commercial documents survive where the language is quite different from its continental counterpart, though it has been shown that many scribes and clerks were aware of the differences. Gower's French is of course highly literary, and the poet was very familiar with contemporary continental writing: his language is an interesting mixture of insular and continental elements. My remarks are limited to the *Balades*, and my examples are not exhaustive. I recommend reading Macaulay's admirable description of language and versification in the introduction to volume one of his editions.[1]

MORPHOLOGY

Declension and flexion. Gower seems aware that there was a two-case system in medieval French, though fast being reduced in most instances to a single case based on the objective rather than the nominative forms. In *Cinkante Balades* Dedication I.16 I find *Vostre Gower, q'est trestout vos soubgitz* where the past participle adjective *soubgitz* retains nominative singular *s*, yet clearly to suit the rhyme pattern he has chosen. Similarly in *Cinkante Balades* IX.4 the poet describes his heart as *Parfit, verai, loial, entalentis*, the last adjective only with *s* rhyming with the following line *amis* as well as other adjectives in the same balade: *vifs, faillis, esbaubis, mendis, poestis*. There is even a form with *s* used in the object case where none would be expected, *Cinkante Balades* IX.36: *tanqu'il m'avera guaris*, again suiting the rhyme. In *Cinkante Balades* XI.2 he writes *li coers* where both article and noun are in the old nominative, without any versificational influence. In *Cinkante Balades* XVIII.1 *Les goutes d'eaue qe cheont menu* might have had *menues*, feminine plural nominative, but again the rhyme (*avenu, defendu*, etc.) forces the poet's hand.

The relative pronouns *qui* and *qe* are both used in the nominative, the latter more frequently. Personal pronouns which maintain nominative, direct and indirect objective forms into modern French are mostly standard, but occasionally there are insular usages: *qe jeo lui aime* (*Cinkante Balades* XXIII.13) where the indirect (also a tonic) form replaces the direct. Another example of AF usage is the neuter demonstrative pronoun as an adjective:

---

[1] Gower, *Complete Works*, 1:xvi–xxxiv. Also still of value for morphology, phonology, and orthography is Pope, *From Latin to Modern French*, part 5. An update of some of Pope's material can be found in Short's *Manual of Anglo-Norman*.

ce/ceo lettre (*Cinkante Balades* II.25/III.23). Possessive adejctives *mon* and *son* are often written *moun* and *soun*. Earlier AN *mun* and *sun* do not appear. The possessive singular *vostre* and plural *vos* can both be found as *vo* without distinction of number. The *a* of feminine *ma* and *sa* can both be elided before a vowel.

Gender distinctions and agreements are not always kept as they would be in standard medieval French and again meter and rhyme can explain some of the examples though not all: *Du providence* (*Cinkante Balades* Dedication I.3), *ce lettre* (*Cinkante Balades* II.25), *corps humeine* (*Cinkante Balades* XIIII.3), *du bouche* (*Cinkante Balades* XIIII.23), *le fin* (*Cinkante Balades* XIX.18), *maint question* (XXIIII.20), *chose humein* (*Cinkante Balades* XXIIII.22), *celle appetit* (*Cinkante Balades* XXVI.21), *le defalte* (*Cinkante Balades* XXVIII.12), *[l]a cliere Estée* (*Cinkante Balades* XXXII.8), *[m]a belle oisel* (*Cinkante Balades* XXXIIII.25), *mon chançoun* (*Cinkante Balades* XXXV.24), *un chaunçon verrai* (*Cinkante Balades* XL.22), *les herbes sont floris* (*Cinkante Balades* XXXVI.4), etc. The definite article *le* is feminine in Picard and often too in AF. The enclitic *du* is sometimes the equivalent of *de*: *Du quelle* (*Cinkante Balades* XLV.10), and perhaps *du bouche* (*Cinkante Balades* XIIII.23, compare the remark on gender). Similarly *au* stands for *a* in *au peine* (*Cinkante Balades* XXII.13).

Verbs. Verbs present little in the way of insular or unusual forms. The older AN distinction between first conjugation verbs ending in -*er* and -*ier* has disappeared in rhyme and often in spelling in infinitives and past participles: *envoier/amer* (*Cinkante Balades* VIII.22/24), *recomencer* (*Cinkante Balades* Dedication II.23), *adrescée/ymaginée* (*Cinkante Balades* VI.17/VI.15), *eslongée/desirée*, (*Cinkante Balades* VII.2/VII.4), etc. Infinitives in the other conjugations are in -*ir* and -*oir*, close to modern endings. One oddly-spelled infinitive used as a substantive is *poair*.

Some first person present indicatives of the first conjugation in -*er* (and thus -*ier*) have acquired a final *e*: *aime* (*Cinkante Balades* XXIII.13), *quide* (*Cinkante Balades* XXIIII.1), etc., but not all: *pri* (*Cinkante Balades* II.19), *asseur* (*Cinkante Balades* IIII.5), *j'aim* (*Cinkante Balades* IIII*.2), etc.; several third conjugation verbs which acquired *s* in the first person during Middle French remain without the *s*: *sui, sai, voi, doi, di, quier*, etc., though I do find *j'escrits* (*Cinkante Balades* LI.25) which is followed by *Henris* in the objective case and thus does not provide a proven rhyme, and *rens* (*Cinkante Balades* I.25) which rhymes with *serementz* (obj. pl., *Cinkante Balades* I.27), etc. More archaic forms are retained in *truis* (*Cinkante Balades* XVI.23), *trieus* (*Cinkante Balades* XXXIX.15), *puiss* (*Cinkante Balades* XVI.21), etc. First person plural can follow the insular and Norman ending -*om(s)*: *joioms* (*Cinkante Balades* Dedication II.26). Second person plurals often end in -*tz*: *avetz, fuissetz, croietz*, etc. Third person plural endings are almost always -*ent* but there are several examples in the *Balades* of the AN/AF ending -*ont*: *vienont* (*Cinkante Balades* II.8), *cheont* (*Cinkante Balades* XVIII.1), *parlont, diont* (*Cinkante Balades* XXXI.22), *provont* (*Cinkante Balades* XL.8), etc.

A number of future forms have an intrusive *e* between *v* and *r* which can or not be counted as a syllable, depending on the line: *averai* (*Cinkante Balades* I.21), *devera* (*Cinkante Balades* V.9), *viverai* (*Cinkante Balades* X.18), etc. In AN this *e* was sometimes an indicator that the manuscript *u* was indeed a *v*. Futures and conditionals of some third conjugation verbs double *r* orthographically but they can rhyme with single *r*: *plerra/semblera* (*Cinkante Balades* II.20/21), *irra/remembrera* (*Cinkante Balades*, II.25/27), *querroie/changeroie* (*Cinkante Balades* V.22/24), etc.

Past tense forms are mostly regular and because of the nature of the text, centered on the present and future, Gower thus uses the present perfect more than the simple past. Of the latter I find such forms as: *di* (< *dire*) *fis* (< *faire*), *esta* (< *ester*), *fuismes, fuist* (confusion of *ui* and *u*), *vi* (< *voir*), *passa*, *eschapa*, etc. Past participles are also regular though gender agreement is not always observed: *qe jeo vous ai amé* (i.e., his lady) (*Cinkante Balades* XXXVII.13): *lié* masc. (*Cinkante Balades* XXXVII.14).

PHONOLOGY AND ORTHOGRAPHY

Gower's text looks very different in spelling from AN texts of the thirteenth and fourteenth centuries, especially in reintroducing dipthongs that had earlier been reduced to simple vowels. Some of this is the result of the influence of continental French, some the characteristics of later AN and AF. For example the *oi* diphthong which had been *ei* or simple *e* is used frequently: *reçoit, doit, esploit, decevoir, manoir, coie*, etc., as in modern French. In earlier AN one might have found *reçeit* (compare English *receipt*), *deit, espleit* or *esplet* (among many others), etc. As I discuss below, the dipthongs *ei* and *ai* are also found before nasals and in rhymes which suggest these are principally orthographic. Gower does retain the insular *ou*, especially before *r* and *s* and in the nasal *oun*. There are few uses, however, of single *u* instead of *ou* or single *o*, a main feature of AN.

Simple vowels. Most simple vowels are unexceptional though there is some orthographical confusion with digraphs: *ie* for *e* in *la* [*n*]*ief* (*Cinkante Balades* XXX.1), [*l*]*a cliere Estée* (*Cinkante Balades* XXXII.8), *miere* (*Cinkante Balades* XLIX.25), etc. Similarly *ui* is sometimes used for *u*: *fuismes* (*Cinkante Balades* Dedication I.6), *fuist* and *ou* for *o*, especially before a nasal: *moun* (*Cinkante Balades* II.10), *soun* (*Cinkante Balades* II.3), *comparisoun* (*Cinkante Balades* XXI.2), *resoun* (*Cinkante Balades* XXI.4), *bandoun* (*Cinkante Balades* XXI.5), etc. The simple nasal *an* is sometimes *aun*: *sufficaunce* (*Cinkante Balades* IIII.11), *fiaunce* (*Cinkante Balades* IIII.12), etc., but *an* is strongly maintained graphically: *plesance* (*Cinkante Balades* I.17), *continuance* (*Cinkante Balades* I.19), etc.

The so-called feminine or weak (atonic) *e* was unstable even in early AN and certainly by Gower's time. Final *e* in particular at word end could be pronounced or suppressed according to meter:

> *Pité, prouesse. humblesse, honour roial*
> *Se sont en vous, mon liege seignour, mis*
> > (*Cinkante Balades* Dedication I.1–2)

Final *e* of a line is not counted in the meter and can even be dropped to assure a rhyme: *conspir* (ind. pres.3)/*plesir* (*Cinkante Balades* XXV.3/1). The loss of *e* can eliminate masculine and feminine distinctions in past participles ending in -*é* and -*ée*; the confusion is evident when one encounters -*ée* for -*é*: *eslongée* masc. (*Cinkante Balades* VII.2): *honourée* fem. (*Cinkante Balades* VII.5), *prée* masc. (*Cinkante Balades* VII.9): *pensée* fem. (*Cinkante Balades* VII.11). An unstressed *e* is written *i* in *chivaler* (*Cinkante Balades* VII.14), etc.

Diphthongs. Diphthong reduction was a feature of AN from the twelfth century on and there is some evidence here of its continuation in rhyme, but mostly diphthongs are maintained or reproduced from contemporary French.

ie is reduced to *e* though often maintained in spelling: *Messager/conter*, (*Cinkante Balades* VIII.12/11), *danger/mirer* (*Cinkante Balades* XII.19/17), *pleniere/amiere* = *amer* "bitter" (*Cinkante Balades* XVI.9/11), *requiere* (*Cinkante Balades* XVIII.16): *matiere* (*Cinkante Balades* XVIII.18): *quarere* (*Cinkante Balades* XVIII.19), etc. There is no graphic reduction before a nasal: *bien*.

ei is almost always found before a nasal where there is often confusion with what was once *ai*: *peigne/compleigne*, compare English *complain* (*Cinkante Balades* III.1/3), *peine/sovereine* (*Cinkante Balades* X.15/17), *peine/humeine* (*Cinkante Balades* XIIII.6/3), *asseine/capiteine* (*Cinkante Balades* XXXIX.9/11), etc. *ei* can also stand for *oi*: *aqueintai* (*Cinkante Balades* X.4), *s'aqueinte/queinte/meinte* (*Cinkante Balades* XLII.2/4/5), etc. *ai* is found for *ei* in *s'oraille* (*Cinkante Balades* XVIII.18).

ai can be written *e*: *jammes/pres*, compare Modern French *jamais* (*Cinkante Balades* II.14/16), *pes/pres*, compare Modern French *paix* (*Cinkante Balades* II.22/24), etc., as well as the expected *ai*: *compaignie* (*Cinkante Balades* IIII.13), *fait* (*Cinkante Balades* IIII.17), *debonaire*, *maire* (*Cinkante Balades* IIII*.6, IIII*.7), etc., and in the verb forms: *amerai* (*Cinkante Balades* IIII*.2), *viverai* (*Cinkante Balades* IIII*.4), *ai* (*Cinkante Balades* IIII*.5), *sai* (*Cinkante Balades* IIII*.9), etc. Occasionally the diphthong is written *ay*: *mesprendray* (*Cinkante Balades* IIII*.16), etc. and *ea*: *ease* (*Cinkante Balades* XIII.7), *peas* (*Cinkante Balades* XLI.7). There is also the more unusual substitution of *ie*: *sciet* (*Cinkante Balades* V.20). Pretonic *ai* is often *e*: *plesance*, *lerra*, *feture*, etc., but not always: *plaisir*, *forsfaiture*, etc.

oi from earlier *ei* (sometimes just *e* in AN) is frequent and helps give the text a more "continental" appearance: *foi*, *quoique*, *ainçois*, *voloir*, *avoit*, *espoir*, etc. (*Cinkante Balades* I.19, I.22). *oi* that comes from Latin *o* < *au* + palatal remains intact: *oisel*, *esjoiera*, *joies* (*Cinkante Balades* II.3, II.4, II.28), etc.

ou, however, did not become *eu* as was the case in central French: *dolour*, *dolçour*, *valour*, *amorouse*, *honour* (*Cinkante Balades* II.24, III.3, III.9, III.1, III.15), etc. In AN *ou* and *o* were often written *u*, a distinctive insular feature of early texts. Gower has few examples of this *u* in the *Balades* but occasionally they are in rhyme: *hure/nature* (*Cinkante Balades* VII.3/1), *plure/figure* (*Cinkante Balades* XII.23/21), etc.

ui is regular in such forms as *sui*, *puis(s)*, *truis* but is sometimes used, as noted above, for *u*: *pluis*, *fuist*, etc.; *ui* for *oi* is found in *vuill*, *bienvuillance*.

True triphthongs are present in *lieu*, *eaue*, etc. but orthographic only in *trieus*, *dieurté*, *scieussetz*, etc.

Consonants. There is little to comment on concerning consonants. As already mentioned, single and double *r* are found in rhyme and *tz* is used for *s* and for *z*: *toutz*, *tormentz*, *tenetz*, *croietz*, etc. Rhymes also show that the palatal nasal *gn* has been depalatalized to *n*: *enseigne/certeine* (*Cinkante Balades* XL.2/4), *pleigne/Heleine* (*Cinkante Balades* XL.7/5), etc., and *gn* is sometimes used for simple *n*: *peigne* (*Cinkante Balades* III.1), *[l]oigns* (*Cinkante Balades* XIX.17), etc. Central French *gu* as in *guardé*, *guarderai*, can be *w*: *rewardise* (*Cinkante Balades* LI.19). Initial *h* from Latin *h* is kept: *humble*, *heritance*, and dropped: *oure* ('hour'), etc. Gower follows the practice of introducing etymological letters recalling the Latin from which the word is derived — or thought to have been — that would be silent in pronunciation: *doulce*, *soubgis*, *sciet* (a confusion of *scire* with *sapere*), *oultre*, *escript*, *longtein*, etc.

🌿 BIBLIOGRAPHY

Alain of Lille. *The Plaint of Nature*. Trans. James J. Sheridan. Toronto: Pontifical Institute of Mediaeval Studies, 1980.

Alghieri, Dante. *The Divine Comedy*. Ed. Charles S. Singleton. 6 vols. Princeton, NJ: Princeton University Press, 1970–77.

Allen, Hope Emily. "The Authorship of the *Prick of Conscience*." In *Studies in English and Comparative Literature*. Boston: Ginn, 1910. Pp. 115–70.

———. "The *Speculum Vitae*: Addendum." *PMLA* 32 (1917), 133–62.

———. *Writings Ascribed to Richard Rolle, Hermit of Hampole and Materials for His Biography*. New York: D. C. Heath, 1927.

Allison, K. J., ed. *A History of the County of York, East Riding*. Vol. 1. London: Oxford University Press, 1969.

Andreas Capellanus. *The Art of Courtly Love*. Trans. John Jay Parry. New York: Columbia University Press, 1959.

Aquinas, Thomas. *S. Thomae Aquinatis opera omnia*. Ed. Roberto Busa. 7 vols. Stuttgart-Bad Cannstatt: Fromman-Holzboog, 1980.

Audiau, Jean. *Les Troubadours et l'Angleterre: contribution à l'étude des poètes anglais de l'amour au moyen-âge (XIIIe et XIVe siècles)*. Paris: Vrin, 1927.

Barber, Malcolm. *The Cathars: Dualist Heretics in Languedoc in the High Middle Ages*. Harlow: Longman, 2000.

Baugh, Albert C., and Thomas Cable. *A History of the English Language*. London: Routledge, 2002.

Benoît de Sainte-More. *Le Roman de Troie*. Ed. Léopold Constans. 6 vols. Paris: Firmin-Didot, 1904–12.

The Bestiary: A Book of Beasts. Trans. T. H. White. New York: G. P. Putnam's Sons, 1954.

Boethius. *The Consolation of Philosophy*. Trans. Richard Green. Indianapolis, IN: Bobbs-Merrill, 1962.

Boffey, Julia. "'Cy ensuent trios chaunceons': Groups and Sequences of Middle English Lyrics." In *Medieval Texts in Context*. Ed. Graham D. Caie and Denis Renevey. London: Routledge, 2008. Pp. 85–95.

Braddy, Haldeen. *Chaucer and the French Poet, Graunson*. Baton Rouge: Louisiana State University Press, 1947.

Burrows, T. N. "The Geography of Monastic Property in Medieval England: A Case Study of Nostell and Bridlington Priories (Yorkshire)." *Yorkshire Archaeolgical Journal* 57 (1985), 79–86.

Burton, Janet. *The Monastic Order in Yorkshire, 1069–1215*. Cambridge: Cambridge University Press, 1999.

Butterfield, Ardis. *Poetry and Music in Medieval France: From Jean Renart to Guillaume de Machaut*. Cambridge: Cambridge University Press, 2002.

Chaucer, Geoffrey. *The Riverside Chaucer*. Third edition. Ed. Larry D. Benson. Boston: Houghton Mifflin, 1987.

Coleman, Joyce. "Lay Readers and Hard Latin: How Gower May Have Intended the *Confessio Amantis* to Be Read." *Studies in the Age of Chaucer* 24 (2002), 209–35.

Colvin, H. M. *The White Canons in England*. Oxford: Clarendon Press, 1951.

Dan Michel. *Ayenbite of Inwyt, or Remorse of Conscience*. Ed. Richard Morris and Pamela Gradon. 2 vols. EETS o.s. 23 and 278. Oxford: Oxford University Press, 1965–79.

De planctu Naturae. See Alain of Lille, *The Plaint of Nature*.

Deschamps, Eustache. *Oeuvres Complètes de Eustache Deschamps*. Ed. le Marquis de Queux de Saint-Hilaire and Gaston Raynaud. 11 vols. Paris: Firmin-Didot, 1878–1903.

———. *L'Art de Dictier*. Ed. and trans. Deborah M. Sinnreich-Levi. East Lansing, MI: Colleagues Press, 1994.

Dickinson, J. C. *The Origins of the Austin Canons and Their Introduction into England*. London: S.P.C.K., 1950.

Echard, Siân. "Designs for Reading: Some Manuscripts of Gower's *Confessio Amantis*." *Trivium* 31 (1999), 59–72.

Echard, Siân, and Claire Fanger. *The Latin Verses in the Confessio Amantis: An Annotated Translation*. East Lansing, MI: Colleagues Press, 1991.

Epistola Alexandri ad Aristotelem. Ed. W. Walther Boer. Meisenheim: Anton Hain, 1973.

Evans, Joan, and Mary S. Sergeantson, eds. *English Mediaeval Lapidaries*. EETS o.s. 190. London: Oxford University Press, 1933.

The Exeter Book Riddles. Ed. and trans. Kevin Crossley-Holland. Cambridge: Brewer, 1989.

Fisher, John H. *John Gower: Moral Philosopher and Friend of Chaucer*. New York: New York University Press, 1964.

———. *The Emergence of Standard English*. Lexington: University Press of Kentucky, 1996.

Gower, John. *The Complete Works of John Gower*. Ed. G. C. Macaulay. 4 vols. Oxford: Clarendon Press, 1899–1902.

———. *The Major Latin Works of John Gower: The Voice of One Crying and the Tripartite Chronicle*. Trans. Eric W. Stockton. Seattle: University of Washington Press, 1962.

———. *Mirour de l'Omme (The Mirror of Mankind)*. Trans. William Burton Wilson. East Lansing, MI: Colleagues Press, 1992.

———. *Confessio Amantis*. Ed. Russell A. Peck, with Latin translations by Andrew Galloway. 3 vols. Kalamazoo, MI: Medieval Institute Publications, 2000–06.

———. *The Minor Latin Works*. Ed. and trans. R. F. Yeager, with *In Praise of Peace*, ed. Michael Livingston. Kalamazoo, MI: Medieval Institute Publications, 2005.

Gratian. *The Treatise on Laws (Decretum DD. 1–20)*. Trans. Augustine Thompson, with *The Ordinary Gloss*, trans. James Gordley. Washington, DC: Catholic University of America Press, 1993.

Greimas, A. J. *Dictionnaire de l'ancien français jusqu'au milieu du XIVe siècle*. Paris: Larousse, 1968.

Guido delle Colonne. *Historia destructionis Troiae*. Trans. Mary Elizabeth Meek. Bloomington: Indiana University Press, 1974.

Guillaume de Lorris and Jean de Meun. *Le Roman de la Rose*. Ed. Félix Lecoy. 3 vols. Paris: Librairie Honoré, 1970–74.

Hanna, Ralph. *London Literature, 1300–1380*. Cambridge: Cambridge University Press, 2005.

Hill, John. *An History of Animals*. London: Thomas Osborne, 1752.

Holmes, Edmond. *The Holy Heretics: The Story of the Albigensian Crusade*. London: Watts, 1948.

The Holy Bible Translated from the Latin Vulgate and Diligently Compared with Other Editions in Divers Languages (Douai, A.D. 1609; Rheims, A.D. 1582) Published as Revised and Annotated by Authority. London: Burns and Oates, 1964.

Homer. *The Iliad of Homer*. Trans. Richmond Lattimore. Chicago: University of Chicago Press, 1951.

Hyginus. *Hygini Fabulae*. Ed. Peter K. Marshall. Stuttgart: Teubner, 1993.

Isidore of Seville. *The Etymologies of Isidore of Seville*. Ed. Stephen A. Barney, W. J. Lewis, J. A. Beach, and Oliver Berghof. Cambridge: Cambridge University Press, 2006.

Itô, Masayoshi. *John Gower, the Medieval Poet*. Tokyo: Shinozaki Shorin, 1976.

Kar, G. *Thoughts on the Mediæval Lyric*. Oxford: Basil Blackwell, 1933.

Kelly, Henry Ansgar. *Love and Marriage in the Age of Chaucer*. Ithaca, NY: Cornell University Press, 1975.

Kirby, J. L. *Henry IV of England*. London: Constable, 1970.

Kittredge, George Lyman. *The Date of Chaucer's Troilus and Other Chaucer Matters*. London: K. Paul, Trench, and Trübner, 1909.

Kuczynski, Michael P. "Gower's Virgil." In *On John Gower: Essays at the Millennium*. Ed. R. F. Yeager. Kalamazoo, MI: Medieval Institute Publications, 2007. Pp. 161–87.

Lapidaries. See Evans and Sergeantson.

Lawless, George. *Augustine of Hippo and His Monastic Rule*. Oxford: Clarendon Press, 1987.

Lewis, C. S. *The Allegory of Love: A Study in Medieval Tradition*. Oxford: Clarendon Press, 1936.

Loomis, Roger Sherman, and Laura Hibbard Loomis, eds. *Medieval Romances*. New York: Random House, 1957.

MacCracken, Henry Noble. "Quixley's Ballades Royal (?1402)." *Yorkshire Archaeological Journal* 20 (1909), 33–50.

Machan, Tim William. *English in the Middle Ages*. Oxford: Oxford University Press, 2003.

Machaut, Guillaume de. *Oeuvres de Guillaume de Machaut*. Ed. Ernest Hoepffner. 3 vols. Paris: Firmin-Didot, 1908–21.

Matthew, H. C. G., and Brian Harrison, eds. *Oxford Dictionary of National Biography: from the Earliest Times to the Year 2000*. Oxford: Oxford University Press, 2004.

McIntosh, Angus, M. L. Samuels, and Michael Bensken, eds. *A Linguistic Atlas of Late Mediaeval English*. 4 vols. Aberdeen: Aberdeen University Press, 1986.

The Middle English Letter of Alexander to Aristotle. Ed. Vincent DiMarco and Leslie Perelman. Amsterdam: Rodopi, 1978.

Morrin, Margaret J. *John Waldeby, OSA, c. 1315–c. 1372: English Augustinian Preacher and Writer, with a Critical Edition of His Tract on the "Ave Maria."* Rome: Analecta Augustiniana, 1975.

Nicholson, Peter. "The Dedications of Gower's *Confessio Amantis*." *Mediaevalia* 10 (1984), 159–80.

———. *Love and Ethics in Gower's Confessio Amantis*. Ann Arbor: University of Michigan Press, 2005.

Ovid. *Heroides and Amores*. Ed. and trans. Grant Showerman, rev. G. P. Goold. Cambridge, MA: Harvard University Press, 1986.

———. *Fasti*. Ed. and trans. James George Frazer, rev. G. P. Goold. Cambridge, MA: Harvard University Press, 1989.

———. *Metamorphoses*. Ed. and trans. F. J. Miller, rev. G. P. Goold. 2 vols. Cambridge, MA: Harvard University Press, 1994.

Peterson, Ingrid J. *William of Nassington: Canon, Mystic and Poet of the* Speculum Vitae. New York: Peter Lang, 1986.

Physiologus. Trans. Michael J. Curley. Austin: University of Texas Press, 1979.

Pliny. *Natural History*. Ed. and trans. Henry Rackham. 10 vols. London: Heineman, 1938–62.

Pope, M. K. *From Latin to Modern French with Especial Consideration of Anglo-Norman: Phonology and Morphology*. Manchester: Manchester University Press, 1952.

Raynaud, Gaston, ed. *Les Cent Ballades, poème du XIVe siècle*. Paris: Firmin-Didot, 1905.

Richardson, Robert. *Commentary on the Rule of St. Augustine by Robertus Richardinus*. Ed. G. G. Coulton. Edinburgh: T. and A. Constable, 1935.

Robert of Bridlington. *The Bridlington Dialogue: An Exposition of the Rule of St. Augustine for the Life of the Clergy, Given through a Dialogue between Master and Disciple*. London: Mowbray, 1960.

Roman de la Rose. See Guillaume de Lorris and Jean de Meun.

Salter, H. E. *Chapters of the Augustinian Canons*. London: Canterbury and York Society, 1922.

Shakespeare, William. *Hamlet*. Ed. Harold Jenkins. New York: Methuen, 1982.

———. *The Second Part of King Henry IV*. Ed. A. R. Humphreys. London: Methuen, 1966.

Short, Ian. *Manual of Anglo-Norman*. London: Anglo-Norman Text Society, 2007.

Stevens, Martin. "The Royal Stanza in Early English Literature." *PMLA* 94 (1979), 62–76.

Strohm, Paul. "Some Generic Distinctions in the *Canterbury Tales*." *Modern Philology* 68 (1971), 321–28.

Thompson, Raymond H., and Keith Busby, eds. *Gawain: A Casebook*. New York: Routledge, 2006.

Virgil. *The Aeneid*. Trans. Robert Fitzgerald. New York: Random House, 1981.

Warton, Thomas, ed. *The History of English Poetry from the Twelfth to the Close of the Sixteenth Century*. 4 vols. London: Reeves and Turner, 1870–71.

Whiting, Bartlett Jere. *Chaucer's Use of Proverbs*. Cambridge, MA: Harvard University Press, 1934.

Wilkins, Ernest H. *Petrarch's Later Years*. Cambridge, MA: Medieval Academy of America, 1959.

Willard, Charity Cannon. *Christine de Pizan: Her Life and Works*. New York: Persea Books, 1984.

Wimsatt, James I. *Chaucer and His French Contemporaries: Natural Music in the Fourteenth Century*. Toronto: University of Toronto Press, 1991.

———, ed. *Chaucer and the Poems of "Ch."* Revised Edition. Kalamazoo, MI: Medieval Institute Publications, 2009.

Yeager, R. F. "English, Latin, and the Text as 'Other': The Page as Sign in the Work of John Gower." *Text: Transactions of the Society for Textual Scholarship* 3 (1987), 251–67.

———. *John Gower's Poetic: The Search for a New Arion*. Cambridge: D. S. Brewer, 1990.

———. "Gower's Lancastrian Affinity: The Iberian Connection." *Viator* 35 (2004), 483–515.

———. "John Gower's Audience: The Ballades." *Chaucer Review* 40 (2005), 81–105.

Stanzaic Guy of Warwick, edited by Alison Wiggins (2004)

Saints' Lives in Middle English Collections, edited by E. Gordon Whatley, with Anne B. Thompson and Robert K. Upchurch (2004)

Siege of Jerusalem, edited by Michael Livingston (2004)

The Kingis Quair and Other Prison Poems, edited by Linne R. Mooney and Mary-Jo Arn (2005)

The Chaucerian Apocrypha: A Selection, edited by Kathleen Forni (2005)

John Gower, *The Minor Latin Works*, edited and translated by R. F. Yeager, with *In Praise of Peace*, edited by Michael Livingston (2005)

Sentimental and Humorous Romances: Floris and Blancheflour, Sir Degrevant, The Squire of Low Degree, The Tournament of Tottenham, and The Feast of Tottenham, edited by Erik Kooper (2006)

The Dicts and Sayings of the Philosophers, edited by John William Sutton (2006)

Everyman and Its Dutch Original, Elckerlijc, edited by Clifford Davidson, Martin W. Walsh, and Ton J. Broos (2007)

The N-Town Plays, edited by Douglas Sugano, with assistance by Victor I. Scherb (2007)

The Book of John Mandeville, edited by Tamarah Kohanski and C. David Benson (2007)

John Lydgate, *The Temple of Glas*, edited by J. Allan Mitchell (2007)

The Northern Homily Cycle, edited by Anne B. Thompson (2008)

Codex Ashmole 61: A Compilation of Popular Middle English Verse, edited by George Shuffelton (2008)

Chaucer and the Poems of "Ch," edited by James I. Wimsatt (revised edition 2009)

William Caxton, *The Game and Playe of the Chesse*, edited by Jenny Adams (2009)

John the Blind Audelay, *Poems and Carols*, edited by Susanna Fein (2009)

Two Moral Interludes: The Pride of Life and Wisdom, edited by David Klausner (2009)

John Lydgate, *Mummings and Entertainments*, edited by Claire Sponsler (2010)

Mankind, edited by Kathleen M. Ashley and Gerard NeCastro (2010)

The Castle of Perseverance, edited by David N. Klausner (2010)

Robert Henryson, *The Complete Works*, edited by David J. Parkinson (2010)

COMMENTARY SERIES

Haimo of Auxerre, *Commentary on the Book of Jonah*, translated with an introduction and notes by Deborah Everhart (1993)

Medieval Exegesis in Translation: Commentaries on the Book of Ruth, translated with an introduction and notes by Lesley Smith (1996)

Nicholas of Lyra's Apocalypse Commentary, translated with an introduction and notes by Philip D. W. Krey (1997)

Rabbi Ezra Ben Solomon of Gerona, *Commentary on the Song of Songs and Other Kabbalistic Commentaries*, selected, translated, and annotated by Seth Brody (1999)

John Wyclif, *On the Truth of Holy Scripture*, translated with an introduction and notes by Ian Christopher Levy (2001)

Second Thessalonians: Two Early Medieval Apocalyptic Commentaries, introduced and translated by Steven R. Cartwright and Kevin L. Hughes (2001)

The "Glossa Ordinaria" on the Song of Songs, translated with an introduction and notes by Mary Dove (2004)

The Seven Seals of the Apocalypse: Medieval Texts in Translation, translated with an introduction and notes by Francis X. Gumerlock (2009)

DOCUMENTS OF PRACTICE SERIES

Love and Marriage in Late Medieval London, selected, translated, and introduced by Shannon McSheffrey (1995)

Sources for the History of Medicine in Late Medieval England, selected, introduced, and translated by Carole Rawcliffe (1995)

A Slice of Life: Selected Documents of Medieval English Peasant Experience, edited, translated, and with an introduction by Edwin Brezette DeWindt (1996)

Regular Life: Monastic, Canonical, and Mendicant "Rules," selected and introduced by Douglas J. McMillan and Kathryn Smith Fladenmuller (1997); second edition, selected and introduced by Daniel Marcel La Corte and Douglas J. McMillan (2004)

Women and Monasticism in Medieval Europe: Sisters and Patrons of the Cistercian Reform, selected, translated, and with an introduction by Constance H. Berman (2002)

Medieval Notaries and Their Acts: The 1327–1328 Register of Jean Holanie, introduced, edited, and translated by Kathryn L. Reyerson and Debra A. Salata (2004)

John Stone's Chronicle: Christ Church Priory, Canterbury, 1417–1472, selected, translated, and introduced by Meriel Connor (2010)

✒ MEDIEVAL GERMAN TEXTS IN BILINGUAL EDITIONS SERIES

Sovereignty and Salvation in the Vernacular, 1050–1150, introduction, translations, and notes by James A. Schultz (2000)

Ava's New Testament Narratives: "When the Old Law Passed Away," introduction, translation, and notes by James A. Rushing, Jr. (2003)

History as Literature: German World Chronicles of the Thirteenth Century in Verse, introduction, translation, and notes by R. Graeme Dunphy (2003)

Thomasin von Zirclaria, *Der Welsche Gast (The Italian Guest)*, translated by Marion Gibbs and Winder McConnell (2009)

Ladies, Whores, and Holy Women: A Sourcebook in Courtly, Religious, and Urban Cultures of Late Medieval Germany, introductions, translations, and notes by Ann Marie Rasmussen and Sarah Westphal-Wihl (2010)

✒ VARIA

The Study of Chivalry: Resources and Approaches, edited by Howell Chickering and Thomas H. Seiler (1988)

Studies in the Harley Manuscript: The Scribes, Contents, and Social Contexts of British Library MS Harley 2253, edited by Susanna Fein (2000)

The Liturgy of the Medieval Church, edited by Thomas J. Heffernan and E. Ann Matter (2001; second edition 2005)

✒ TO ORDER PLEASE CONTACT:

Medieval Institute Publications
Western Michigan University
Kalamazoo, MI 49008-5432
Phone (269) 387-8755
FAX (269) 387-8750
http://www.wmich.edu/medieval/mip/index.html

Typeset in 10/13 New Baskerville
and Golden Cockerel Ornaments display
Designed by Linda K. Judy
Manufactured by Cushing-Malloy, Inc.

Medieval Institute Publications
College of Arts and Sciences
Western Michigan University
1903 W. Michigan Avenue
Kalamazoo, MI 49008-5432
http:/ /www.wmich.edu/medieval/mip

 WESTERN MICHIGAN UNIVERSITY